Theories of Reading

In loving memory of my grandmother,
Margarete Schutz, who made this all possible.

Theories of Reading

Books, Bodies, and Bibliomania

Karin Littau

polity

First published in 2006 by Polity Press

Polity Press
65 Bridge Street
Cambridge CB2 1UR, UK

Polity Press
350 Main Street
Malden, MA 02148, USA

ISBN-10: 0-7456-1658-5
ISBN-13: 978-07456-1658-2
ISBN-10: 0-7456-1659-3 (pb)
ISBN-13: 978-07456-1659-9 (pb)

A catalogue record for this book is available from the British Library.

Typeset in 10.5 on 12 pt Bembo
by Planman I:TES India Ltd.
Printed and bound in India by Replika Press Pvt Ltd

For further information on Polity, visit our website: www.polity.co.uk

Contents

List of Illustrations   ix

Acknowledgements   x

Introduction: Anatomy of Reading   1
    Books   3
    Bibliomania   4
    Bodies   8

1 A History of Reading   13
    From reading aloud to reading silently   14
    From monastic to scholastic reading   15
    Reading in solitude   17
    From intensive to extensive reading   19

2 The Material Conditions of Reading   23
    Expressive function of print   25
    Instability of the textual object   27
    Histories of textual transmission   29
    From manuscript to typographic culture   32
    From print to hypermedia culture   33

3 The Physiology of Consumption   36
    Side-effects of reading   37
    Reading-fever   39
    Reading addiction   42
    Modernity and the assault on the senses   45
    Eye-strain and eye-hunger   49
    Film-fever   50

Dazzling the audience   52
Dizzy in hyperspace   53
(Dis)embodied in cyberspace   57
Passive consumers   58

4   The Reader in Fiction   62
Dangers of reading   63
The tearful reader   65
The frightened reader   69
The passionate reader   72
Pathology of reading   74
Reading games   76
The danger of a future without books   77
Multisensory media   79

5   The Role o`f Affect in Literary Criticism   83
Reading with/without pathos   84
Docere–delectare–movere   86
From reader to author to text   90
Disinterested and contemplative reading   92
Close reading   96
Reading for sense rather than sensation   98

6   The Reader in Theory   103
(Un)readability   105
A priori conditions of reading   107
Controlling readers' responses   108
Reading expectations   109
Conventions of reading   111
Interpretive communities   113
Failure of reading   116
Misreading   119
The reader as writer   120
The politics of difference   122

7   Sexual Politics of Reading   125
The resisting reader   127
Black women readers   128
Empirical audiences   131

Active consumers   134
'Low-/middle-/highbrow' reading   137
Embodied reading   142
Reading as/like a woman   148
The feminization of the reader   151

Conclusion: *Materialist* Readings   **154**

Notes   **158**

References and Bibliography   **168**

Index   **186**

List of Illustrations

Figure 1   Print shop, by Mathias Huss (Lyons, ca. 1500):
           British Library, IB.41735   1

Figure 2   Woodcut of a monk, by Heredi di Phi. Giunta
           (Florence, 1529): from Sotheby & Co., *Catalogue
           of Valuable Italian Books of the 15th and 16th
           Centuries*, 6 May 1970, p. 222   13

Figure 3   Reading machine, by Jean de Gourmont II
           (Paris, 1588): British Library, 48.f.15   23

Figure 4   'Tales of Wonder', by James Gillray (1802):
           George G. Harrap & Co. Ltd, 1930   36

Figure 5   A side-effect of reading, from *Belgravia* (1868):
           British Library, P.P.6004.gn   62

Figure 6   A scene from Homer, by John Flaxman (ca. 1800):
           British Library, 1760 A8   83

Figure 7   The readability of a text:
           www.nlg.nhs.uk/orthoptics/images/print.gif   103

Figure 8   *Ex libris*: author's collection   125

Acknowledgements

My interests in theories of reading go back to my student days, and an essay I wrote for a bewildering MA course on literary theory with what seemed at the time a rather voguish title, 'Making Sense of Reading/The Reading of Sense'. It was written under gruelling circumstances, between several operations to remove a shattered radial head from my elbow, and perhaps my interests in reading and the body first found their inspiration then. I owe much gratitude to the staff at the University of Warwick not only for their caring attitude to their budding graduate students, but also for the vigorous academic environment which helped shape my subsequent intellectual life. I am especially grateful to Susan Bassnett, who has been a great inspiration in how to think comparatively, for planting the idea in the head of a theory-mad student that, as our reading lives mature, we gradually work our way back to the histories of those theories. She was right. This book pulls in both directions, looking back at the history of reading, and wondering about its future.

I should also like to thank the British Academy for their willingness to fund me not just as a student but as an academic too. The one-year sabbatical made possible by their grant and the generosity of the School of English at the University of the West of England could have brought this book to publication years ago. Instead, I used this invaluable year to rethink what should have been a study of contemporary theories of reading into a study of the history of those theories, and I hope the book, as it stands now, is the better for it. Kate Fullbrook, my then Head of Department, gave unfailing support in the early parts of this project, and I am saddened that her own career as a fine thinker was cut short by the cruelty of illness. I would also like to thank my colleagues at the University of Essex for embracing their now not so new colleague with such warmth, and for their continuing interest in my work. Specifically I would like to thank Kay Stevenson, in whose presence I always believed that I was a theorist with the makings of a scholar, and Jeffrey Geiger, Maria Cristina Fumagalli, John Haynes and David Musselwhite for their encouragement at low points of writing this book. I also wish Francis Barker was still with us, arguing and disagreeing with me about theory, under hefty clouds of cigarette smoke. Last, but not least, my gratitude goes to Jonathan White, who took the time to read my manuscript while in the last stages of his own book. This was a true act of generosity and friendship.

To my students past and present, but especially to those who chose 'The Gutenberg Galaxy' course and whose openness and inquisitiveness about my ideas has been a joy, I owe thanks. They will no doubt recognize much in this book, including my enthusiasm for new technologies, at least in theory, if not always in a practical context. Research for *Theories of Reading* greatly benefited from conversations with Helen Boden, Gerry Carlin and Paul R. Sealey, as well as the patience and kindness of the staff at Polity Press, especially John Thompson, Gill Motley in the early stages, and Andrea Drugan, who saw the project through to the end. An author could not have wished for more understanding editors in a climate of increasing pressures on university life. I should also like to thank the reader of the initial proposal and the reader of the manuscript, whose helpful suggestions for chapter 7 were much appreciated. Finally, I could not have finished this book had it not been for Iain Hamilton Grant, the most well-read, thoughtful and loving person I know.

Introduction: Anatomy of Reading

Figure 1 Print shop, by Mathias Huss, Lyons, ca. 1500, illustrating that the printed word, unlike the flesh, is immortal.

Strictly speaking, the book you hold in your hands is not one but two books. As the scholar Cathy N. Davidson reminds us, these two books 'are not the same', because one is a 'manufactured artifact', the other a 'conveyor of meaning' (1986: 15). To conceive of a book as two kinds – one material the other ideational – marks the dividing line between two fields of study: cultural history and literary theory. Whereas cultural historians are interested in the word in all its technological innovations, handwritten, printed, and digitalized, literary theorists are concerned predominantly with textuality. When literary theorists therefore approach the 'thousands of possible relations' a reader has to a text (Cixous 1990: 3), they rarely take into account the one factor which, apart from historicity, is central to cultural historians of reading: materiality.[1] This is because for literary theorists both the text and the reader are abstractions. For cultural historians, by contrast, texts are embedded in objects and reading is a concrete bodily act (cf. Chartier 1988a: 12; 1988b: 307). By bringing together these distinct lines of enquiry, one into the technical apparatus of the written text, the other into processes of textual signification, it is possible to see how material production impinges on meaning production. When we read we interpret semantic content and, insofar as poetic or narrative structure gives form to content, we enter into a deeper level of interpretation. Texts are therefore conveyors of complex and multi-layered meanings. Since a text is also, however, an embodied material object, this object's materiality and physical organization conditions our readings. Thus conceived, texts bring into contact *content*, *form* and *matter*, and readers respond to linguistic and literary codes as well as bibliographical and medium-specific ones (cf. McGann 1991: 13).

This is just one line of enquiry I pursue in this book. The other concerns the physicality of reading. The relation a reader has to a book is also a relation between two bodies: one made of paper and ink, the other flesh and blood. This is to say, the book has a body, evident even in the use of terms such as footnotes and headers, but so does the reader. We are apt to think that reading is comprehension and occurs only in our heads. In literary circles, especially, we think of reading as a 'bracing mental exercise' (Q. D. Leavis 1932: 135); and yet, as cultural history has shown, physicians once regarded reading as a form of physical exercise. Reading aloud exercises not just the vocal chords but also the lips as they mouth and murmur the sounds of words. It was even said that it is of cardiovascular benefit because it 'sets our blood in motion' (Bergk 1966 [1799]: 69). As a practice of reading it has a much longer history than reading silently, with our eyes only, which is the mode of reading most familiar to us in modern times. Therefore, reading is historically variable and physically conditioned – two factors easily ignored if we regard the relation between text and reader as a relation between an ideal or transcendent work and a idealized or universal reader.

But reading aloud is not the only evidence we have of reading as a labour of the body. Literary history is filled with stories of book reading as a deeply affecting experience. Whether what is produced is tears of sorrow, bellies filled with laughter or hair-raising terror, such symptoms belong to the body. Our own age deems such reactions trivial. Two centuries ago the sublimity of rapture or the tenderness of sentiment were either acclaimed critically or condemned as dangerously irrational. For the ancients, moreover, poetry's capacity for generating affect was a testament to the greatness of the poet. In the classical and neo-classical traditions the production of affect was something poets found worth emulating, critics worth studying, and audiences worth experiencing. The dispassionate, disinterested pleasure we now take in art is far removed from those passionate encounters which for centuries justified aesthetic theory and practice. Literature has become, as Jane Tompkins observes, an 'occasion for interpretation' (1980: 206), and contemporary theorists only occasionally remember that, for their predecessors, drama, poetry and prose fiction offered 'occasions of feeling'.[2] This is because before the arrival of formalism, which has dominated critical practice since the twentieth century, 'it was doubtful', Tompkins argues, that critics 'would recognize "meaning" as a critical issue at all' (ibid.: 203).[3] Overall, then, the history recounted in this book points to a split between modern literary study, which tends to regard reading as a reducibly mental activity, and a tradition reaching back to antiquity which assumed that reading literature was not only about sense-making but also about sensation.

Books

Apart from the human body, the book is the longest serving medium for the storage, retrieval and transmission of knowledge. It also remains, alongside other, more modern recording media such as film and the computer, one of the principal means by which to give expression to the imagination: storytelling. Whether once etched in human memory, scratched into stone, clay or wax, penned onto papyrus, printed on wood pulp, or now saved electronically at the touch of a button, the production and distribution of literature is unthinkable without these material carriers, and culture unthinkable without media. What this suggests is that literary communication is a confluence of the physiological, the material and the technological – three strands which continually weave their way through the fabric of this book. While much of the history of writing survives because it has been inscribed onto durable surfaces, or copied again and again for later generations, reading is much more evanescent. And yet, its history too survives in written records. Reading notes, marginalia, diaries, autobiographies, critical works, literary texts, trial transcripts, subscription lists, membership lists for reading societies, etc., all these sources can be used to give us a glimpse of practices of reading across the ages. The research of historians of reading, such as Roger Chartier and Robert Darnton among others, has taught us much about who read what, when and where, and why people read. What this research also indicates is that the way people read, and even the experience of reading itself, depended on the technologies by which they received the written word. Or, to take this one step further, media technologies have altered not just our relation to writing and reading but our perception of the world, and perhaps even, as theorists of new media would suggest, perception itself.

  Three significant technological innovations in modern times have redefined Western societies' relation to the written word, and in the process altered our sensibilities: the invention of the printing press in the mid-fifteenth century, the invention of the cinematograph at the end of the nineteenth century and the invention of the computer in the mid-twentieth century. Print first ushered us into modernity, of which cinema is the culmination and embodiment, whereas computer technology has propelled us into postmodernity. The printing press facilitated an unprecedented increase in the production of books, creating large readerships, and was instrumental in the rise of the genre of the novel. While film in many respects has challenged the novel as the main form of mass entertainment, raising suspicions of a bookless future, the computer promises new environments for fiction, but also engenders the fear that we are nearing the end of the book.[4] By reflecting on our previous encounters with once new technologies, including how each technology has shaped our culture's artistic output, it is possible to chart connections between the *effects* of old media on their consumers and the *effects* of the new media on their users. Given that we inhabit a rapidly changing mediascape, we need to make such connections in order to help us understand our being-in-the-world. Therefore, what we can learn from these connections, and what kinds of directions such enquiries might lead us in, is one of the key concerns of this book.

When we examine the history of print culture, it becomes clear that the full effects of print were only felt several centuries after its invention. Once calibrated, mechanized, and more efficiently industrialized, the printing press had produced so many books, pamphlets, magazines, and other paper trails in the course of the eighteenth century that Immanuel Kant complained of 'parchment-headed' men and women who, because they read so much, had lost the capacity to think for themselves (1963: iii). Kant was not the only one to make this point. In England, Samuel Johnson worried that the sheer proliferation of printed matter would make readers rush into print, becoming writers themselves: 'there was never a time when men of all degrees of ability, of every education, of every profession and employment were posting with ardour so general to the press' (qtd. Nunberg 1995: 33) – a complaint often rearticulated by critics of the Internet, who worry that its unregulated use allows 'anyone' to put their writings into the public domain. From the eighteenth century onwards, and right through the nineteenth century, countless warnings are heard about a newly emerging mass culture of reading which print, coupled with increasing levels of literacy, had created, and which had spread as fast as an epidemic. In the periodical press, but also in philosophical treatises and works of fiction, writers warned of too much print, too much writing, too much reading. Bibliomania had infected Western societies and become, as a French dictionary defines it in 1740: 'une des maladies de ce siècle' (qtd. König 1977: 92).[5]

Bibliomania

One form this sickness takes is the so-called reading-fever. It is an addiction associated with excessive and obsessive reading, which hurries readers from one novel to the next. Its social manifestations include general idleness, work-shyness, and lofty notions of romance. In the course of the nineteenth century its effects had become so alarming and widespread 'that it was construed as a disease to be treated by medicine – "the novel-reading disease"' (de Bolla 1989: 264). Its medical symptoms range from constipation, a flabby stomach and eye and brain disorders, to nerve complaints and mental disease. Too much print and too much reading thus went hand in hand not only with feeding but with overfeeding those hungry for fiction. Regarded as a consumer product, to be read swiftly, then discarded, the novel – like the cinema later – provided short-lived bursts of entertainment, filled with cheap sentiments or thrills and, as William Wordsworth saw it, 'deluges of idle and extravagant stories' (1974 [1800]: 128). Insofar as ferocious novel reading also fostered disconnected and 'higgledy-piggledy' practices of reading (Hoche 1794, qtd. Schenda 1988: 60), it was thought that, 'if persisted in', it would have the effect of 'enfeebling the minds of men and women, making flabby the fibre of their bodies and undermining the vigour of nations' (Austin 1874: 251). Like all addictions, those afflicted demanded more and more of the same: more to read, more excitement, more tears, horror and thrills. Bibliomania is therefore part of a larger cultural *malaise* specifically associated with modernity: sensory overstimulation. From the perspective of a theory of reading it shows that reading, insofar as it is either bad or good for the reader's health, is in both instances conceived in physicalist terms.

While novelists catered for this hunger for fiction, many also thematized the ill effects of novel reading in their work. Indeed, Cervantes' *Don Quixote* (1605, 1615), generally regarded as the first modern novel,[6] already contains a critique of the novel by featuring a character whose excesses of reading have flung him into madness whereby he mistakes fiction for reality. This kind of quixotic reader appears with added frequency as levels of print production increase, only to be replaced as a trope by similar concerns voiced about the absorbing effects of narrative film, and more recently about the out-of-body experience promised by virtual reality (VR). The forgetting of oneself and becoming other than oneself while immersed in the world of fiction are not the only indicators of a pathology of reading. Uncontrollable weeping, inflamed passions, and irrational terror are some of the sensory stimuli one might experience during reading. These too are pathological insofar as they are illustrative of a mind unable to rein in the impulses of the body. Unlike serious book reading, which 'lifts the reader from sensation to intellect' (Hannah More 1799, qtd. de Bolla 1989: 269), novel reading, because it can 'produce effects almost without the intervention of the will', as Samuel Johnson saw it (1969 [1750]: 22), was feared to operate in reverse: gratifying the baser instincts by appealing less to the reader's faculty for sense-making than his or her sensations, thus reducing or eliminating the reader's capacity for action.

If therefore considered in the light of Friedrich Nietzsche's premise that art is intoxication (1967– [1888]: 328), the consequences of severe bibliomania are the negation of the autonomy of the subject and, with it, the humanist ideal of rational agency. This is why the questions I pose repeatedly in this book have to do with agency. Are our rational faculties in control of our bodies? What effects does fiction have on the reader, and are they beyond his or her control? Does art affect us sensually before we can respond intellectually? And, relatedly, are humans in control of technology? Again, Nietzsche's observation that 'our writing instruments contribute to our thoughts' (qtd. Kittler 1990: 210) is instructive insofar as it suggests that technology – here the typewriter – is not a neutral apparatus or a transparent medium, but has a physical effect on us, changing not only how we write, but how we compose. Accordingly, as Friedrich Kittler argues, 'humans change their positions – they turn from the agency of writing to become an inscription surface' (ibid.). This redefinition of the relation between human subject and technological instrument reopens the problem of technological determinism, questioning the premise of humanism by which humans are in control of their use of technology. The reader will therefore notice an anti-humanist argument which runs through this entire book, and which plays off a Nietzschean aesthetics-as-physiology against a Kantian aesthetics of rational disinterestedness. By extension, a similar argument is deployed with regard to the question of whether technology is an agent of cultural change, or whether it is culture that is responsible for technological change, thus playing off Marshall McLuhan's insights against those of Raymond Williams.

The confluence of the technological, the physiological and the medical indicates that the relation between media and consumers is not just about the acquisition of knowledge, wisdom and understanding, or the reception of meanings alone. Rather, the study of the consumption and reception of literature within the remit of material cultures allows an insight into the ways in which technology shapes sensibilities and thinking itself. This marks a difference between the study of literature within the framework of the humanities, literally as the *Geisteswissenschaften* ('the sciences of the spirit'), and the study of literature as part of media history and aesthetics. I am not suggesting that literature be studied according to the model of media studies as conceived within the tradition of British cultural studies, namely looking at popular culture from the perspective of those who are politically disfranchised, or from the perspective of 'ordinary' people's everyday life interests. Rather, it seems to me that approaches to the interfaces between media, as implicit in the writings of Walter Benjamin, proposed by Marshall McLuhan, and also practised by Friedrich Kittler, provide a much broader framework through which to tackle the relations between art, aesthetics, aesthesis and technology than is currently the case in media-related studies which focus exclusively on contemporary mass media, and exclude literature on the grounds that it is too 'arty' or too elitist. By contrast, Benjamin, McLuhan and Kittler draw on canonical and popular art forms in equal measure. Although *Theories of Reading* is concerned primarily with the consumption and reception of literature, I also make reference to newer media such as film and the computer so as to provide a framework by which we might compare the way in which newer media differ from, but also remediate,[7] those very conditions for consumption and reception. Thus, although not in the scope of this book, I have gestured towards a study of comparative media[8] as a means by which to connect the history of practices of reading with emerging new practices of receiving texts.

When Kittler, for instance, explores the relations between literature and cinema he asks what difference the cinema has made to our reading experience of literature.

As long as a book was responsible for all serial data flows, words quivered with sensuality and memory. It was the passion of all reading to hallucinate meaning between letters and lines [...] And the passion of all writing was (in the words of E.T.A. Hoffmann) the poet's desire to 'describe' the hallucinated 'picture in one's mind with all its vivid colors, the light and the shade', in order to 'strike [the] gentle reader like an electric shock'.

(1999: 10)

The cinema is situated at the very cusp of the electric age, looking back at a culture based on paper and already anticipating a culture based on the screen. Since the cinema, as the dream machine, is able to translate, by technologically reproducing, hallucinatory images onto the screen, then writing and reading as we know it, Kittler implies, has changed forever. It is not just that film has remediated aspects of the great realist novel, but it has amplified, even electrified (metaphorically and literally), what was once specific about the relation to the alphabet and print. This is to say the new representational technology tries to supplant the old representational technology by creating illusions even more enticing, or 'dangerously delusional', than was the case previously (cf. Murray 1997: 18). What Johann Ludwig Erwald in 1789 called 'novel-fever' (Erwald, qtd. König 1977: 104) turns in 1922 for Max Prels into 'film-fever' (Prels, qtd. Hake 1993: 52), displacing the danger of reading with the danger of watching images. That science fictions already warn of the dangers of VR is an index of another representational technology on the horizon which, if ever perfected, would undoubtedly change the conditions of consumption by creating the kind of hallucinatory space that, in theory at least, makes it impossible to distinguish between fiction and reality, machine and body, the 'I' and the 'not I'.

New media invent not just new forms of fictions, but also new means of perceptual manipulation. As such they present audiences with new opportunities for experiencing fictional worlds. When F. R. Leavis complains in *Mass Civilisation and Minority Culture* that films 'provide now the main form of recreation in the civilised world' (1930: 9-10), his fear is that the new medium gives the masses what they want. Films, he writes, 'involve surrender, under conditions of hypnotic receptivity, to the cheapest of emotional appeals, appeals the more insidious because they are associated with a compellingly vivid illusion of actual life' (ibid.: 10). In a similar vein and around the same time, Thomas Mann wonders why the cinematic experience is synonymous with outpourings of emotions: 'Tell me, why is it that in the movies we are always crying or weeping like servant girls?' (1978 [1928]: 164).[9] For Mann, film is a rival form of entertainment to the novel. It is neither the product of high culture, nor does it qualify as art because, unlike literature, which requires mental effort, it appeals to the emotions. 'Art is a cold sphere' (ibid.: 165), Mann explains, a comment which reveals what he regards not only as genuine art but also as an appropriate response to art. Cinema, by implication, is *a hot sphere* (an odd presaging of Marshall McLuhan's distinction between 'hot' and 'cool media'),[10] bringing out responses in the audience best kept suppressed, or reserved for the darkness of the auditorium. What underlies critiques of the cinema by literary critics and writers is a concern that film so entrances spectators that they react to, rather than reflect on, what they see. This is because, as a medium which bombards viewers with the quick succession of moving pictures, it 'assaults every one of the senses using every possible means' (Kracauer 1987 [1926]: 92). The way in which the technology works, then, makes it difficult to procure the necessary moment of tranquility for spectators to contemplate the image at their leisure. Film overpowers the senses, and thus stimulates the body before it can stimulate the mind. Or, as F. R. Leavis finds, the motion pictures offer 'passive diversion', making 'active recreation, especially active use of the mind, more difficult' (1930: 10).

At the high end of culture, it is the sublime, of course, which is associated with art's capacity for generating affect. According to Jean-François Lyotard, the sublime overpowers the recipient with 'the event of a passion, of a suffering for which the mind won't have been prepared', and thus 'suspends the activity of the mind at least for an instant' (1991: 301-2). That this is potentially dangerous for those who succumb to its turbulence is not just a crucial concern in Kant's theory of aesthetic judgement, but also an issue which Nietzsche captures perfectly when he refers to 'the physiological danger of art' (1967– [1888]: 327). Whereas Nietzsche celebrates rapture, for Kant it must be resisted, which is why the relation to art must be one of cognitive *apatheia* and not *pathos*. Given the etymological interlacing between 'pathos', 'sympathy', 'passion', 'passivity', 'patient' and 'pathology', it is not surprising why to be carried away by the unruly passions, or to submit passively to pathos, might be deemed pathological. To watch a film or read a novel with pathos means being acted upon, that is, to receive passively, and thus forsake self and reason. The sublime is therefore a reminder that the purpose of a work of art had once been inseparable from the unleashing of great passions, and that the purpose of criticism had once been to instruct the poet how best to incite those passions. What modernists such as Mann and Leavis forget, then, is that genuine art had been *a hot sphere*, so much so that Plato dismissed the poetic altogether because, unlike philosophy, it 'feeds and waters' the passions, hampering and corrupting the rational faculty (*Republic* 606d).

Bodies

With each invention of a new medium – film, digital technologies, or the novel – it is the reinvention of affective response which gives critics cause for concern. While affect is a central theme in this book, I have not provided an overview of different theories, differentiated amongst types (such as sadness, joy, fear, startle, excitement, disgust, etc.), or constructed my own theory of affect. Nor have I given an account of how affect as a concept has changed historically. Suffice it to say that in contemporary theory it is taken as a given that affect is discursively constructed – a premise which is historical itself, insofar as the specification of affect as constructed is just one stage – the most recent – of its history (cf. Sedgwick 2003: 109–11). Rather, the history of affect recounted in this book is a history of its demise as a once valuable cultural and aesthetic category. This devaluation is nowhere more clearly articulated than in W. K. Wimsatt's and Monroe C. Beardsley's essay 'The Affective Fallacy', first published in 1949. Famously, this essay articulates the reasons why the figure of the reader should be excluded from literary enquiry, reasons based entirely on the assumption that art and art criticism belong in the 'cold sphere' (1954: 31). Citing Thomas Mann's observations in support, Wimsatt and Beardsley argue for critical distance as a means of protection from emotional contamination, and make a case against the surrender to affect. Their critique turns against a tradition of affective criticism which goes back to Gorgias, Horace and Longinus, and was still of moment in discourses on the sublime in the eighteenth century, whereby the greatness of literature was judged by its capacity to *move* its audience. What Wimsatt and Beardsley argue for is a criticism detached from affect, a criticism which 'will talk not of tears, prickles, or other physiological symptoms, of feeling angry, joyful, hot, cold, or intense, or of vaguer states of emotional disturbance' (ibid.: 34). This is because the new critic they envisage is not concerned with what a text does to a reader, but what a text means, how it signifies: it is not a 'tabulator of the subject's responses' but 'a teacher or explicator of meanings'. Accordingly, great art must leave the reader cold, and great criticism must refuse to countenance readers' affective responses.

I am not arguing that Wimsatt and Beardsley single-handedly ousted an entire audience-oriented tradition of criticism and replaced it with a text-centred criticism, since the formalist seeds of this thinking had already been sown with Kant's notion of the autonomy of the work of art. Rather, I want to draw attention to another fallacy which Wimsatt and Beardsley, as well as their most ardent critics, commit: the cognitive fallacy. Even Stanley Fish, who rejects a text-centred criticism and proposes a theory of reader-response, does not, despite claims to the contrary, embrace affect, but its opposite, cognition, exactly as Wimsatt and Beardsley had done. When Fish insists in his manifesto piece 'Literature in the Reader: Affective Stylistics' (1970) that 'I include not only "tears, prickles," and "other psychological symptoms" but all the precise mental operations involved in reading' (1980: 42-3), this is not the case. As the reader-response critic Jonathan Culler has pointed out, despite Fish's claim to 'include not only "tears, prickles," and "other psychological symptoms" that Wimsatt and Beardsley's fallacy sets aside', he never actually 'mentions tears or prickles' again (1983: 39-40). Instead of accounting for readers' emotions and sensations, he makes literature an 'occasion for interpretation', emphasizing not an affective but a cognitive response to literature.

What interests me about both Fish's and Culler's critical engagement with 'The Affective Fallacy' is that it is based on a misquotation. Wimsatt and Beardsley did not describe 'tears and prickles' as '*psychological* symptoms', as Fish and Culler do, but as '*physiological* symptoms' (my emphases). The misquotation could, of course, be the result of a typing or printer's error, the kind of physical corruption which, as bibliographers know only too well, can change minimally the meaning of a sentence and maximally the significance of a book. However, since Fish was not the only one to have made this mistake insofar as Culler compounded it, I am tempted to interpret the misquotation as a slip of the tongue, less to do with a typographical oversight than with a conceptual blindness. To have translated '*physiological* symptoms' (which manifestly belong to the body) into '*psychological* symptoms' (which manifestly belong to the mind) betrays a mentalist bias that informs much of contemporary criticism and theory.

Thus, the bulk of twentieth-century reader-oriented theories, with some notable exceptions from within feminist theory, are concerned predominantly either with how readers make sense of a text (Culler, Fish, Iser, Jauss, Gadamer), how texts frustrate readers' attempts at making sense (de Man, Miller, Hartman, Bloom, Derrida), or how readers resist the meanings of certain texts (Fetterley, Radway, Bobo). Thus, even when theorists turned away from an overly textualist approach to a more contextual, or politically engaged, approach, the production of meaning is still the primary concern. By contrast, theories of reading before the twentieth century were also concerned with readers' sensations. 'Contemporary' theory empowers the reader: he or she is not someone who undergoes passions passively, but an active producer of meaning, thus operating with the Cartesian division of body and mind. Even the members of 'real' audiences interviewed within the remit of cultural studies are never flesh and blood, but subjects from whom ethnographic researchers elicit subversive meanings and counter-readings. Whether the figure of the reader is therefore conceived as a textual entity, an ideal abstraction or a universal, as theorists variously did in the 1970s and 1980s, or whether the reader is reconceived as socially situated, as theorists did in the 1980s and 1990s, that is, marked among other factors by gender, sexual orientation, class, race, ethnicity, this reader tends to be a disembodied mind rather than a physiological being sitting at the edge of his or her seat, tears welling up inside, pulse racing, spine tingling. As Susan Sontag has argued in *Against Interpretation*, we live '[i]n a culture whose classical dilemma is the hypertrophy of the intellect at the expense of energy and sensual capability', and it is for this reason that 'interpretation is the revenge of the intellect upon art' (1987 [1967]: 7). Reading is synonymous with sense-making, and reading for sensation, the critical concern for centuries, has come to an end.

Theories of Reading: Books, Bodies, and Bibliomania presents a historical overview of a great many theories of reading, comparing long-forgotten ones with little-noticed and canonical accounts, so as to call attention to a decidedly modern, and moreover modernist, bias towards reading as a predominantly mentalist activity. My approach is not that of a micro-analysis, drawing conclusions on the basis of certain case studies, as the historian might do. Rather, I tell an overarching narrative, fully aware of the pitfalls that such an approach entails. The postmodernist suspicion of grand narratives is justified insofar as generality works at the expense of specificity and does injustice to the marginal. In my defence I would have to say that the overarching story I tell is one which highlights what contemporary literary theories of reading have systematically marginalized, excluded or ignored: the body of the reader.

Accordingly, although I tell a grand narrative, the reading strategy deployed in this book is in crucial respects indebted to feminist thought. On the one hand, feminist theories have brought the body back into the theoretical arena since, in addressing sexual difference, they have also had to negotiate questions of physiological difference. But this is only one reason why feminist theorists have been attentive to the body. A second reason concerns the re-reading of history from the perspective of what feminists see as history's exclusions. A considerable corpus of feminist criticism has sought to expose the systematic hierarchies that have worked to privilege reason over passion in the history of Western philosophical thought. It is the privileging of head over heart, and by extension its alignment with the masculine over the feminine, which informs my argument throughout the book, and which is addressed directly in the concluding chapter. Here, I explore more fully the historical alignment of woman with the other of reason or, conversely, the alignment of man with rationality – an alignment which, I demonstrate, has fuelled feminist distrust of the confirmation of mind, with its concomitant denial of body. A theory of reading such as is offered by Hélène Cixous, for instance, which not only focuses on the bodily relation between reader and text but also takes into consideration the physicality of writing and the materiality of the written text does so in order to highlight the links, which also exist etymologically, between *materialism, mater* and *matrix* (cf. Butler 1993: 31).

There is another reason, however, why I think we should take materialism seriously. In this respect it is instructive to go back to Aristotle, and especially to the *Physics*. It is here that he outlines four causes, causes which he uses to explain how a thing (in our case literature) comes to be a thing. The first cause is material, designating that 'from which a thing is made'; the second cause concerns form, whether in terms of a specific or a generic pattern; the third, which Aristotle calls 'efficient', names the 'devisor of a plan' – here the author; and the fourth and final cause, because it asks for the purpose or goal of a thing, refers to the audience (194b23-32). It seems to me that, while the study of literature takes into account three of these causes, at different times emphasizing one cause over another, it is the first cause, the very substance from which the producer[11] causes form to emerge, which has largely been ignored. Book history (cf. Chartier, Darnton) and the discipline of bibliography (cf. McKenzie, McGann) have already pointed the way towards the importance of a consideration of the first, material cause. Literary theory, however, has hardly engaged with the matter of matter, with the exception, although to a limited extent, of feminism. While literary theory, feminism included, has bequeathed to us the importance of recognizing the exclusions and hierarchies operative in our critical traditions, exposing and deconstructing them, there is one exclusion which remains to be addressed: the exclusion of the material and the physical. But it is this exclusion which also confronts us with a hierarchy which might well turn out to be non-reversible: without nature to produce human animals there can be neither culture nor politics, whereas without culture and politics there still can be nature. It is this series of dependency relations which haunts the edges of this book.

1 A History of Reading

Figure 2 This woodcut of a monk, by Heredi di Phi. Giunta (Florence, 1529) in 'Savonarola (Girolamo) Libro della vita Christiana tradocto in volgare', shows him reading with his right index finger what he has already written. Such a corporeal mode of reading was often also executed with a 'reading tool', so that ink and gold would not be smudged by a sweaty finger.

Whether you are sitting studiously at your desk or curled up comfortably on your sofa, whether you are in a public library or in the privacy of your home, the likelihood is that you are reading these words silently. To read silently, rather than aloud, is a relatively recent phenomenon. Far from having always been conducted in the same way, reading – like the form of the book itself – has been subject to many variations over the course of its history. As historians of the book have shown,[1] the materiality in which writing comes to us – whether in the form of engraved tablets, scrolls, bound pages for the codex, mass-produced printed copies, or on-line hypertexts available anywhere by anyone – is an important factor in shaping our relation to the written word. It is also an important factor in terms of how we conduct our reading, even where we read, what kinds of literatures we read, and how much we read. As we shall see in this as well as the next two chapters, the experience of reading a printed book, unalterable and easily reproducible, is not the same as that of reading a unique handwritten artefact whose blank margins invite glosses, or an electronic copy whose hyperlinks allow users to reconfigure that text. How a work is therefore produced, circulated, and made public, and that this was different before and after print, before and after the computer, are all factors which have to be taken into account when considering a history of reading. That various technological innovations have altered our modes of communication is evident to anybody living in our current digital age. The way in which our exposure to different modes of communication (oral, handwritten, printed or virtual) has influenced not just the culture of reading but all levels of Western culture is the topic of this chapter. What follows then is a history of the changing technologies and cultural forms of reading in the West.[2]

From reading aloud to reading silently

When the alphabet first came to ancient Greece from the Phoenicians in the eighth century BC, writing was a tool with which to aid one's memory, merely recording the spoken word for later reference. As an oral culture deeply steeped in disseminating knowledge in the mode of the lecture as a public performance, its mode of discourse relied primarily on sound, dialogue and the public debate. What was written down on clay, wooden or wax tablets, and later on rolls of papyrus or parchment, was neither as transportable nor as easily readable as the handwritten codex or the printed book. While the nature of the writing surfaces made inscription cumbersome, but also led scribes to cram together letters and words so as to fill up the available space economically (cf. Landow 1996: 217), even the more pliable scroll exerted constraints on processes of reading and writing. Since the roll was unfolded from right to left, and had to be held with two hands, it did not allow one to read and make written notes at the same time.[3] Moreover, given that what was written was with virtually no word separation or punctuation for breathing,

ITMADEITALTOGETHEREASIERFORREADERSTOCOMPREHENDASCRIPT BYREADINGITOUTALOUDINORDERTOLISTENWHEREBREAKSMIGHTOCCUR,

and where sense would emerge between the unbroken, continuous stream of words (cf. Ivan Illich 1992, qtd. Gauger 1994: 31).

Little changed in Europe until the high Middle Ages. Despite the appearance of the codex in the third and fourth centuries (cf. Martin 1994: 59), which brought with it a more organized layout through pagination and indexes, thus facilitating the leafing through of pages and the retrieval of knowledge, it was not until the introduction of interword spacing in the seventh century and its more systematic use from the eleventh century onwards that a less corporal mode of reading began to be fostered which, rather than using lip movement and murmuring, was both silent and visual (cf. Saenger 1997). Allowing one to read more quickly or even speed-read with the eye, and therefore to read more, silent reading was a practice adopted in institutions of learning by the twelfth century and, two centuries on, also by the lay aristocracy (cf. Chartier 1995: 15-16; 1989c: 124-5). Although paragraph breaks, chapter headings or the numbering of psalms, all of which made reading as well as learning easier, came to be customary features of a book's layout over the following centuries,[4] and silent reading became increasingly widespread among educated readers (and is undoubtedly the dominant mode of reading nowadays), it by no means follows that all readers adopted this practice or that all texts were produced in this new manner, whether they were handwritten or printed. While poetry continued to be sung, literature was recited and the works of Rabelais, the tales of Boccaccio or the multi-volume novels of the seventeenth century were still printed with few blank spaces (cf. Martin 1994: 317), the practice of reading aloud, particularly for others, was not only often implied in literary texts themselves, such as in the numerous references to a listening reader in Cervantes' *Don Quixote* (1605, 1615), but continued to be a favoured mode of reading, perhaps even until as recently as the invention of television, to provide entertainment for the family or in a social circle.

From monastic to scholastic reading

What we can discern therefore is a crucial shift in the way readers read, which must be understood in conjunction not only with changes in book production but also with changes in people's relationship to the written word. While a book's format was clearly dependent on the availability of certain materials, such as papyrus from the Middle East or paper, the technology for the production of which came to Europe from China, or the invention of the printing press by Gutenberg in the mid-fifteenth century,[5] factors which all contributed to an altogether more portable book with an increasingly more organized and systematized layout, it would also be true to say that the emergence of the universities (Bologna 1119; Oxford 1214; Sorbonne 1255) with their libraries led to an alteration of the function both of reading and of writing. While devotional literature was the object of study in monasteries, and was almost exclusively the reading matter of those that were literate even up until the eighteenth century, a monastic model of writing and reading, according to Roger Chartier, gave way to a scholastic one around the twelfth century, when 'writing ceased to be strictly a means of conservation and memorization and came to be composed and copied for reading that was understood as intellectual work' (1995: 16). Rather than keeping manuscripts locked in cabinets, as monastery libraries often did, university libraries gave access to their holdings at all times (cf. Martin 1994: 186-8), marking a period of increased study and a concomitant increase in demand for books. A further expansion of the university sector in the fourteenth century (Prague 1348; Krakow 1364; Vienna 1365; Heidelberg 1386; Cologne 1388; Erfurt 1392) under the direction of secular authorities rather than the Church also meant that the newly emerging professionals in towns and cities, such as lawyers for instance, could not only be trained locally but also be served with reading materials useful for their trades.

Still, very few books were in circulation. In 1338, the library of the Sorbonne had the largest holdings in Christendom, with 338 books chained to reading desks and a total stock of 1738 for loan (cf. Martin 1994: 154), but few private individuals were wealthy enough to own their own copies, and those who could, or had learned to read, usually read only the Bible. Much of the reading that was done therefore, be it silently or aloud, in private or in public, was constrained to a limited number of books, often in the form of a collection of notes or copies that a given person had made for their own use, which were then circulated among a relatively small circle of their friends and acquaintances. When copies were made, either privately by an interested reader or by professional copyists, texts were altered in the process: details might be omitted and commentaries added, or mistakes were simply made in the flurry of trying to meet the demand for further reading matter. In the age of the manuscript, each book was therefore a unique artefact, with few anxieties besetting those that copied a text to be faithful to its letter, or those that imitated its spirit not to have produced something utterly new and original. Since there was no mechanism 'to distinguish between composing a poem and reciting one, or writing a book and copying one' (Eisenstein 1980: 121), this is why in the Middle Ages '[a]ny reader', according to J. David Bolter, 'could decide to cross over and become an author' (1991: 149), and why any author, if esteeming a given work highly enough, could plagiarize from it.[6] This goes to show not only that 'manuscript culture had taken inter-textuality for granted' (Ong 1982: 133), a condition that postmodern literature now plays on, but also that the modern conception of authorship, with its trappings of originality and propriety over one's work, is a relatively new development. One reason for this was 'the common classical and Christian view of poetic inspiration', in accordance with which 'the poet does not originate the poem but is the inspired channel for a divine act of creation' (Selden 1988: 303). In pre-print culture an author, or auctor, was therefore less a creator of a given work than its assembler, whose rights to the work extended merely to the physical object of the manuscript he or she had produced in the first instance, rather than the text as the fruit of his or her private consciousness, as is the case in the copyright law now.

With the invention of print technology between 1445 and 1450 much more than just the medieval notion of authorship changed. Although the earliest printed books imitated the writing styles of manuscripts, and were initially still finished off by hand, their typography and overall shape, just as much as the grammar and language in which the texts were written, became more and more standardized. On the other hand, the printed book also fixes or rather 'imposes its form, structure and layout without', as Chartier adds, 'in any way presupposing the reader's participation'. This is because the reader of the print-ed book can 'only insinuate his or her own reading in the virgin spaces of the book', those spaces in other words, 'that have been left free of printing', whereas the reader or copyist of the manuscript, not unlike the reader of the new electronic media, 'can construct collections of original texts whose exis-tence and organization depend on the reader alone' (1995: 20). If 'writing and the reproduction of writing' were conflated in the Middle Ages 'under the gen-eral conception of "making books"' (Rose 1993: 10), after the invention of the printing press the production of writing, its manufacture, and its consumption emerge as distinct activities, and therefore also in due course as autonomous professions: those of the printer (sixteenth century), the bookseller (seventeenth century), the writer (eighteenth century) and the publisher (nineteenth cen-tury), as well as the professional reader, such as the critic (eighteenth century) or the theorist (twentieth century).

The new print medium, which slowly turned itself into a viable commer-cial enterprise over the course of the next three centuries, did revolutionize habits of reading in other ways too. As a technology for the 'serial production of multiple copies of texts by means of movable type', following Henri-Jean Martin's definition of a printed book (1994: 182), it was able to meet the increasing demand for reading material among a rapidly expanding urban bourgeoisie. Since books tended more and more to be printed in the vernac-ular, the language of the people, rather than in Latin, the language of learning and the learned, this also meant that they could reach a less formally trained audience of readers (this of course Martin Luther already understood when, spreading the word of reform in the sixteenth century, he had the Bible printed in German). Thus, the sheer endless repeatability of the printed word allowed for more people to afford their own books and read more, and the more portable format allowed a reader to take the book to a place of their choosing (the bedroom was to become a favoured place or, monies permit-ting, one's own library) to do their reading in privacy.

Reading in solitude

Although silent reading had preceded the invention of print and was there-fore not a consequence of it, the shift towards reading in solitude must be attributed to a technology which, on the one hand, made this possible and which, on the other hand, was also readily adopted by the emergent theology/ideology of Lutheranism. The rise of Protestantism between the sixteenth and seventeenth centuries, with its emphasis on the direct, private and internalized relation between the word of God and the individual[7] – and its rejection therefore of Catholicism's adherence to the public function of the pope or priests as mediators of the Word – in effect encouraged the solitary reading and re-reading of the scriptures, thus leading not only to more individualized practices of reading but also to another mode of reading altogether: 'the eventual internalization of interpretive authority'. For, as Matei Calinescu has shown, once the encounter with the Word of God became primarily a private affair, the Bible was seen as a 'self-interpreting' text, where 'ultimate responsibility devolved on the ordinary individual reader, who was now both free and obliged to understand the Bible according to its internal logic as this logic disclosed itself in the process of repeated reading' (1993: 86), rather than dependent, as is the case in Catholicism, on the interpretive mediation of the scriptures by a priest. As such, solitary reading is already an index of the individualism which eventually takes Europe by storm in the seventeenth century and which in literary terms, as we shall see, generates that form – the novel – which not only can establish a more intimate relation between text and reader, but which is also the very genre, in Mikhail Bakhtin's view, 'that "authorizes" the reader as an interpreter' (qtd. Davidson 1986: 45).

The circulation of texts within the newly flourishing economy of book-selling and trading, where individuals would obtain books for their own reading in private, and where authors were increasingly dependent on such private sales, saw a sharp rise from the sixteenth century onwards; while in German-speaking areas, for instance, the fifteenth century was producing around 800 titles, the sixteenth century 100,000, and the seventeenth century could already boast up to 200,000 (cf. Gauger 1994: 37), France saw a 'tripling or quadrupling of book production between the beginning of the century and the 1780s' (Chartier 1991: 90), with secular literature, especially light fiction (but also periodicals and newspapers), eventually outstripping the demand for devotional reading material. Once money was to be made from writing, authors' names began to appear on their works (which had not always been the case in the Middle Ages), thus signalling not only the emergence of writing as a profession but also the need to safeguard the fruits of this labour in the cut-throat marketplace of rogue booksellers, illicit book smugglers, and foreign publishers trading in unauthorized, pirated editions.[8] With the introduction of copyright (in England its first statute was enacted in 1710; cf. Rose 1993: 4, 36), such a safeguard was given. As a legal definition of literary propriety and originality, it also prepared the ground for a new, individualistic conception of authorship, not based on the medieval notion of the assembler but what was to emerge as the Romanticist notion of the creative genius, an ideal which has remained with us until this very day. While writers would still have been dependent on a patron in the seventeenth century and sometimes even as late as in the nineteenth century (cf. Darnton 1990: 298) – a wealthy lord or king in whose service they would write, to whom they might address their work and to whose friends, often not unknown to the author, they would publicly present their work, receiving in return comment on this work, providing immediate feedback and judgement – the rapid expansion of commercial printing finally severed this personal relation of a writer to a specific audience (cf. Tompkins 1980: 210-14).

What emerges as a result is not only a notion of the author as a lonely, if extraordinarily gifted, human being, set apart from ordinary men and women, but also a conception of literature, not as an activity deeply embedded in the social and political context of the day but as an autonomous and aesthetically driven pursuit, that is, literature as 'an "end in itself" loftily removed from any sordid social purpose' (Eagleton 1983: 21). This is to say, once writing is not directed to a known constituency but produced by an impersonal author for an anonymous consumer's private response, its potential social and moral effect becomes less important than its effect on the psychology of the individual reader, leading to new literary expressions – among which Jane Tompkins cites 'sentimental novels, Gothic novels, the poetry of sensibility', which were 'designed to give the reader certain kinds of emotional experience rather than to mold character or guide behavior, and [were] aimed at the psychic life of individuals rather than at collective standards of judgment on public issues' (1980: 215).

From intensive to extensive reading

With the eighteenth century the entire landscape was therefore beginning to change, setting in motion a reading culture which very much resembles our own. Here, reading is less a medium for learning or improving oneself than an activity which on the one hand enables aesthetic appreciation (especially poetry) and on the other hand keeps one entertained (especially the novel). What characterizes the eighteenth century above all, as the book fair catalogues of both Leipzig and Frankfurt show, is the increased demand for belles-lettres, with poetry in the period between 1740 and 1800 rising at a ratio of 1:13, and the novel in the period between 1750 and 1805 at a ratio of 1:32 (cf. Schön 1987: 44). This indicates that the novel emerges as the period's most popular form of escape from the drudgeries of everyday life. Given the clear demarcation between work and free time that the bourgeoisie now experienced, and its concomitant division of labour between the roles of male breadwinner and his housewife, eighteenth-century reading is primarily for leisure and pleasure, with men, according to Schön, as readers predominantly of newspapers and non-fiction literature and women as avid readers predominantly of the novel (ibid.: 42). Thus, rather than devoting oneself to the reading and re-reading of the Bible for religious instruction, the reader of this era not only reads more, and moreover different kinds of literature, but also reads differently (ibid.: 50). The shift therefore from religious to secular literature, from sermon to fiction, is a shift which Rolf Engelsing has also referred to as one from 'intensive' to 'extensive reading' (1974: 182-3). What amounts for him in effect to a 'reading revolution' ('*Leserevolution*') he locates towards the second half of the century, when the kind of intensive reading that had previously and piously been deployed *vis-à-vis* the one book owned by the family – invariably the Bible – gave way to frequent, hence extensive, reading which, in order to fill one's spare time, moves quickly, in the search for amusement, from one book (or newspaper article, or periodical essay) to the next. Thus people began to read many a novel superficially rather than re-reading the Word in depth.

While it is true to say that religious reading receded in that period and that readers no longer followed the strictures of the religious calendar but chose their reading times at their own leisure (cf. Calinescu 1993: 86), and while it is also true that people read more, and more quickly, reading for distraction rather than instruction, the charge that extensive reading is superficial reading is not borne out, for example, by the spate of suicides apparently committed by readers of Goethe's *The Sufferings of Young Werther* (1774), following the deeds of the novel's hero to the letter.[9] Instead, if we accept Roland Galle's thesis as to the 'emergence of a tender, sensitive and empathetic reader' who, as Calinescu points out, is 'actually the opposite of Engelsing's extensive reader' (1993: 291), then what the so-called Werther-fever in Germany (or the 'Pamela-fever' in England, or the 'Emile-fever' in France) illustrates is that reading is not without its dangers, for it affects, it was felt at the time, precisely those readers with a more delicate disposition, such as the man of feeling or those with a rather gullible disposition, such children or women.

Since the novel is a genre which encourages a strong identification between readers and characters, it becomes the object of widespread critique from the mid-eighteenth century onwards. As Kate Flint has shown with reference to Victorian and Edwardian practices of reading in *The Woman Reader 1837–1914* (1993), the private activity of reading, with its tendency towards 'self-absorption', indicates not only a given reader's 'vulnerability to textual influence, deaf and blind to all other stimuli in her immediate environment' (1993: 4), but also that it is dangerous for women in particular, given their apparent predilection for over-identification, which, it was feared, would lead them, not unlike Cervantes' Don Quixote, to act out, or at least act upon, fancy ideas encountered in reading. The distrust therefore of novels with a romantic twist, which might leave 'the gentle sex' with false expectations about marriage, and result in a sense of dissatisfaction with the reality of their own lives compared to a book's world of fantasy, is based on the assumption not only that reading is a form of escapism but also that reading might 'teach politically seditious attitudes, especially, but not exclusively, challenging the role of the family and the position of woman in relation to authority' (ibid.: 24). The argument then that reading fiction could be dangerous, and squandered time which might otherwise have been used for praying (or housework), continues well into the nineteenth century, only to be superseded at the beginning of the twentieth century by similar attitudes voiced about early (and especially female) cinema spectators (see chapter 3), and more recently in terms of the debate about violence on TV, which addresses itself to the potentially negative effects of screen images on minors.

The passage from the eighteenth century, which paved the way for modern habits of reading, into the nineteenth was one not of qualitative but of quantitative difference (cf. Schön 1987: 51). The expansion of book production, made possible by the invention around 1860 of pulp, made no longer from rags but from an endless supply of wood (cf. Martin 1994: 402), providing the raw material for cheap, mass-produced novels, not as artefacts to be preserved but as affordable products to be consumed and then discarded (cf. Raven et al. 1996: 8-9), for an increasingly more literate population and an accordingly broader readership, marked the beginnings of the kind of a mass society whose 'Philistine' tastes would later be deplored by critics such as Matthew Arnold or F. R. Leavis (see chapter 5). Thus, popular forms of entertainment, whether in the form of the serialized novel or pulp fiction or in the experience of the variety format of picture palace programmes, catered for a population whose common denominator – the reformers of the time suspected – was geared towards pleasure-seeking or thrills rather than moral edification. What the industrialized nineteenth century with its machinery relentlessly working around the clock, and its systems of transportation steadily spreading across the land and the globe, created was an environment which by the end of the century was characterized by a 'neurotic' population in 'urgent need for stimuli' (Benjamin 1973 [1939]: 132). Here, reactions are physical rather than contemplative (see chapter 3), and entertainment stirs the emotions or, as is the case with the moving pictures in particular, 'assault[ing]', in Kracauer's view, 'every one of the senses using every possible means' (1987 [1926]: 92). If the cinema cashed in on a growing mass audience by the beginning of the twentieth century, it could already draw on a new reading public which had demanded not only more, but also new kinds of narratives for entertainment. A new consumer audience emerges from the 1850s onwards, one that by the twentieth century, as Clive Bloom has shown, cuts across classes in its mutual hunger for reading new stories and genres, be they horror, sensation, or detective fiction, thus changing the contents of fiction over the course of the century as well as 'stripp[ing] it of its *style*', with its '*utility* function [...] no longer in its moral trajectory but in its offering practical aid towards relaxation and escape' (1996: 69).

This alliance between technology, market forces and aesthetics is perhaps nowhere more evident than in the rise of the motion picture industry. If 'the novel is the only literary genre to have been invented since the invention of printing, and its literary history is inseparable from the history of its publication' (Feather 1988: 57), film is the art form which provides the first stepping stone towards a culture based on the screen rather than paper. The technological devices at the cinema's disposal, which draw its audiences into the reality-effect of the screen image and provide an escapism unmatched by the printed word, and have therefore raised from its very inception debates about the dangers and lures of the image, culminate most fervently in the effacement between seen and lived experience which virtual reality technology now offers and will no doubt soon perfect. If two centuries ago critics began to deplore the psychological and physiological effects that over–identification with a character in the world of fiction can have on a given reader, a century hence critics might well point to the devastating physical dependencies that the 'lived' sensory simulation might yet exert on us (see chapters 3 and 4). Whether virtual reality will one day be an art form or a dangerous hallucinatory space, how it will affect the way we see and think, how and what we will be reading in an age dominated by digital technology, and what such a future holds is not to be settled by the historian of reading, but might better be glimpsed from the science fictions of current cyberpunk writers such as William Gibson or Bruce Sterling. That practices of reading will alter with the increased use of electronic hypertext, which allows readers interactively to engage with, assemble, rewrite and in effect 'author' or 'auctor' new versions of virtual texts, so much is clear. That the form of the book is currently entering a new phase is also clear, not least because a story-on-a-floppy, such as Gibson's *Agrippa*, which erases itself as part of the reading process, is a testament to this. However, if scientists are currently still busy reading cyberpunk pulp fictions as blueprints for their own inventions, then neither the so-called end of the book nor the exhaustion of reading is yet in sight, despite many a gloomy prediction (cf., for instance, Lyotard 1988: xv) and despite the euphoria as to what the new media can offer.

2 The Material Conditions of Reading

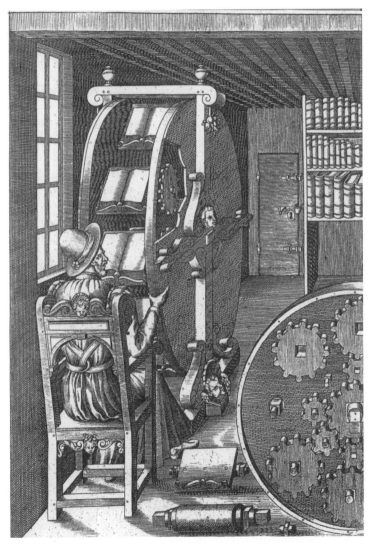

Figure 3 This reading machine is illustrated in Agostino Ramelli's *Le Diverse et Artificiose Machine* (Paris 1588; copperplate by Jean de Gourmont II).

It is simply not true to say that 'in reading a printed text the individual letters and verbal signs do not have individual qualities for us; they simply do not matter', as Roman Ingarden claims (1974: 20n.). The metaphorical usage of 'matter' merely elides the actual material constitution of the printed sign. In bracketing this out, Ingarden formulates a programme for the mentalist determination of the literary object as a transparent vehicle for the meaning and interpretive acts in which the text consists *for* consciousness. There could be no clearer statement of the fact that, for Ingarden, as for many other literary theorists, the book we hold in our hands is invisible to us. One of the lessons we can learn from historians of print is that books have bodies and letters have form. If we do not choose to see this, then it is because we assume that a reader's engagement with a given work operates solely at a linguistic level. In literary circles we are apt to think of textuality, reading and interpretation as conceptual issues, and tend to ignore that all written texts bring into play *content, form and matter*, that is, they engage not just 'linguistic' but also 'bibliographical' (McGann 1991: 56-7) as well as medium-specific codes. Roger Chartier's point 'that there is no text apart from the physical support that offers it for reading (or hearing), hence there is no comprehension of any written piece that does not at least in part depend upon the forms in which it reaches its reader' (1994: 9), is an insight which has serious implications for the study of literature. For Chartier, a historian of the book, any given text's meaning is inextricably bound up with its material manifestations, and, if this is so, it is clearly not sufficient to focus exclusively on a text's verbal, poetic and narrative patterns; rather, attention must equally be paid to a text's oral incarnation (its embodiment by a speaker), or its anatomy (its physical inscription on the page) and morphology (the changing forms as part of its history of transmission). This is to say, we should never ignore a 'book's total form' (McKenzie 1981, qtd. McDonald 1997: 107), whether it boasts this or that typography, appears in this or that edition, or is the product of a hand-written artefact, a printed copy, or an electronic version, because all these factors have an effect on the contents of our readings as well as the forms themselves that our practices of reading take, whether we read aloud or silently, monastically, scholastically or for leisure, publicly or in private, intensively or extensively.

The thesis that the book's materiality has an impact on the contents of our readings is very much the grounding insight of textual criticism, a discipline concerned with how the physical forms of a text (page layout, typeface, book design, even punctuation) affect not just a given text's meaning but therefore also the way in which it can be interpreted – an effect, textual critics illustrate, which is further amplified with each successive (re-)editing and (re)printing of a given work. This is distinct from saying that the materiality of the book affects modes of reading, an insight derived from the history of the book, a discipline which traces the evolution of the book, examining the ways in which its different physical forms – handwritten, printed, electronic – have impacted on our experience of reading – indeed, have altered our habits and practices of reading over time. Whereas historians of the book are very concerned with what reading meant in the lives of (ordinary) people, what they read, where, and when, and even how they read (the forms their practices of reading took), textual critics[1] are concerned with the life-cycle so to speak of a text's history of physical transformation, as well as the kinds of meanings readers therefore construe from a text. In any case, what matters to both are the material processes which underpin the production, distribution and reception of the written word.

Chapter 1 drew on insights of historians of the book to show how '[t]rans-formations in the book and transformations in reading practices necessarily went hand in hand' (Cavallo and Chartier 1999: 15). This chapter returns to material considerations, albeit from the perspective of textual criticism, in order to demonstrate how the transformations of a given text by its editors and the transformations at the level of the contents of the readings them-selves necessarily go hand in hand. While the material conditions of reading are the focus here, in chapter 6 I turn to the philosophical conditions of the possibility of reading; and, when we do so, we should keep in mind – because theorists tend not to – that a book's material forms, just as a text's physical 'formatting', have very palpable effects on interpretation and reading. This is by no means to suggest that literary-theoretical approaches do not yield important insights about readers and reading. Such theories can tell us a lot about the ways in which readers make sense of texts, or conversely how texts resist readers' attempts at deriving meaning from them. What they do not touch on, however, are issues to do with materiality or physicality. Not only is the body of the reader resolutely excluded from such theories, but the body of the text is ignored too. What historians of the book and textual critics largely offer, then, is an alternative to the work of reader-oriented literary the-orists, since, unlike the latter, they do not approach texts and readers as if both were without material circumstance or immune to historical contingency.

Expressive function of print

With works as obviously ornamented as Blake's illuminated texts, as typo-graphically striking as Apollinaire's *calligrammes*, or as subtly visually composed as Pound's *Cantos*, it is manifestly not the case that the 'formatting' of the page has nothing to do with these works' meaning.[2] This, literary critics, literary theorists and textual critics would certainly agree on. And with similar conviction it can also be said that poetry in particular, and very deliberately, exploits the physical features of the page through layout and typeface, just as the novel is not exempt from print's expressive function as a carrier of meaning. This latter point is perhaps less important to literary critics and theorists than it is to historians of the book, who see the novel's rise as a genre indissociable from the mode of its production as a portable book, a format which was made possible by Gutenberg's invention of the printing press (see chapter 3). That certain novels very self-consciously 'comment physically on their material existence', and that the 'physical form of the novel' is therefore a crucial aspect of their meaning as texts, is also something which Michael Kaufmann argues many critics are not willing to concede (1994: 14). However, just as the marbled, black, blank and missing pages in Laurence Sterne's *The Life and Opinions of Tristram Shandy* (1759-67) play a crucial role in that work's signification, so a careful reading of James Joyce's *Ulysses* (1922) will reveal the interplay between materiality and ideation in the ways in which Joyce used pagination as an integral part of the novel's symbolic meaning (cf. John Kidd, summarized in McKenzie 1999: 58-60). As these cases indicate, it would only ever be a partial view of literature then to say that (narrative or poetic) form is inseparable from content. But can literary critics and theorists go one step further, and take on board that the message is as inseparable from the medium as content is from form, thus supplementing form and content with matter? And what if matter did not merely *affect* meaning but, taking a McLuhanite path, as the print historian D. F. McKenzie seems to, if it were the case that 'forms *effect* sense' (1999: 18; my emphasis)?[3]

Let me present then the case in the manner in which a textual critic such as Jerome J. McGann would, and say that 'the advent of meaning as a material event [...] is coterminous (in several senses) with its textual execution' (1991: 11). If we take the issue to heart that a particular physical form in which a given text appears affects both that work's meaning and our reading of it, what if that same text were to appear in a new object, whose forms had also changed? This is, of course, at the centre of the project of textual criticism, since its concerns, as I have already said, revolve largely around issues to do with a work's history of textual transmission, that is, how a work is materially and therefore also conceptually changed by those who (re-)edit and (re)print it. Let me ask this, then: are the editions which Sterne had prepared for *Tristram Shandy's* original publications still the same works as those of contemporary editions, say, by Penguin (1967, 1997)? For a start, Sterne's novel was published serially, and not in one volume. If we were to compare the contents of these editions with the modern paperback, aside from the immediate differences in book design, we would find that the Penguin edition does with only minor alterations follow the verbal text of the first serial volumes. It also includes the marbled, black, blank and missing pages, which numerous other editions simply miss out but refer to in their edition's textual apparatus. Clearly, the Penguin editor did not share the stance of many other editors that the medium of print is of secondary importance to this work's meaning. And yet, the Penguin marbled pages, mass-produced as they are, are reproduced uniformly across the entire print-run in black and white, and therefore lack the specificity of the colourings which were produced for the first edition of the third volume of *Tristram Shandy*. How then might this be said to have impinged on the interpretation of this novel?

As McKenzie has shown, the marbled pages of Sterne's editions are unique by virtue of having been done by hand: this is not only because they are a product of chance, and therefore a radically indeterminate sign within each edition of the work, but also because they are necessarily different from one edition to the next. This is not the case, of course, once these very pages are mass-reproduced. If in the original editions they symbolized a uniqueness through which its author commented on his work as an artefact rather than as a run-of-the-mill printed copy, it follows that the inclusion of these pages might well have sought 'to embody an emblem [...] of the very instability of text from copy to copy' (McKenzie 1999: 36). To print the marbled pages uniformly in black and white is to remove this particular level of the work's signification, while to leave them out altogether is to curtail the reader's active participation in producing the novel's meaning. Since the said pages cannot but interrupt a reader's reading of the content of the narrative, not only do these features therefore foreground the materiality of books, and with it the artifice of the narrative, but they also invite the reader to fill in those narrative gaps which are quite literally left open by an empty or absent page. What the existence of different editions of Sterne's novel illustrates is that neither a text nor its meanings are ever stable, for what ostensibly is the 'same' text, namely the work entitled *The Life and Opinions of Tristram Shandy*, is in effect a number of different texts, each of which prompts a reader's responses in distinct ways.

For a textual critic to say that a text or meaning is unstable is very different from the same claim made by a literary theorist. As noted in chapter 6, the Yale critics regard all texts as unstable because of 'a built-in fatality of language' (Miller 1989: 157-8) and not, as is the argument here, because of a text's changing material conditions. As McGann illustrates this issue in *The Textual Condition* (1991), when a book gets edited, printed and reprinted, changes to its material condition invariably occur, which do alter this work's respective comprehensions. This is, of course, amplified in such cases as when there exist competing manuscripts and/or editions by an author of 'one' of his or her particular works, and an editor has to decide which copy-text to adopt for the new edition. But it is not only authors who rewrite their own work (as is evident from the existence of multiple manuscripts), thereby changing a given work's potential meanings. Editors too are rewriters (cf. McKenzie 1999: 2, 25).[4] This is because '[e]very new edition', as McGann says, 'is an act of re-imagining and redefining a text's audience(s) and its ways of interacting with those audience(s)' (1991: 66-7). It would therefore be a mistake to think 'that editors "establish" the texts that critics then go on to "interpret"'; rather, it is the case that '[a]ll editing is an act of interpretation' (ibid.: 27).

Instability of the textual object

Take Christa Wolf's *Cassandra*, for instance, of which two different editions, each appearing in different countries (under the different political imperatives which formerly divided West from East Germany), resulted in changes to the sequencing of the work's internal structure, which produced very different meanings for each respective edition. Wolf's narrative of

Cassandra is a feminist rewrite of the myth, in which Cassandra, the prophet who is silenced because she is not believed, is given a voice by the well-known GDR writer. This voice itself was first heard in the form of five lectures which Wolf delivered at the University of Frankfurt in 1982. The first four lectures (two travelogues, a diary and a letter) recount the genesis of Wolf's Cassandra project, and culminate in the fifth, a story in the form of a monologue by Cassandra; together they unfold a portrait of a female figure whose world is torn apart by wars and violence. While the impetus behind the work was to show up the parallels between Cassandra's world and the contemporary arms race in its relation to patriarchal structures, the force of the writing comes by way of bringing together different genres (such as auto-biography and epistolary and travel writing), many of which are specifically drawn from conventions associated with women novelists. As Edith Waldstein has pointed out, this is done to allow a woman character to find the 'maximum of expression' in a world where women have systematically been silenced for 3000 years (1987: 197). The sequence in which the lectures were given, and subsequently published in East Germany by Aufbau-Verlag in 1984, is crucial in terms of understanding the innovations to literary form that Wolf undertook in writing *Cassandra* as a work which deliberately inter-laces the critical with the creative. However, when the work first appeared in the West German edition by Luchterhand in 1983, it was only available as two books. No longer 'one' work, assembled from fragments and different styles, it had become neatly separated into a more readily recognizable literary format: literary-critical essays in one volume (*Voraussetzungen einer Erzählung: Kassandra*) and the story in the other (*Kassandra: Erzählung*).[5] Similarly, the English edition, by Virago (1986), undertakes an equally subtle literary revision as regards the physical form of the book: in placing the Cassandra mono-logue at the opening, that is, before the four lectures which it was meant to follow, and by omitting the bibliography which Wolf provided at the end of her work, this edition deliberately privileges the fictional part, while para-doxically overlooking, and as a consequence even undermining, the sense of the work as an innovative novel – a kind of novel-as-draft. Precisely because the sequencing and order of the chapters, just as the themes explored within the work as a whole, place an 'emphasis on process, on coming to authorship' (Waldstein 1987: 197), which both the Virago edition and the two West German volumes ignore, neither presents what is so important to Wolf's writ-ing aesthetic: the search for a means, via the 'mixing and untraditional use of genres' (ibid.), of giving women a voice in literature and society.

As the publications of Wolf's *Cassandra* show, the original did not remain fixed, but its physical form changed, changing in turn what was once an innovative literary form, playing with the conventions of the novel form, into a more conventional literary form. The mistake made by literary critics, in McGann's view, is to approach literary works as if they never varied, as if 'originals' remained 'fixed for good' (1991: 184). For McGann, as the editions of *Tristram Shandy* just as those of *Cassandra* illustrate so well, the opposite is true: 'no such stability in the material object can be assumed with respect to texts' (ibid.: 185). Nor – crucially – for that matter are different interpretations of a text, according to McGann, the consequence of variations between readers. While for literary theorists of reading meaning is not inherent in texts but is produced by readers, for McGann, taking a stab against this very argument, 'variation' is not located in the reader but is 'the invariant rule of the textual condition' (ibid.). This is why '[i]interpretive differentials (or the freedom of the reader) are not the origin or cause of the variation, they are only its most manifest set of symptoms' (ibid.). What he is suggesting here is that prior to the activities of particular readers, and prior to the production of particular readings, the very possibility of reading is conditioned by the physical form that the book-as-artefact takes. The kind of form will therefore determine the kind of reading, and the range of readings possible for or available to readers. McGann offers a means of accounting for specific readings, not on the basis of an ideal reader's responses to an unchanging set of marks on the page, but of a reader whose readings vary historically (and in the case of *Cassandra* even nationally) according to the changing material conditions of a text.

It is this aspect of textual criticism which is crucial not only for the study of a text's production history but also for its reception history. Not only does this mean that a text is always subject to *mediation* by authorities other than the author him- or herself, but it also means that we would be quite wrong to assume that the *medium* in which a given text comes to us is a transparent conduit for that work's linguistic, poetic or narrative meanings only. Rather, it is as impossible to disengage the materiality of the text from its meaning as a work as it is to disengage the understanding of a work from the physical forms in which we receive it.

Histories of textual transmission

Perhaps nowhere has the *mediation* of a body of texts been debated more than with Shakespeare, a writer whose work is so contested that a play of his could now hardly be treated as 'a single, recognizable object' (Dawson 1995: 4). And perhaps nowhere is the dependence of a work on the *medium* in which it has been published quite so prominent as with Shakespeare, given that his plays were once theatre texts to be performed (the quarto editions), were preserved after his death as dramatic literature to be read (the first folio edition), and are now kept up to date as hypertexts to be interacted with (the MIT Shakespeare). Since the effort to present a Shakespeare play which resembles most closely or faithfully the original authorial intention is marred by many difficulties, not least because in Shakespeare's case there is no surviving manuscript from his hand but in many cases several competing editions of the 'same' play, theories abound as to exactly which versions of his work are to be seen as authoritative. More crucially in the context of this chapter is the issue, however, of what differences the physical organization of a Shakespeare text makes not only to the meanings readers derive from different editions of the 'same' work, but also how entirely different formats imply diverse readerships as well as new practices of reading. What difference, for instance, does the phys- ical form of the folio make as opposed to a quarto edition, not just to the kind of reading available but to who is likely to read these different formats? I will take these two issues in turn.

It is a well-known fact that John Heminge and Henry Condell, the first recognized editors of Shakespeare's plays, produced the first folio edition (1623) of his collected works several years after the bard's death. By claim- ing that their edition was 'Published according to the True Originall Copies', copies which they say in their preface were based on 'fair' rather than 'foul' handwritten papers, their aim is to represent the folio as the authoritative Shakespeare, with the bard's words now finally 'offer'd to your view cur'd, and perfect of their limbes' (Norton facsimile edn, 1968: 7).[6] In other words, Heminge and Condell mistrust the quarto editions which appeared during Shakespeare's lifetime of nineteen of his plays, which were usually sold at thea- tres and often without his name. This is because there was little certainty as to whether the quartos were penned by Shakespeare himself or stitched together from performances, and thereby also corrupted, it is said, either by a spectator or by a troupe of actors who reconstructed a given play to provide them with a prompt book. A close look at Shakespeare's 'Hamlets' bears out only too well the nature of the controversy.

And yet, even the first folio, despite Heminge and Condell's claim, is hardly an edition of perfect limbs. The folio in which the plays were set posed certain problems for its compositors, given that its format sometimes made it necessary to waste space, at other times to gain it, issues which, in D. C. Greetham's view, have impinged on critical interpretation. Following Charlton Hinman's insights, Greetham demonstrates that on some occasions this meant that compositors set prose as verse, since the latter takes up more space, while on other occasions it meant dropping lines altogether, creating gaps, or rather interpretive fissures, which might now only be bridged, and guessed at, by the reader. Indeed, questions surrounding the surprisingly 'rough, free and irregular' verse in the later plays might best be explained in terms of the physical nature of the folio as a format. As Greetham elucidates the problem, 'it may be that some of this irregularity (of verse-length if not of internal metrics) may in fact be the result of the setting of these verses within the much narrower columns of a folio (as compared to the relatively wider quarto columns), so that lines would have to be "broken" by the com- positor [...] not necessarily by the author' (1992: 287).[7] From such instances we can see that the Shakespearean texts were always subject to mediation by authorities other than himself, here the compositors. Moreover, as these examples also illustrate, we would be mistaken to assume that the format in which a text comes to us never interferes with that work's poetic form or narrative content, and therefore also with the ways in which a reader inter- prets a given work.

The respective formats of the quartos and the folio also bring home to us the close link between a 'book's total form' and its effect on modes of reading, insofar as the difference between a quarto edition and a folio edition can be defined in terms of a certain 'hierarchy of formats'. As Chartier explains, each format is associated with a certain kind of text, and therefore also with a specific practice of reading: while the folio 'must be set down to be read' and 'is, therefore, a university and reference book', the 'more manageable quarto [...] offers the classic texts as well as the new literary texts' for a more leisure oriented rather than scholarly reading (1988b: 310-11). In other words, the different formats of these books are designed to cater for diverse audiences. This opens up yet another question: what effect did the folio edition, addressed as it is to a more scholarly audience, have on the long-term reception and comprehension of 'Shakespeare'? To answer this question, consider the following argument by Andrew Murphy. Interested in the ways in which Shakespeare became invented as a modern author, Murphy illustrates how this process involved delimiting what was 'singular' and 'definitive' about his work as a whole:

As far as the Shakespeare text is concerned, this process begins as early as 1623, when we find the First Folio text staking a claim to authority by declaring that the singular texts it provides are 'absolute in their numbers, as [Shakespeare] conceived the[m]', thus centralising the author as the unique source of a unique - and definitely stabilised - meaning.

(2000: 198)

Given that the quarto editions were put together from performances, this makes their function twofold: they preserve what was *spoken* in the performance, and they serve as written texts for future stage versions. In either case, they are intimately linked with the forms of the theatre, not least because, as critics have pointed out as regards *Hamlet* for example, it is the first quarto which presents a more actable, if not to say more action-based, text (cf. Dawson 1995: 23, 27). The folio edition, though, in presenting the author's complete body of works, has another function altogether: it seeks to preserve the Shakespearean oeuvre for literature's canon and to reserve for its author a certain literary status. As its editors, Heminge and Condell, confirm in their preface, 'His mind and hand went together: And what he thought, he vttered with that easinesse, that wee haue scarse receiued from him a blot in his papers. But it is not our prouince, who only gather his works, and guie them you, to praise him. It is yours that reade him' (Norton facsimile edn, 1968: 7). Although they were actors themselves, it is as if Heminge and Condell present the first folio as dramatic literature to be read in print, whereas the quartos are part of a mode of collaborative textual production associated not only with theatre practice, but with manuscript culture per se. This signals something of the wider cultural transition in the Renaissance: 'between oral and manuscript culture on the one side and typographic culture on the other' (Martin Elsky 1989, qtd. Murphy 2000: 196). The difference then is one between an oral and a manuscript culture, which is at ease not only with collaboration as a mode of translating stage onto page, or even as a mode of original writing, but also with the existence of divergent multiple copies and a typographic culture which seeks to unify the corpus of an author and with it his role as sole creator of this work. The one harks back to a medieval notion of authorship where an 'author authorizes the circulation of his text and permits new copies to be made outside his control' (Chartier 1988b: 318), while the other already looks forward to a modern conception of authorship in tune with the dictates of print culture.

From manuscript to typographic culture

To put this slightly differently, if Shakespeare was working within a Renaissance theatrical practice that was essentially collaborative, which is why we would be mistaken to expect there to be a definitive or completed version of a Shakespearean play (cf. Orgel 1981: 3, 6), and was also comfortable with reworking materials already in circulation, as was certainly an accepted literary convention at that time (cf. Murphy 2000: 193), then we might even say that, compared to Heminge and Condell, Shakespeare still belongs to a manuscript culture, whereas the former already belong to an emergent print culture. It seems therefore that Shakespeare the author and his friends and editors Heminge and Condell sit at different ends of a publishing tradition, because he seemed to care less about adding his name to his publications (borne out by the fact that only one of the quartos published before 1600 carried his name on its title page; cf. Murphy 2000: 200) than they did: 'It had bene a thing, we confesse, worthie to haue bene wished, that the Author himselfe had liu'd to haue set forth, and ouerseen his owne writings' (Norton facsimile edn, 1968: 7). Since the effects of print culture came to be felt fully only in the eighteenth century, it was then that the very seeds which Heminge and Condell sowed truly began to flourish: to make one of Shakespeare where there had previously been many.[8]

What the appropriation of Shakespeare for the theatre (through the quarto editions) or for literature (through the folio editions) highlights is this: literary interpretation cannot be divorced from the physical forms which embody it, just as the meaning an author might hold for a culture cannot be divorced from the modes in which this author has been published. In this sense it would not be too far-fetched to say that Shakespeare's works, as well as Shakespeare's worth, have been successively manufactured by copyists, editors and printers alike. And it is here that the project of historians of the book, concerned with physical form at the level of the medium itself, and the project of textual critics, concerned with physical form at the level of a given text's 'formatting', both converge and diverge.

While the former focus on medium-specific questions, in terms of the effects a book's changing forms have had on practices of reading, but also on larger cultural and intellectual activity, the latter have sought 'to record and explain the physical forms which mediate meaning' (McKenzie 1999: 61), particularly as these forms, and with them the meanings they mediate, are altered through successive versions of the 'same' text. Although both approaches share a conviction regarding the importance of the materiality of the *book*, or the physicality of *text* respectively, historians of the book see the written word as a bearer and shaper of cultural meanings, whereas textual critics (something they share with literary critics and theorists) interpret the written word for its literary meanings. This difference is crucial insofar as the object of their analyses is driven by diverging concerns: one with the shifting context from oral to typographic culture and beyond, the other with the shifts that occur in a given work from one textual edition to another; one with the material forms of the medium of the book, the other with the mediation of literary form and content by material form. This is to say, to read Shakespeare within the context of the Renaissance at the cusp between manuscript and print culture is to read cultural-historically; to read the changing editions within the context of authorship is to read literary-historically. Both concerns meet insofar as changing notions of authorship are unthinkable without the shift from manuscript to print culture.

From print to hypermedia culture

If Shakespeare lived in an era that saw a transition from manuscript to print culture (and Christa Wolf wrestles with an oral culture in the age of print),[9] we are currently witness to another shift in modes of communication, namely a shift from paper to screen, from the material to the virtual. What then of modern editions of Shakespeare, say editions produced not in Gutenberg's medium but for a computer environment? For the study of drama in particular, since it hinges on the complex relations between scripted text and its staged versions, hypertext seems an altogether more suitable medium for approaching a literature that is in effect written to be performed (or written down after the performance) than is that of the printed book. This is because an electronic medium can successfully combine the textual and the visual, that is, can bring together the words of drama and the gestures of theatre. The MIT Shakespeare Electronic Archive Project directed by Peter Donaldson, Larry Friedlander and Janet H. Murray, for instance, is a videodisc project which seeks to link not only a variety of modern editions and photofacsimiles of early Shakespeare editions and give access to multiple performances of selected scenes as well as their filmic adaptations, but also to allow users to put together their own staging of scenes on a computer simulation programme (cf. Friedlander 1991; Murray 1997: 286). The advantage of such a collation of textual, visual and auditory materials over a printed variorum edition lies precisely in the comprehensiveness of the available documents and the ease with which the new technology can bridge the gap that many a scholar in an English department has wrestled with in the classroom for years, between the bard's plays as dramatic literature *and* theatre.

But is any given Shakespeare play still the 'same' work when it appears in a hypermedial environment? As we shall see in chapter 3, the mode and experience of reading a hypertext is different from the mode and experience of reading print. Therefore, reading a hypertextual version of Shakespeare is surely a different experience from reading a play of his in printed form, with readers encountering very different Shakespeares in each medium. The great majority of Shakespeare editions in print are, of course, heavily annotated. Despite the textual apparatuses that such editions carry, editors tend to follow the conventions of a single or clear reading text which requires a sequential mode of reading. Accordingly, an edition will be printed in the form of one textual variant, with additional information about other variants either in the footnotes or in a textual apparatus which is carefully separated from the main reading text, by being placed at the beginning or the end of the publication. Hypertext, by contrast, is an open environment, which can display the 'work in progress', that is to say, it can make visible a text's entire history of production and transmission in a windows environment, and can therefore present multivariant versions simultaneously. The vantage point for reading a given literary work in a hypertext environment would then be its facility to call up multivariant versions simultaneously, which might be compared and annotated, but also reworked into the user's own hybrid version. In other words, not only would this reader engage with the texts in a non-linear fashion via the practice of comparative intertextual reading, but the reader would also become an editor him- or herself, insofar as the technology enables readers to assemble or rather 'version' their own, customized edition.

Here the full force of insights from historians of the book, as of futurologists of the book and theorists of New Media, comes into view. Not only does a hypertext environment change our conception of what editing is, but it is also, as George P. Landow has argued, 'an almost embarrassingly literal embodiment' of the poststructuralist claim that readers are writers (1992: 34). For, if the reader versions his or her own text, this undermines the critical assumptions about authorship, originality and textuality which are based on Romanticist notions of the unified artwork as the unique and original expression of a gifted individual. If anything, the hypertextual reader is more at home in the age of the manuscript than in the age of print, since the spaces in the margins of the codex belonged to the medieval scholarly reader (cf. Bolter 1991: 162), who would add comments in those margins of a page – comments which a scribe might later even assemble into the main text of a new manuscript. A medieval manuscript, already a palimpsest of illustrations, lemmata and other glosses, makes it as difficult to maintain the hierarchy between centre text and marginal notes, or that of authoring and commentary, as it does in a hypertext environment, mainly because in both cases it makes it hard to delineate the borders between individual contributions which make up such a script.[10]

Chartier is quite right then to say that '[w]hen it passes from the *codex* to the monitor screen the 'same' text is no longer truly the same because the new formal devices that offer it to its reader modify the conditions of its reception and its comprehension' (1994: 90). The electronic edition of *The Works of Shakespeare* by Oxford University Press (1990) is not the same as a printed edition, and even when the typeface is captured and emulated in electronic form, as is the case with Michael Lesk's electronic replica of the first edition of *Tristram Shandy* (cf. Alston 1998: 283-6), Chartier's point is still valid. Whereas the printed text is physically unalterable by its reader (bar annotations in the margins, or underlinings), an electronic text by comparison allows its user to reconfigure that text, or any multitude of texts, on the computer screen. Therefore, the relation an electronic environment, as opposed to the printed medium, forges with its reader is entirely different, insofar as this new technology promotes this new kind of interactive 'reader-author' (Landow 1992: 117). The reader is akin to a writer, because he or she is not the passive consumer of a finished *product*, but – very literally – a collaborator in the *process* of text production and therefore also an active *producer* of meanings. In a hypertext environment it makes little sense to hold on to a notion of the strict division of labour between creating a text, reproducing it and distributing it, a division which came about only with the industrialization of the printing press. In this respect, computer technology is not just transforming both our concept of what a text is and what it is to make books, but also changing our experience of reading and writing. Several hundred years ago it was print which transformed reading and writing in Western societies. The fact that it is now the computer which is bringing new changes means that technology – to announce the topic of the next chapter – is a constitutive element of the reading experience.

3 The Physiology of Consumption

This attempt to describe the effects of the Sublime & Wonderful is dedicated to M.G. Lewis Esq.' M.P.

TALES of WONDER!

Figure 4 This illustration by James Gillray (1802), 'Tales of Wonder' (repr. in Cruse 1930), shows the effects of reading Gothic fiction. The women are listening to a reading of M. G. Lewis's *The Monk* (1801).

Few would disagree with the suggestion that reading can be 'a bracing mental exercise' (Q. D. Leavis 1932: 135); most of us, however, would be rather startled if our doctor advised us, as the medical profession in ancient times might well have done, to take up reading 'as a form of physical exercise on an equal level with walking, running, or ball-playing' (Jean Dom Leclercq 1961, qtd. McLuhan 1962: 89). In our own times reading is regarded primarily as an activity of the mind, and if exertion occurs at all then it is mental, not physical. Given our tendency to measure civilization and culture by their very distance from the body, we hardly ever concede that there is a corporeal dimension to reading. And yet, as Roger Chartier reminds us, '[r]eading is not uniquely an abstract operation of the intellect: it brings the body into play, it is inscribed in a space and a relationship with oneself or with others' (1994: 8). What I want to chart in this chapter is a history of reading which does not 'exclude the body from the site of reading' (Camille 1997: 40), but makes the flesh and blood reader a central concern.[1] My argument is guided by two assumptions: reading is not primarily an act of interpretation, but an activity, to borrow Maurice Merleau-Ponty's words, 'accessible to inspection by the body' (1962: 320); secondly, books are carriers of meaning, but first and foremost they are also material objects which determine modes and habits of reading.

Even if modern literary theory too readily falls into a Cartesian dualism, privileging mind over body, or ideation over matter, the history of literary criticism (chapter 5) provides ample examples of readers who are not disembodied minds, or solely makers of meaning, but are sensitive and sensual. Indeed, as Samuel Johnson saw in 1750, that reading fiction might 'produce effects almost without the intervention of the will' (Johnson 1969: 22) was a widespread fear in the eighteenth and nineteenth centuries, and did not disappear until the birth of the cinema, which became the new target for such concerns. Implicit in such critiques is a cultural anxiety that reading or, later on, that watching films and TV would amuse rather than instruct, or stimulate the body rather than the mind. It is attitudes such as these, culled from a mixture of what would now be regarded as dubious voices, and certainly largely forgotten ones, together with some canonical ones (as Johnson's voice certainly is), that will inform the bulk of this chapter.

Side-effects of reading

The most visible form of bodily involvement in reading was that of reading aloud, the kind of rhetorical performance where the whole body 'sway[s] to the cadence of sentences' (Manguel 1996: 45) and labours to express through voice, intonation and pitch the sense of a phrase. In silent reading, by contrast, the body is immobilized, even if the heart is moved. We remember from chapter 1 that it was the introduction of interword spacing which brought about the shift from reading aloud to reading silently, thus 'altering the neurophysiological process of reading' (Saenger 1997: 13). Once reading is conducted silently, the reader's relation to the written word becomes internalized, locating reading in the private, interior space of the mind. Since from the eighteenth century onwards reading aloud was no longer a dominant practice, the question becomes whether the bodily aspect of reading is lost among the newly emerging silent novel readers, whose only movements consist in the use of their eyes.

Whereas reading aloud was thought to have benefits similar to taking 'a stroll in the fresh air' (Bergk 1966 [1799]: 69), reading silently was feared to defraud readers of 'their proper amount of exercise, get[ting] their muscles relaxed and their health out of gear', not least because readers would 'sit over the fire and read a new novel or pore over a dreary journal' rather than 'take a good walk' (Austin 1874: 256). Even though silent readers show few outward visible signs of physical activity during reading, this does not mean that the body is not affected by reading. This is evident from countless treatises written by educationalists, reformers and critics in the eighteenth and nineteenth centuries, who thought that reading caused a whole host of ill effects. Karl Gottfried Bauer, writing in the context of sex education, blames 'the enforced position and absence of all bodily motion during reading, in conjunction with the altogether violent alternation of ideations and sensations', as causal agents of 'lethargy, congestion, wind and constipation' (1791, qtd. König 1977: 102). If immobility is unhealthy, because it leads to 'flabbiness of the whole body', to read 'horizontally' comes with its own dangers. Thus, three-quarters of a century later, a commentator in *Sharpe's London Magazine* gives vent to this concern: 'to read when in bed, is to inflict a great evil on yourself without an equivalent. It is to injure your eyes, your brain, your nervous system, your intellect' (Anon. 1867: 317). Here, as elsewhere, physiological concerns are immediately conjoint with ideological ones insofar as reading in bed is not merely immobile reading, but secluded reading. In the context of women this sparks particular social anxieties, as it engenders images of young ladies withdrawing quietly to the privacy of their bedrooms, so that they might lose themselves to the world of the forbidden pleasures of novel reading while safely removed from public, paternal or patriarchal scrutiny.

The writings of this period show that attention to the physicality of reading is now centred less on the mechanics of the body as a tool for expressive reading than on the involuntary physiological reactions in the body to reading. Reading 'horizontally', reading unsuitable material (particularly secular literature, i.e., the novel), reading too engrossedly, or just reading too much, are practices which trigger concerns about the dangers of reading and its many ill effects. These range from physical to psychopathological complaints, and cover everything from exhaustion, which Diderot experiences reading Richardson's *Clarissa* (1761, qtd. Watt 1957: 228), to fits of uncontrollable weeping over Rousseau's *La Nouvelle Héloïse* (cf. Darnton 1985: 242), to attacks of 'brightness', which Kant suffers as it 'suddenly spreads over the page, confusing and mixing up all the letters until they are completely illegible' (1992 [1798]: 211), to more serious afflictions of 'hysteria and nervous diseases', which a health report on women finds to be the case 'among the highest of classes' (E. J. Tilt 1851, qtd. Flint 1993: 58). Symptoms seem to intensify or multiply when it comes to excessive reading. In the case of the seventeenth-century scholar Peter Heylyn, it was thought to have caused his actual 'blindness as the "*Laboratory*" of his brain overheated and destroyed the crystalline humor of his eyes' (Johns 1998: 383); and in Johann Georg Heinzmann's assessment of 1795, excessive reading is responsible for the following ailments:

susceptibility to colds, headaches, weakening of eyes, heat rashes, gout, arthritis, hemorrhoids, asthma, apoplexy, pulmonary disease, indigestion, blocking of the bowels, nervous disorder, migraines, epilepsy, hypochondria, and melancholy.

(qtd. Darnton 1990: 171-2)

In an age which conceives of the world less according to the laws of Newtonian mechanics than in terms of a proto-Romanticist sensibility – where the world forms itself in relation to its environmental stimuli and the reciprocal growth of its own parts, and where man and woman need to be nurtured – the list of illnesses above, on the one hand, are explicable in the context of this emphatically organicist-physiological world and, on the other hand, account for a growing anxiety regarding the physical effects of print culture.

Reading-fever

Accordingly, the many diagnoses of the 'epidemic rage for reading' (J. H. Campe 1785, qtd. König 1977: 93) that swept across Europe in the eighteenth century must be understood as responses to the increase in book production which occurred during this period. It is not just that more readers could read; in addition, readers read more, that is, they read more extensively, particularly with regard to secular literature, but they also read more intensively, in the sense that they read with unbridled passions. These habits of reading are intimately tied up with the rise of the novel, which itself was a 'product of the age of printed publication' (Feather 1988: 150). As a medium for private consumption this new genre was to encourage total immersion in a world of fabrication and fiction. Thus, the many sensitive, passionate readers, who displayed an 'overwhelming desire to make contact with the lives behind the printed page' (Darnton 1985: 244), bring into focus a new attitude to reading and a new relation of readers to the book. The so-called *Wertherfieber* [Werther-fever] in Germany, or the 'Pamela-fever' in England, bears this out. Robert Darnton's research on the impact of Rousseau's *La Nouvelle Héloïse* (1759) in France also shows just how much readers abandoned themselves to their sensations. In floods of tears, with heart-felt sighs and pounding hearts, readers again and again wrote to Rousseau himself to report how his book, and in particular Julie's fate at the end of it, choked them with emotion (cf. Darnton 1985: 243). It is not just that readers tended to over-identify with the material, as if to live out the novels they had read, but the sensitivity of their reactions displays a deeply bodily experience (see chapter 4). The call therefore 'to inoculate novel-fever [*Romanfieber*]' (Johann Ludwig Erwald 1789, qtd. König 1977: 104) constitutes a moral response not just to a social disease, but to a veritable physiological condition. Critics analyse symptoms and suggest cures in an attempt to deal with a full-blown 'novel epidemic' [*Romanseuche*] (Heinzmann 1795, qtd. Schenda 1988 [1970]: 110), where '[e]verybody reads novels, including the lowest ranks' (Christian Viktor

Kindervater 1787, qtd. Schön 1987: 46) and where everything is being devoured with little discernment for quality.

Books speak to the heart just as much as to the head, and reading is food for stomachs just as much as it is food for thought. This is perhaps nowhere more evident than in the many eighteenth-century dietetic addresses to reading, where the language of physiology is not a gloss but acquires a literal explanatory force. One such treatise is Johann Adam Bergk's *The Art of Reading* (1799), which couches moral and aesthetic concerns in a language that makes it clear that reading matter is absorbed, or ingested, through the body:

> Never before has so much been read in Germany than right now. The majority of read-
> ers devour the poorest and most tasteless novels with such voracious appetite [*Heißhunger*,
> literally 'heated hunger'], in such a way that they debase head and heart. [...] The conse-
> quences of such tasteless and uninspiring literature are therefore senseless squandering,
> insurmountable shunning of all exertion, limitless predilection for luxury, suppression of
> the voice of conscience, world-weariness and an early death.
>
> (1966 [1799]: 411–12)

In a vibrant literary market where the novel had become the most popular form of entertainment, Bergk's critique of reading is directly related to the dangers it presents as a genre which encourages escapism and reading for pleasure and leisure. Although the novel became more respectable as a genre during the nineteenth century (cf. Lyons 1999: 314), gaining 'widespread cultural acceptance, though not exactly aesthetic legitimacy' (Brantlinger 1998: 2), it nevertheless continued to be cast as wicked, sentimental and delusional, at once the object of blame for inflaming readers' passions and the explanation for readers' evasion of, or escape from, societal duties.

By casting novel reading as a form of eating, critics such as Bergk align it with a 'lowly' bodily function. It is a critique not just of the genre but also of its indiscriminate readers. As Patrick Brantlinger has pointed out, the entire rhetoric of devouring – or consuming – fiction 'places novel-reading in the emergent category of mass consumption' (1998: 11). References to gluttonous novel eating can therefore often be understood as a means by which critics then, as now, distinguish 'the brutal sphere of textual consump-tion' from the 'gentler world of textual reception' (Klancher 1987: 137), as well as a means by which they draw a hierarchical distinction between low and high cultural production. By extension, this suggests that *the material sphere of consumption* is a consumption through the body, whereas the *more spiritual sphere of reception* is the reception through the critical faculties. However, since references to 'book eating' were not confined to examples of 'tasteless' novels, but were also used in conjunction with 'wholesome' litera-ture, this indicates that the rhetoric of eating goes beyond the distinction between low and high cultural production. For Carl Wald, for instance, an editor from Berlin, 'a wholesome, nourishing and authentically German diet' of books (1889, qtd. Schenda 1988 [1970]: 66) is a prerequisite for a healthy Germany. Hence, literature worthy of reading is also worthy of 'eating', because it has nutritional value. Insofar as 'wholesome' works of literature, just as 'tasteless' ones, have an effect on the body, the fact that reference is made to 'both effects', as Nina Baym has found, 'shares a conception of the novel as a substance taken into the body, there to work an effect beyond the reader's control' (1984: 58). This is also the reason why reading in her view operates in a very 'physical way' (ibid.). Textual reception cannot therefore be conceived solely as an act of mind, with the subject conscious and in control of what he or she reads, but extends to sensory stimulation – in this instance, as an ingestion through the stomach. After all, why else would Kant have it that 'thinking – whether in the form of *study* (reading books) or *reflection* (meditation and discovery) – is a scholar's food' (1992 [1798]: 199), or Friedrich Burchard Beneken compare memory to a stomach (1791, qtd. König 1977: 100) and Nietzsche recommend that one read like a 'cow' so that ideas might be mulled over slowly, ruminated, consumed twice (1967 [1887]: 23)? In all these comments, reading and thinking are processed physiologically insofar as ideas from reading are directly absorbed into the body's organism.

Such language cannot be understood solely in terms of metaphors. As Dominik von König has argued with reference to debates on reading-fever, these 'speech-patterns have moved beyond the level of comparison [...] and lead us directly towards the psychopathology of reading' (1977: 101). Similarly, Nina Baym finds, albeit with reference to mid-nineteenth-century reviewers in the American periodical press, that 'this language, whether of gustatory or sensual appetite, goes far beyond the elaboration of the submerged metaphor of literary taste' (1984: 60). In her view this:

testifies to the reviewers' belief in the compelling impact of the novel on its readers, an impact the novel seldom has in our own era of far more explicit stimulations. Both the subject matter and also the reading process itself were believed to be sources of an intense pleasure that reviewers distrusted yet had to accept as the basis of the novel's success.

(Ibid.)

Kelly Mays too reaches this conclusion *vis-à-vis* the stances adopted by essayists in the British periodical press between 1860 and 1900. Contemporaneous deliberations on 'whether the craving for books may not be a disease' (Doubleday 1859: 110) or whether 'reading [...] may be positively injurious' (Anon. 1867: 322-3) seem to confirm that such concerns were very real rather than just figures of speech. Indeed, 'these essayists insisted', Mays remarks, that 'the correlation between reading and disease is far from metaphorical. That correlation was instead both literal and directly causal' (1995: 174). This line of argument is all the more persuasive in the light of Nietzsche's claim that a metaphor was once a 'nerve stimulus', at least that is before metaphors became so removed from their sources that they 'have been drained of sensuous force' (Nietzsche 1988 [1871]: 82-4). So, even if we were to understand references to book reading as book eating in terms of tropes rather than of a pathology of reading, the physical in both instances presents a continuum of the physiological and the metaphorical as regards cultural consumption.

Reading addiction

When Alfred Austin comments on the way in which fiction 'is not read merely, it is devoured', for, straight after 'having finished' one book, 'they hunger for another' (1874: 253), he likens such a practice of reading to 'a vulgar, detrimental habit, like dram-drinking' (ibid.: 251). What he is describing therefore is no longer a *habit of reading* but a *reading habit* in the form of a bodily addiction, seemingly well 'beyond the reader's control'. This assessment of reading habits in England shares a lot with that of the vicar and schoolmaster Johann Rudolf Gottlieb Beyer in Germany over eighty years earlier. For Beyer, the 'voracious appetite' for reading matter is nothing other, we might say, than an all-consuming compulsion to consume more works of fiction, which is precisely why one can see:

> men and women book readers, who get up in the morning and go to bed in the evening with a book in their hand, who sit down at the table with it, who put it next to them at work, carry it with them on walks, and who cannot separate themselves from it, until they have finished reading it. But they have hardly devoured the last page of a book, they are already greedily eyeing up, where they might get the next one from [...] and devour it with a voracious appetite [*Heißhunger*]. No smoker, coffee-friend, wine-drinker, gambler could be so addicted to their pipe, bottle, games or coffee table than many a book-hungry reader [*Lesehungrige*] is to his reading.
>
> (1795, qtd. Schenda 1988 [1970]: 60)

Beyer's and Austin's avid readers are not characterized as healthy readers in search for wholesome food. In each case, the hunger is so voracious that it goes beyond a basic physical need; nor is the thirst for the next book anything other than an unholy dependency on the 'vice' of 'novel-drinking' (Austin 1874: 253). What strikes us in all these examples is that the behaviour is as compulsive as consumerism itself and as addictive as any other substance abuse. Indeed, there seems to be little doubt in the mind of the reviewer from *Sharpe's London Magazine* that 'the leaves of a book are as sure an opiate as the petals of the poppy' (Anon. 1867: 317-18). Once more, then, descriptions such as these point to a condition where psychophysical needs determine readers' behaviour. The term most readily used to sum up this condition in German discussions of the 1780s and 1790s was reading addiction [*Lesesucht*]. It is a term, according to von König, which has its roots in book addiction [*Büchersucht*], the manic amassing of books also known as bibliomania, which as an illness is also closely related to writing rage [*Schreibwut*]. When *Lesesucht* was first introduced as a new word, in volume 3 of the 1809 *Wörterbuch der Deutschen Sprache*, it was defined in terms of an 'unbounded, unregulated [...] craving to pleasure oneself through reading books' and the first stage of a more serious affliction, namely, reading rage [*Lesewut*] (qtd. König 1977: 92).

It should be remembered, however, that reading is by no means a bad habit *per se*. Only when it becomes excessive does it turn into a disease. As Johann Gottfried Hoche explains:

Reading addiction [*Lesesucht*] is a foolish and harmful abuse of an otherwise good thing, a truly great evil, which is as infectious as yellow fever in Philadelphia [...] One reads everything in a *higgledy-piggledy* fashion without aim, one savours nothing and devours everything, nothing is put in its proper order, and everything is *read fleetingly* and just as fleetingly then forgotten, which with some of course is a useful thing.

(1794, qtd. Schenda 1988 [1970]: 60; my emphasis)

This analysis not only highlights how contagious a disease reading addiction is, but also underlines another crucial aspect of the *reading habit* which brings about *new habits of reading*. The 'higgledy-piggledy' reading practices of the Englishman Sidney Smith, who apparently 'read four books at a time' so as to 'avoid the gloom which proceeds from hanging a long while over a single book' (qtd. Cruse 1930: 255), is not just an early nineteenth-century example of both 'superficial' reading (Amy Cruse's term) and 'extensive' reading (to use Rolf Engelsing's term); his need for overstimulation bears all the hallmarks of a compulsive reading that is as restless as it is nervous. In this sense it is also truly modern. The figure of the 'excited reader', described in *Blackwood's Magazine*, perhaps best personifies this modern reader, 'who tears his way through books, that appear to put him through the whole gamut of passions'. Not only can '[y]ou see him clutching nervously at the pages as if he would precipitate himself forward and anticipate conclusions', but he also 'rolls his eyes, and clenches his fists, and snarls in the concentrated energy of indignation', or 'he reads with rippling smiles, varied by occasional spasms of approving laughter' (Shand 1879: 255). If reading addiction drives readers to read more, that is, to take bigger and bigger doses to satisfy their addiction, it also drives them to read more 'fleetingly', in which case the overload means that little of what is read is truly taken in or digested, and little of what is read is therefore held onto in the mind.

Reading 'fleetingly' picks up speed in the course of the nineteenth century, as if 'readers were reproducing the speed of production, in the speed of their own reading' (Mays 1995: 171). The comment made by A. Innes Shand, that in the print-free pre-Gutenberg era '[t]here was no wear-and-tear of the mental fibres, and, consequently, there were none of those painful brain and nerve diseases that fill our asylums [now]' (1879: 236), must therefore be understood in the context of a mania made possible by the more efficient industrial means for the production of the book. In this respect it is also instructive to compare the analysis by Hoche from 1794, cited above, with that made by Shand nearly a century later:

With printing and the promiscuous circulation of books the mischief that had broken out in Germany was spread everywhere by insidious contagion, like the Black Death of the fourteenth century. But unlike that subtle and deadly plague, it has gone on running its course ever since, and diffusing itself gradually through all classes of the community. The ferment of thought, the restless craving for intellectual excitement of some kind, have been stimulated; till now, in the last quarter of the nineteenth century, we are being driven along at high-pressure pace; and it is impossible for any one who is recalcitrant to stop himself.

(1879: 238-9)

What is clear from this description is that the pace of reading, just as the pace of life, has accelerated to the extent that the very structure of experience has undergone a change: 'restless' and 'driven', but also fragmentary and discontinuous. The mind can barely keep pace with the tempo of modern times.

At the start of this chapter I suggested that a book's mode of production has an impact on its mode of consumption. We can now qualify this claim to suggest that print as a mode of mass production changed modes of consumption insofar as 'the promiscuous circulation of books' in the post-Gutenberg era brought about what Samuel Taylor Coleridge in 1818 had called the '*mischief* of unconnected and promiscuous reading' (1987: 40); that is, print not only determined how much readers were able to read and what they read, but also the ways in which they read. Since the novel is the literary genre whose fortunes were most closely tied to changes in modern book production (cf. Feather 1988: 96-7, 150), not least because unlike poetry (which given its size can be circulated easily) and unlike drama (which is intended for theatrical performance) it relies for its public existence on being printed, bound and mass-produced (cf. Lodge 1986: 156), much of the critique that was levelled against excessive reading cast it as the culprit of readers' ill effects. Since novels tended to be read silently and by readers who were on their own, a factor which helped forge an intimate relation between book and reader, such intimacy had only become possible as a result of print. Seclusion depends, at least in part (besides architecture, leisure time, income, etc.), on a reader being able to carry their book to a private corner of the household. Insofar as it was Gutenberg's invention that helped the manufacture of books small enough to be portable in the first place, the rise of the novel and its subsequent literary history cannot be divorced from this particular feature of its production (cf. Ong 1982: 131). If so, the materiality of the medium, in this instance the novel's size, had a bearing on matters of consumption.

Since the speed of production, another enabling factor of mechanized print technology, fed the rate of consumption, and was therefore responsible for the afflictions modern readers suffered, the impact of technology on physiology becomes incremental. This impact was by no means direct or linear, insofar as Gutenberg could not have predicted how his invention was to change the production, distribution, circulation and consumption of the book. Only retrospectively is it possible to see what effects this technology had on readers, or any technology has on society. The industrial age, with its increasingly efficient mechanisation – including that of print – must have seemed to those that were driven along by it like the train Émile Zola describes in his novel *La Bête humaine* (1890): an engine that hurries along the rails 'like a fierce storm sweeping all before it' (1977: 58). Technology is like a runaway train: we do not know whether it will accelerate and crash, or slow down; and even if we got off the train, refused ever to board another, this would not mean that railway travel were never to affect daily lives again. Our whole environment and our lines of communication have changed with travel, as they have with print.[2] Technology is a network, quite literally like that of the railways, which is as fundamental a part of modern society as is the central nervous system itself to our bodies (cf. McLuhan 1964: 53). In effect, this understanding of the relations between humans and machines is cumulative: the impact, or determining factors, of print (machine) on readers (humans), or of the railways on travellers, which have both brought about new modes of perception, are so interstitched with each other and us, and appear now so 'natural' to our way of life, that it is impossible to unknit physiology from technology.

The task for the remainder of this chapter is to outline the ways in which the age that Charles Baudelaire characterized in 1863 as 'an immense reservoir of electric energy' (1964: 9) was to amplify the physical assaults on those who inhabited it, so that we might draw a connective line between the technology of print, with its *transportable* and *movable* books, and other new technologies which transport us literally, and virtually, from A to B, or figuratively into a world of fantasy, to move us internally, stirring our emotions or putting our nerves on edge. The technologies I am referring to are railway travel, the motion pictures and the information highways.

Modernity and the assault on the senses

Everything associated with the modern age – industrialization, mobility and consumerism – and everything this entailed, from overpopulated urban centres, machinery working around the clock and the deafening noise of trains, to shopping as a new form of addiction, were factors in shaping a sensibility that had become, according to Friedrich Nietzsche in 1888, 'immensely more irritable' (1968: 47). Just as modernity's urban fabric is rent by shocks, fits and jostling, decomposing the social collective, so the reader is 'decomposed' by the constant demands on his literary attention. As one reviewer put it in 1859, '[p]laced among the countless shelves of modern libraries, we are like men with many acquaintances but few friends [...] there are so many new comers that a reader felt himself called upon to give up his best friend, to step across and chat with the smartly dressed crowd of strangers' (Doubleday 1859: 110). No longer does the reader get to know the book intimately, no longer does the city dweller know his neighbour, or the train traveller his companion in the compartment. Just as there is little time to make out one face among many in an anonymous crowd, or one image from the next when it is glimpsed from behind a window of a speeding train, so reading is increasingly marked by a fleeting familiarity that knows little of the contemplative tranquility of earlier times. It is as if there is now little time for the reader to think, reflect at their leisure, or truly digest. The mass production together with the mass consumption of books brought about the kind of 'unsettled reading' which Richard Steele of *The Guardian* criticized as far back as 1713 because it 'naturally seduces us into as undetermined a manner of thinking' (qtd. Watt 1957: 53), and which by the time Alfred Austin writes is in full flow: '[r]eading, as at present conducted, is rapidly destroying all thinking and all powers of thought' (1874: 252). As a 'practice' which, according to Doubleday, 'has rather gone out of late' (1859: 111), thinking, or at least original thinking, is no longer necessary when readers' minds are filled with the thoughts of others, or when men and women 'read, not for the sake of reading, but for the want of thought' (*Monthly Review* 1761, qtd. de Bolla 1989: 257).

That such an environment should create a 'restless craving' for excitement is a tendency which William Wordsworth found himself in the midst of in 1800, when he bemoaned what he saw as his age's 'thirst after outrageous stimulation' (1974: 130), an index of which he found in the extent to which the 'invaluable works of our elder writers', such as for instance Shakespeare and Milton, had been 'driven into neglect by frantic novels, sickly and stupid German Tragedies, and deluges of idle and extravagant stories in verse' (ibid.: 128). What Wordsworth is offering in the Preface to *Lyrical Ballads* is not only a critique of popular literature, as Doubleday offers again nearly sixty years later when he says that '[y]oung men now-a-days [...] read neither their Bible nor their Shakespeare enough' (1859: 110), but a glimpse of a culture which is yet to make itself fully felt:

For a multitude of causes unknown to former times are now acting with a combined force to blunt the discriminating powers of the mind, and unfitting it for all voluntary exertion to reduce it to a state of almost savage torpor. The most effective of these causes are the great national events which are daily taking place, and the encreasing accumulation of men in cities, where the uniformity of their occupations produces a craving for extraordinary incident which the rapid communication of intelligence hourly gratifies. To this tendency of life and manners the literature and theatrical exhibitions of the country have conformed themselves.

(Wordsworth 1974 [1800]: 128)

Wordsworth's observations on modernity share similarities with those of many later thinkers, such as Baudelaire, Nietzsche, Simmel, Kracauer and Benjamin, albeit that the latter tend to embrace, rather than resist, the intensity of physical and mental stimulation that an urban, and increasingly technologized, environment induces in its population. Sensory overload in Wordsworth's view is precisely that which has contributed to the *blunting* of the modern mind, just as the abundance of books together with the speed of consumption overstimulated readers to the extent that it *enfeebled* their minds.

Eighty-seven years after Wordsworth's diagnosis of modernity, Nietzsche gives his own, rather similar, account of modernity, even emulating its tempo and rhythm in the fragmentary nature of his style:

Modernity in the perspective of the metaphor of nourishment and digestion. – Sensibility immensely more irritable [...] the abundance of disparate impressions greater than ever:

cosmopolitanism in foods, literatures, newspapers, forms, tastes, even landscapes. The tempo of this influx *prestissimo*; the impressions erase each other; one instinctively resists taking in anything, taking anything deeply, to 'digest' anything; a weakening of the power to digest results from this. A kind of adaptation of this flood of impressions takes place: men unlearn spontaneous action, they merely react to stimuli from outside. [...] *Profound weakness of spontaneity*: the historian, critic, analyst, the interpreter, the observer, the collector, the reader – all of them *reactive* talents – all science!

(1968 [1887/8]: 47)

Life presents so many new and unseen spectacles, the passage seems to be suggesting, that these have become altogether too fleeting to absorb in anything but fragments. Since the very hallmark of modernity is 'the ephemeral, the fugitive, the contingent' (Baudelaire 1964: 13), it is this that sets into motion a different relation to, and perception of, the world.

This comes across in Edgar Allen Poe's short story 'The Man of the Crowd' (1840), whose narrator is seated by a window in a café and watches urban crowds milling through London. But when he tries to read significance into their faces, gestures and movements he finds that the 'rapidity with which the world flitted before the window, prevented me from casting more than a glance upon each visage' (1986: 183), thus frustrating his endeavour to give any order to what he sees. If the ebb and flow of movement is therefore too fugitive to be fully legible, or if shop window after shop window overwhelms with its confusing array of consumer goods on display (cf. Zola's *The Ladies' Paradise* [1883]), the speed at which the landscape flits by from the moving carriage of a train only goes to exaggerate the sensation recounted by Poe, namely that it 'gave an aching sensation to the eye' (ibid.). Thus, when Russell Reynolds, in an article on 'Travelling; its Influence on Health' (1884), says of the experience of looking out of a moving train that '[t]he eyes are strained, the ears are dinned, the muscles are jostled hither and thither, and the nerves are worried by the attempt to maintain order' (qtd. Schivelbusch 1986: 118), this in effect serves as a microcosmic experience of the industrialized age as a whole. Modernity not only leaves its populus irritable, it also makes great demands on the organ of looking, making itself felt, according to Reynolds, as it 'pull[s] at the eyeballs on looking out of the window'. In a flash the landscape recedes, and what the traveller sees are 'no longer flowers',Victor Hugo writes,'but flecks, or rather streaks of red and white' (qtd. Christie 1994: 16).What we see out of the window of a train, just as what we see of a moving train, Zola suggests in *La Bête humaine* (1890), remains impressionistic.This is a hasty kind of looking, where faces on a passing train go past so quickly that 'she was never quite sure she really had seen them; all the faces got blurred and merged one into another, indistinguishable' (1977: 56).What fiction writers such as Poe, Hugo and Zola give expression to is a modernist perception of the world, marked by a sense of agitation.

It is this agitation which for Georg Simmel makes the experience of modernity synonymous with an 'intensification of nervous stimulation' (1997 [1903]: 175), a diagnosis which tallies with Nietzsche's quasi-neurological, that is, a *physiological* explanation of the modern 'sensibility' as having become 'immensely more irritable'. Equally, Nietzsche's characterization of modernity as an 'abundance of disparate impressions greater than ever' shares Simmel's sense of the fast pace of metropolitan life, which confronts its dwellers, strollers and travellers with the 'rapid crowding of changing images, the sharp discontinuity in the grasp of a single glance, and the unexpectedness of onrushing impressions' (ibid.). What Simmel implies here is a direct correlation between city life and the cinematic experience, insofar as the experience of seeing crowds move hurriedly through traffic is just as applicable to the experience of seeing a landscape race past from the compartment of a moving train as it is to the dizzying sensations of watching the new technology of the motion pictures. Crucially, it is also applicable to the experience of reading 'fleetingly':

> in reading the mind is often in nearly a passive state, like that of dreaming or reverie, in which images flit before the mind without any act of volition to retain them. In rapid reading it is nearly in the same state as yours is when you are whirled through a country in a railway-carriage or post-chaise.
>
> (Anon. 1867: 317)

Reading has become hasty and impressionistic. Its socio-physiological conditions are *proto-cinematic*, in the sense that reading is now distracted, the kind of 'eternal distraction' which, in Friedrich Burchard Beneken's assessment, means that 'never a thought can be held onto entirely' (1791, qtd. König 1977: 101). The most striking aspect about this last remark, made by a critic who saw distraction as a direct outgrowth of 'reading rage', is the way in which habits of reading in 1791 uncannily compare with Siegfried Kracauer's descriptions of cinematic experience at the beginning of the twentieth century. The cinema-goer is *'addicted to distraction'*, says Kracauer (1987 [1926]: 93), because he or she inhabits the kind of restless environment where big-city living is as fast and intoxicating as the speed of onrushing impressions in the cinema itself. Thus, when Kracauer writes that, in the cinema, 'the stimulations of the senses *succeed each other with such rapidity* that there is no room left for even the slightest contemplation to squeeze in between them' (ibid.: 94; my emphasis), it is as if one technology replays the characteristics of another. Or, it is as if Kracauer, writing about film, has borrowed, or remediated, the words of C. H. Butterworth, writing about print: like the moving pictures in the cinema, so 'books of travel, science, poetry, history, fiction, *succeed and overwhelm one another with such alarming rapidity*, that the man who stops for a moment to take breath and reflect, is lost' (Butterworth 1870: 501). This brings us back to Nietzsche's point that readers, and we might also add the film spectator to his list, are 'reactive talents'. In an environment where distraction is the rule, this leaves little room for contemplation: here, responses are necessarily 'reactive', and the capacity to reflect is its casualty. It follows that, in such an environment, reactions are felt first of all at the level of sensations before they enter the conscious mind as reflections; that is to say, a reader's or a spectator's responses are immediate and visceral before they are mediated critically by the mind.

Just as Gothic, horror, and sensation fictions made their readers' blood curdle, 'quicken[ing] the beatings of the heart' (Mary Shelley 1992 [1831]: 7-8), and just as contemporary 'page-turners of cramp-inducing intensity' (Golder 2000) affect their readers' senses, so Kracauer has argued that the cinema 'assaults every one of the senses using every possible means' (1987 [1926]: 92). That discourses on the physiology of reading should be rehearsed in those on film watching bears witness to a certain correlation between the two media of entertainment. First and foremost, however, it is indicative of a history of reception, which foregrounds not just aesthetic considerations, or activities confined to the critical faculties, but also gives weight to what might be called a physiology of consumption. At this juncture it is worth pursuing the way in which the early silent cinema, a medium without recourse to the spoken word, makes use of, as well as makes itself felt in, the body, so as to chart connections between the *effects* of old media, such as print, and those of the new media on their consumers.

Eye-strain and eye-hunger

The claim that film is 'the simple, direct, and legitimate continuation of the book – Edison the new Gutenberg' (Behne 1978 [1926]: 162),[3] can be understood in several senses. While print ushered us into modernity, cinema with its restless succession of moving pictures became *the* art form to embody the modern pace of life. And while print culture, unlike oral culture which dominated the ear, began to tyrannize the eye (McLuhan 1962: 17), it is screen culture which puts an unprecedented strain on viewers' eyes. Fixed to the screen, 'the eye is overloaded', as 'skin, nose, ears, all remaining senses are shut out' (Bloch 1984 [1914]: 315). Repeatedly, then, film viewers complain about 'sleepiness, inflamed eyes, and headaches' (Schönhuber 1918, summarized in Hake 1993: 49), and reformers warn that film might 'permanently destroy the eyesight' because of producing 'an irritation of the retina caused by the confusion of images' (Dr Campbell 1907, qtd. Kirby 1997: 48). Such physiological accounts or medical treatises are all too familiar from earlier concerns about the ill effects of reading. Whereas Kant merely expressed concern for 'the pathological condition of [his] eyes' (1992 [1798]: 211), which he felt were 'harassed from all sides by the wretched affectations of book printers' (ibid.: 209), and consequently called for a change in the typesetting and page layout of books, Konrad Lange, a professor of aesthetics, has 'no doubt that the cinematograph has enriched us with a new means of promoting short-sightedness and nervousness' (1912, qtd. Schlüpmann 1990: 203). As this claim indicates, it is not just eye-strain which affects the spectator; the cinematograph is also a 'strain on the nerves' (Gorky 1985: 229). Undoubtedly this is one of the reasons why those addressing the ill effects of the cinema, such as the neurologist Robert Gaupp, saw little option but 'to demand that the state remove the *poison* that undermines the health of our growing youth' (Gaupp and Lange 1912: 12; my emphasis), a sentiment which echoes the nineteenth-century complaint that books are a poisonous 'opiate'. What is evident in such critiques, one to do with the dangers of reading, the other with the danger of the cinema [*Kinogefahr*], is that both dangers are explained from the viewpoint of physiology.

Indeed, the fear that the moving pictures either have a detrimental effect on the health of spectators or, at least, affect them in very physical ways is as old as the cinema itself. Audience reaction to the cinematograph, when it was first introduced by the Lumière brothers in 1895, is very telling in this respect. What the now legendary story of audiences fleeing the scene of the screening of *Arrival of a Train at la Ciotat* illustrates is not so much that they mistook the screen image of the oncoming train for a real train which would run into them, but that they reacted on bodily impulse. They experienced visual pleasure as physical sensation (cf. Littau 2003, 2005). Whether audiences thought the onrushing locomotive would turn them into a 'sack full of lacerated flesh', as Maxim Gorky thought when he attended the Lumière screening in Russia (1896, qtd. Leyda 1983: 408), whether '[p]eople leaped up. Some rushed toward towards the exit', as the film director Yevgeni-Barkov remembers (qtd. Tsivian 1994: 136), whether the Lumière train made them 'recoil in horror', as one reviewer reported in Lorraine, or utter 'cries of terror', as another witnessed in Switzerland (qtd. Bottomore 1999: 187), or whether spectators at the Lumière premiere sat there 'with gaping mouths', as George Méliès said he did (qtd. Gunning 1994: 119), what is common to all these responses is that they are first registered, involuntarily, by the body. This makes the response to a possible danger pre-rational: not the result of a naïveté which mistakes the illusion for reality, but the result of a forgetting of the conscious self in favour of the physical self, and as such an index of the way in which film 'affects primarily the spectator's senses, engaging him physiologically before he is in a position to respond intellectually' (Kracauer 1997 [1960]: 158), before he or she has the presence of mind to recognize, appreciate or analyse the artistry of effect.

Film-fever

Whether audiences satiate their eyes on the carnage of limbs in *Explosion of a Motor Car* (Cecil Hepworth 1900), sense the terror of *How it Feels to be Run Over* (Hepworth 1900), or get giddy from the kinesthetic motion of the phantom rides,[4] they will leave the picture programme satisfied that they have experienced a 'nerve-wracking thrill' (Hans Rost 1916, qtd. Hake 1993: 13). The cinema's penchant for spectacle did not go unnoticed in the early years of its appearance. Already, then, critics could foresee how a visual culture might come to replace a culture based on print: how 'the lust of the eyes [*Schaulust*], which intensifies in the cinema, diminishes our joy of reading' (Lux 1978 [1914]: 93). This is how one reviewer analyses the impact of the new medium on the pastime of book reading:

No longer do we want to string together prosaic letters into words, which tax the mind [...], but we want to enjoy our reading in pictures, do it with ease and at a glance [*flüchtig*].

[...] The joy for images abounds; we are now better disposed towards watching than reading, which is why everybody streams willingly and just as hypnotically into the cinema [...]. The public has put the dry book on the shelf; the newspaper gets skimmed fleetingly [*flüchtig*], and in the evening the hunger for images is satisfied in the cinema.

(Anon. 1978 [1910]: 41)

This passage is interesting in two respects. While it adumbrates the ways in which the book industry will come to share the market of entertainment with the film industry, and later on the home entertainments of television, VCR and DVD, the reviewer also harks back to the kind of hunger for entertainment which Wordsworth deplored as his age's 'thirst after outrageous stimulation'. Thus, just as readers were once hungry for words, or addicted to the pleasures of 'novel-drinking' (Austin 1874: 253), so movie-goers too are hungry for images.

Many critics feared that the hunger for stimulation, or lust for sensation [*Sensationslust*], had grown stronger than ever before. This is because, having become used to the pace of modernity and largely desensitized to its effects, modern men and women, Maxim Gorky explains, are 'reacting less and less forcefully to the simple "impressions of daily life" and thirst more and more eagerly for new, strong, unusual, burning and strange impressions' (qtd. Singer 1995: 99). That this is precisely, as Gorky concludes, what '[t]he cinematograph gives you' is also echoed by the German writer Friedrich Freska:

Rarely has a time suffered so much from eye-hunger [*Augenhunger*] as ours. This is because the telegraph, newspapers, and lines of communication have brought the whole world closer together. Here, working people, bound to their chairs, are assaulted by a welter of images from all sides [...]. That is why we suffer from eye-hunger; and in order that we at least materially satisfy this hunger, there is nothing so fitting as the cinematograph. Eye-hunger is just as important for us in our time as once was the potato, which made it possible to feed the rapidly amounting mass of people.

(1984 [1912]: 98)

The association Freska makes between film watching with eating is reminiscent, of course, of the discourses which likened reading with eating, suggesting therefore that film too – to rephrase Nina Baym's point about the novel – is *a substance taken into the body, there to work an effect beyond the spectator's control*. It is not just that 'the film-theatre is a fast-food restaurant for eye-hunger' (Strobl 1984 [1911]: 52), and that it serves up a 'bloody diet' (Döblin 1978 [1909]: 38), but that its unwholesome food is unhealthy for its consumer. Thus, movie-goers who 'suffer' from the condition of 'eye-hunger' are also often either 'dipsomaniac' [*trunksüchtig*] (Hardekopf 1984 [1910]: 45), or so 'hungry for pleasure', as Dr Edwards Rees points out, that it soon leads to the 'Picture habit' – a habit, moreover, of which he says that it is more damaging than other forms of addiction: 'not drink nor even gambling is so potent an instrument for the undoing of a people' (1999 [1913]).

We seem to have come full circle: what plagued the health of the nation in the late eighteenth century still plagues it in the early twentieth century.

We need only to compare what Rees says about the 'habit of "the pictures"' with what is said about 'reading addiction' [*Lesesucht*] around 1800 to know that novels and films have similar effects. Therefore, whether readers in 1789 are infected by what Beneken calls a 'reading epidemic' [*Lese-Seuche*] and what Erwald in the same year refers to as 'novel fever', or whether more than an entire century later spectators are affected by a 'cinema epidemic' [*Kinoseuche*] (Adolf Sellmann 1912) and have been attacked in their thousands by 'film-fever' (Max Prels 1922),[5] and are therefore either 'febrile' and 'feeble in self-direction', as Rees says about films (1913), or left with a 'flabby' and 'flaccid' mind or an 'enfeebl[ed]' brain, as Austin says about print (1874: 257, 251) – in all these cases the addictions, afflictions and diseases work effects beyond their consumers' conscious control.

Dazzling the audience

The assumption throughout this chapter has been that reading with the eyes, be this of words on a page or images on screen, is not exclusively about sense-making, but also about the experience of sensations. Neither book reading nor film watching therefore involve first and foremost an act of interpretation. Rather, as history has shown us here, they are activities of which Merleau-Ponty might well have said that they call upon 'the whole of my body as a system of perceptual powers' (1962: 319). Since the technologies of print and cinema echo each other at the level of perceptual modalities, it would appear that the technology of each age embodies its perceptual-physiological condition to which consumers respond. This is not to say that readers no longer feel affected by books, especially the novel, which in its current form has been around for several centuries, or that film spectators are immune to the effects of cinema. It is manifestly not the case that only the early cinema, when it was a new medium, affected viewers in the way they said it did. Contemporary action, disaster or special-effects films prompt bodily responses in their audiences too. One of the reasons why the cinema has been able to sustain and even intensify the visual shocks that send tremors through the body of its audiences is in no small measure owing to the kind of special-effects technology that another new medium, namely the computer, is able to generate. With this technology there has been a visible increase in spectacular film footage, so much so that those films which make use of such technology are often bereft of narrative content, subordinating the story to the thrill. What counts is the quick succession of spectacular images rather than the psychologically motivated plot lines associated with realist narrative techniques.[6] Once again, then, a technology without which our modern age is unthinkable promotes reaction over reflection. Fears that such forms of entertainment dumb down an audience are neither surprising nor new, insofar as Wordsworth had already associated the 'blockbusters' of his day with the enfeeblement of our minds. Had Wordsworth lived to see the projections of the 'cinema of attractions' (Gunning 1990) or its modern-day equivalent, the dazzling computer-generated hyper-real special-effects blockbuster, he might well have found his worst fears come to life on the big screen.

Commenting on the new visual digital forms, which are able to endow the film image with a hitherto unseen 'register of illusionist spectacle', Andrew Darley has this to say: '[t]hey are direct and one-dimensional, about little, other than their ability to commandeer the sight and the senses' (2000: 107, 76). In a similar way to computer games, such films create 'virtual realities', which are changing not just what we can see on the screen but how we experience what we see. Special-effects films are above all about movement and speed, hurrying us from one feast for the eyes to the next, prompting the question which C. H. Butterworth asked in 1870: 'what mind is not is not [*sic*] likely to be thrown into a state of nightmare and ferment by this dancing among disconnected items of temporary intelligence?' (1870: 503). Although Butterworth was talking about the innumerable items printed in the press, his observation that 'this hurrying at lightning speed from one part of chaos to another without one interval to arrange one's thoughts or sift all these strange stories into their proper places' (ibid.) is worth remembering in the context of digital culture, not least because it helps us to understand that technology does have effects on physiology, and that this is so across a whole range of different media: print, cinematograph, computer.

Dizzy in hyperspace

The twentieth century, framed as it is by the cinema's success in the early decades and the computer's in the closing ones, marks the transition from a culture based on paper to a culture based on the screen. Just as the introduction of the printed book brought about changes in the transmission, dissemination and consumption of texts, so the new digital technologies, given the immediacy with which we can now access, retrieve and publish materials globally, are altering the ways in which information is circulated and how communication takes place. And just as the moving image brought new forms of entertainment through film and new avenues for education through TV, so the computer is changing how we amuse ourselves and learn. Since the computer is a relatively recent technological innovation, the question becomes how much this technology has already affected the ways in which we write, read, even think.

The computer has brought new forms of art and entertainment, but whether e-fictions will become a new genre to challenge the novel, whether the 'cyberspace playhouse' will succeed the cinema,[7] or whether cyberspace, as imagined by science fiction writers and film-makers, will be more than a fiction, are futures which we can currently only imagine, since they are yet to be engineered. What we can state with certainty for the moment is that the computer makes possible two trajectories for the future of reading and our engagement with artificial worlds: one in the form of hypertext or hypermedia systems, which give users access to texts, images, film and sound by typing commands or clicking the mouse; the other in the form of virtual reality environments (VR), where users become actors immersed in cyberspace. The distinction that new mediologists have drawn here is broadly one between the computer as a 'symbol manipulator' and the computer as 'perceptual manipulator'. As Jay David Bolter explains:

> As a symbol manipulator, the computer is a writing technology in the tradition of the papyrus roll, the codex, and the printed book. As a perceptual manipulator, the computer extends the tradition of television, film, photography, and even representational painting.
>
> (1996: 257)

In hypertext the reader is akin to a writer who manipulates texts and images on the flat screen, whereas in VR the viewer becomes an actor whose senses are manipulated by neurological interface with a computer-simulated environment. According to this line of thinking, one medium, to adopt Marshall McLuhan's terminology, uses technology as an extension of the body; just as the writing quill is an extension of the hand, the other uses technology as an extension of the senses (McLuhan 1964: 99; McLuhan and Fiore 1967). This suggests that hypertext is primarily narrative, whereas VR is primarily sensory. Further support for this distinction can be found when considering the different implications these two electronic environments have for their respective recipients. In hypertext access to reading matter is mediated by a PC screen acting as a barrier between on-line world and user (an altogether more apt term than reader or even recipient in this context), whereas access to the simulated world in VR is unmediated given the direct response to the stimuli of the virtual environment in which users find themselves. In addition, one medium is based mostly if not exclusively on the alphabet (not least because of the reliance on the computer keyboard), and is two-dimensional just as print is, while the other medium is based predominantly on images, just as the cinema is, and appears as three-dimensionally, as the IMAX does. In this regard, hypertext is interactive and VR is immersive.

Conversely, it could be argued that all technology is immersive, because we inhabit a technologically saturated environment that is as 'imperceptible as water to fish' (McLuhan 1969: 22). Moreover, the technology of print does not merely manipulate symbols on a page, which we as readers then make sense of, as Bolter is suggesting. True, as I. A. Richards said, 'a book is a machine to think with' (1960, qtd. Duguid: 1996: 78), and a novel 'is a machine for generating interpretations', as Umberto Eco once also said (1994: 2), but a book is not just a production mechanism for ideas and meanings, it is also a technology which, as the history of print has amply demonstrated, manipulates its readers perceptually insofar as it affects our sensibility and sense experience. Although print, cinema and computer forge very particular relations with their users' bodies, and as such induce radically different 'reading' experiences for their consumers, the point is that all these media alter our sensory relationship to the world. Before we can speculate about the perceptual effects of VR, let me first say something about the way in which hypertextual systems manipulate our sense-perceptions.

The term 'hypertext' was first used by Theodor H. Nelson in the 1960s to highlight the new possibilities afforded by electronic text processing, a system most fully realized with the development of the World Wide Web (Landow 1996: 227). Unlike text printed and published in book form, hypertexts are virtual texts which contain prompts in the form of hyperlinks, allowing users to navigate their own pathways through a given text or corpus of material to create networks with other related texts or images, each link leading to another, ad infinitum. Whether hypertexts are designed in the form of self-contained CD-Roms, as disks or as networks available on-line, the reading practice they foster is not linear, but connective. For, although we read a given block of text on the screen in this way, we do not proceed through hypertext sequentially, as if it had a beginning, a middle and an end; rather, the hypertext reader moves 'multisequentially', jumping from one reading unit (called a 'lexia') to another, each textual segment joined to the other via hyperlinks, thereby producing ever new and unexpected connections between texts (cf. Landow 1992: 4). As such, readers of hypertext read *both* intensively *and* extensively (to borrow the terminology used by Rolf Engelsing to describe the shift in eighteenth-century reading habits; see chapter 1), insofar as the technology allows them either to study closely a given text's intra- and intertextual links or to zap through texts at great speed.

Hypertext technology makes a virtue then of what critics feared was already a widespread practice in the eighteenth and nineteenth century, namely that of reading 'fleetingly' (Hoche 1794, qtd. Schenda 1988: 60) or 'higgledy-piggledy' (Butterworth 1870: 501). For to jump between or call up different texts at the touch of a button, and be able to read several texts on the screen simultaneously, conjures up the figure of Sidney Smith, whose neurosis it was to 'read four books at a time' (qtd. Cruse 1930: 255). It is as if Smith was an early nineteenth-century practitioner of what a late twentieth-century technological invention makes possible on a global scale. Smith also, of course, epitomizes what a critic in 1859 sums up in the following phrase: '[t]he danger in this much written-for age is that of reading too much' (Doubleday 1859: 110), a danger which on the one hand translated itself into a widespread fear that books were being read indiscriminately and on the other was explained as a consequence of 'the great modern discovery that anybody can write saleable fiction' (Shand 1879: 243). It is of note that complaints about the ease with which 'anyone' can put themselves into print resonate with present-day assessments which either deplore or embrace the ease with which 'anyone' can produce and circulate documents on the Internet. Fears that 'printing and the *promiscuous* circulation of books' (ibid.: 238) made the reader into an 'accomplished skimmer' (ibid.: 255) in the nineteenth century are therefore in evidence once more with regard to the promiscuous circulation of texts on the Internet: according to Howard Bloch and Carla Hesse, '[e]lectronic reading necessarily evokes images of uncontrollability, of promiscuity even' (1995: 5).

When George P. Landow goes so far as to state that '[l]inking across the borders of books produces electronic libraries, not electronic books' (1996: 226), his statement is suggestive of the dream of the universal library as a 'never-ending book', to which any number of readers may simultaneously log on from anywhere. At this juncture the future possibilities of electronic text processing have also been interpreted as a nightmare. Although users are given increased choices as to what they read and how they read at any given moment, their 'nomadic roaming' through hypertext runs the risk of disorientation, according to Patrick Bazin (1996: 162). Just as nineteenth-century critics drew attention to the 'superabundance' of printed matter (Austin 1874: 255), which they feared made the reader's 'head' turn 'dizzy' (Butterworth 1870: 502), so twentieth-century critics fear that the loss of bearing in the information age is similarly a consequence of too much sensory overload, particularly because one 'cannot literally grasp an electronic text in its entirety' (Nunberg 1995: 18). Whether the electronic library can create the kind of order that will 'make it possible for readers to respond to the dizzying boundlessness of knowledge itself' (Bloch and Hesse 1995: 6), or whether it will only serve to amplify disorientation, is clearly an issue of concern. It is interesting to note therefore that a volume edited by Bloch and Hesse, entitled *Future Libraries* (1995), contains essays that, according to its editors, 'offer reassurance that we will not be entirely at a loss in the spaceless, authorless, bookless, and readerless libraries of the future' (ibid.: 12). Besides disorientation and dizziness, there is a further, more profound effect we can envisage as a consequence of turning our printed world digital.

If knowledge is no longer *contained* in the printed book shelved physically in the library, but *spread* across networks, this clearly changes the routes by which we learn (the acquisition of symbolic literacies); it also affects the way in which we think (the induction of cognitive behaviours). In hypertextual systems readers acquire knowledge by ceaselessly making connections between related as well as disparate data, a 'connectionist' modus operandi which Bazin says promotes interdisciplinarity. As Landow explains, 'the emphasis upon linking materials in hypermedia stimulates and encourages habits of relational thinking in the reader' (1991: 83), a point also echoed by Sadie Plant, who sees 'connectionism' as a hallmark of a system such as the net, or for that matter, the brain. As she puts it, '[t]he virtual library is a complex communications system in which contacts and junctions function like [Donald] Hebb's synapses, reinforced and strengthened every time they are made. Unused links may fade into the background, but nothing entirely disappears' (1996: 207). If, for Landow, the new technologies affect the way in which we think, for Plant they might be said to be changing what constitutes our hardware: the brain. Since any system, be it the brain as a neurochemical system of synapses or the net as a cybernetic system of hyperlinks, 'is modified by every connection it makes' (Plant 1996: 204), it follows that the net, just like the brain, is a self-organizing system where 'material modification and learning become continuous processes' (ibid.: 204-5). What Plant suggests here is a correlation between the way the brain and a 'parallel' machine operate and, by extension, a certain continuity, if not a blurring, between 'natural' human intelligence on the one hand and 'artificial' machine intelligence on the other. By implication, the suggestion is that a linear medium such as print cannot represent the complex synergetic operations by which the brain, as a massively parallel neural net, processes data. Or, to put this the other way around, the implication is that print, a medium which promotes linearity, has straight-jacketed us into a mode of linear thinking that was unthinkable in a pre-Gutenberg oral culture. It would appear then that the computer, because it is recharting the ways in which knowledge is organized and reproduced, is not only changing the routes by which we learn, but is also affecting our mental activities quite literally by rewiring our brains. Far from simply regarding technology as having an *effect* on physiology, Plant's thesis places the computer and the brain on a physical continuum. This indicates that the differences between hypermedia and print technology cannot solely be cast in terms of their different uses or of their very different effects on their users, but must be approached in terms of the different perceptual-physiological organizations the use of each technology entails.

(Dis)embodied in cyberspace

Hypermedia environments are virtual, and virtual reality especially, it is assumed, fulfils a desire to leave behind the material body in order to exist as pure consciousness in a space which is both virtual and immaterial. This emphasis on disembodiment, as if the body were excess baggage when floating in cyberspace, is born of a mentalist attitude, which has all too swiftly adopted a Cartesian privileging of consciousness over matter. What this ignores is that users do experience bodily sensations when interfaced with computer technology, whether a particular user is immersed in cyberspace or just tapping away at the PC's keyboard. We should not therefore forget that the computer as a window to the virtual world is as material an object as the physical book itself, nor should we forget that technology has real physical effects, a point elided by claims that see computer technologies in terms of what Jean Baudrillard, in *Symbolic Exchange and Death*, calls the shift from the 'tactile' to the 'digital' (1993: 61).

Virtual reality is a technology which promises to deliver what Howard Rheingold calls a 'combination of mimesis and mesmerism' (1992: 310). Equipped with helmet, gloves and body suit, the VR user is neurologically spliced into a fictional world. This is how Randal Walser, a VR programmer for Autodesk, analyses what virtual reality can offer that other forms of entertainment do not:

Whereas film is used to show a reality to an audience, cyberspace is used to give a virtual body, and a role, to everyone in the audience. Print and radio tell; stage and film show; cyberspace embodies [...] Whereas the playwright and the filmmaker both try to communicate an idea of an experience, the spacemaker tries to communicate the experience itself.

(1990, qtd. Rheingold 1992: 189, 286)

It is these qualities that have led critics to equate VR with an electronic out-of-body experience, a means by which users might wish to escape from the drudgery of their everyday existence. As an artificial reality, virtual reality alters our awareness of conventional reality, but in addition it presents an alternative to reality, hence the escapism which in theory at least it makes viable. VR is often referred to as a hallucinatory space, or described as a form of 'electronic LSD' (cf. Rheingold 1992: 353), since it is feared that users might become addicted – as reformers once feared of novel readers and cinema-goers – to what a simulated world rather than a real one can offer. An example of such addictive behaviour is also evoked in the following episode from William Gibson's novel *Count Zero* (1986), when the character Bobby Newmark describes the physiological effects 'simstim' (simulated stimulation) has on his mother: 'she'd come through the door with a wrapped bottle under her arm, not even take her coat off, just go straight over and jack into the Hitachi, soap her brains out good for six solid hours. Her eyes would unfocus, and sometimes, if it was a really good episode, she'd drool a little' (1986: 54).

What Bobby Newmark's mother experiences is typical of how immersive technologies are envisaged. In artificial realities, Brenda Laurel explains, 'the potential for action is cognitively, emotionally and aesthetically enhanced' (1991, qtd. Rheingold 1992: 286). This is because the distance between the fictional world and the recipient's real world gets erased. It is also because the subject itself is physiologically, medically and technologically enhanced or 'extended'. Unlike a book reader or a film spectator, Martha Newmark – surgically enhanced with a computer port in the back of her head – is literally hybridized with the very technology she is using. Thus, the human–machine interface which electronic hypertexts initiated as their readers typed or clicked their way through their e-fictions on their keyboard or mouse turns the erstwhile user of immersive media, whether 'simstim' or VR, into technologically enhanced flesh, an interface between body and machine. Martha Newmark is neither solely human nor solely machine: she is a cyborg.

Passive consumers

In this chapter I have suggested several potentially contentious points: a) that material objects determine practices of reading; b) that readers are not just sense-makers but read for sensations; c) that cinema promotes reaction over reflection; d) that technology reorganizes our cognitive and perceptual modalities. Since all these points adhere to an argument that it is technology and not human agency which ultimately has effects on, or even determines, cultural practices such as reading, writing and thinking, I might well be accused of practising a form of 'technological determinism', of which Marshall McLuhan is held to be one of the main modern proponents. Such an argument opposes, of course, the ideological stance taken by Raymond Williams, and subsequently adopted within cultural studies, which rejects the idea that technology could be an agent of cultural change and stresses instead how it is certain cultural conditions which make possible technological change.[8] This is how Williams puts the issue:

> If the medium – whether print or television – is the cause, all other causes, all that men ordinarily see as history, are at once reduced to effects. Similarly, what are elsewhere seen as effects, and as such subject to social, cultural, psychological and moral questioning, are excluded as irrelevant by comparison with the direct physiological and therefore 'psychic' effects of the media as such.
>
> (1990 [1974]: 127)

For Williams it is not technology that has determining effects, as if it stood outside a given cultural and historical context, but, rather, technology is itself an effect determined by socio-historical, i.e., finally human, causes. By contrast, I think that we would be mistaken to assume that culture depends solely on how humans make use of technology. Inherent in this argument is a humanism which increasingly sits ill with technological development, which neither has foreseen uses (as Williams also concedes) nor has intentions, but does, I contend, induce effects beyond its users' control. Williams's assumption therefore that *we* make use of technology or interact with it, or even that as humans we are solely responsible for having invented it, is too narrow a conception of its effects. At every point of our lives, particularly in the First World, are we immersed in it. We cannot escape technology, nor stand outside it as if it was simply a matter of pulling the plug. Rather, so immersed are we within it that it is hardly a question of how we make use of technology, or how we might master it, but that it has already invaded us. It is precisely for this reason that I have treated print, cinematograph and computer as objects of medical, neuropathological and neurophysiological enquiry, and have considered how each medium perceptually – and not symbolically – manipulates its user. The primary concern was not with an enquiry into the contents of each medium (what story this or that novel tells, or the kind of narrative told in images, or what kind of texts, images or fictions the computer has or might engender), but with how the medium itself affects those that interact with it or, rather, how the medium acts on its users. For a long time in the history of criticism we have examined the form and content of texts. Perhaps it is time now to turn our attention to the matter of matter.

Where Williams pitches technology against human agency and culture against physiology, I have been gesturing towards another kind of argument altogether: since no human culture is possible without an enabling physiology and a possibilizing technology, those terms are not mutually exclusive but, on the contrary, necessarily inclusive. Between the uses and the effects of paper and pen, the printing press, the cinematograph and the computer, there is not a gulf but a passage. And what this passage teaches us is that machines have made us what we are, just as we have made machines. I think it would be true to say that much of what comes under current debates in popular culture has in effect created this gulf.

Perhaps the argument which best illustrates this is that of Janice Radway, whose critique is directed against cultural critics in the twentieth century who assume that consumers of mass-cultural products digest books largely unthinkingly. When she analyses the ways in which 'the consumption metaphor', which casts reading as a form of eating, has been deployed by those who seek to differentiate low cultural production from high cultural production, she finds that '[t]he methodology that has arisen from the equation of processes of *comprehension* with those of digestion is one that centers on the particular object that is allegedly being digested unwittingly by *passive* consumers' (1986: 11; my emphasis). Firstly, her stance implies that reading is primarily an activity of mind, a process of mental comprehension. Secondly, she infers that such an 'equation' necessarily renders the consumer passive. While this latter point is certainly true, if we proceed from the assumption that all that readers do is make meaning ('active' readers), in the sense that they might even resist dominant meanings (cultural studies' favoured 'resisting reader'), or do not make meaning (passive dupes), then this is the only logical conclusion for a politically engaged 'mentalist' argument. What such an argument overlooks is the body as a site of knowledge, be this in terms of readers' pre-rational, carnal or sensory responses to what they read. Although Radway concerns herself primarily with the ways in which 'actual people' read, it is not the sensations of the flesh and blood person which interest her, but a consumer's capacity for sense-making; no wonder then that references to reading as eating are interpreted along literary lines, that is to say, are read figuratively: as *metaphors* of consumption.

Like Raymond Williams, Radway also rejects the determining effects of material objects or, by extension, 'technological determinism'. Consider the following passage which critiques 'deterministic' approaches to audience study:

> Not only are cultural objects assumed to be fixed and determined in advance in the sense that their meaning is given to them by their creators, but they are thought to be determining as well. That is to say, they have the power to dictate or to control not only how they are perceived and understood by their purchasers but how they are used. Human beings are concomitantly conceived as passive and somnolent, indeed virtually mindless. They are reduced to purely physical entities that are either mechanically moved by the objects that come in contact with them or chemically transformed by those that they consume.
>
> (1986: 11)

The aim of this chapter was to point to a whole history of writing that emphasized the ways in which consumers have been 'chemically transformed' by their reading matter. The issue, however, was never approached from the perspective of humanism, which either stresses the input of creators in processes of meaning production or, conversely – as Radway does here – puts the emphasis on the audience, who in her view have much more actively negotiated responses than are allowed for by the kind of elitist assumptions that deem their input 'virtually mindless'. In this respect it never was a question of how creators influence their consumers, since it is not the creator but the technology itself which transforms consumers. This does not imply that readers are therefore necessarily passive creatures who read books silently and without passion or emotion, or that spectators are passive dupes, immobile and motionless; rather, the 'physiological tempests' which rage within them (Gilbert Cohen-Séat 1946, summarized in Kracauer 1997 [1960]: 159), and which express themselves with each tear, jolt, gulp, scream or hollow feeling in the stomach, are signs of just how much, to use the words of a medieval Englishman, 'the whole body labors'.[9]

4 The Reader in Fiction

Figure 5 This image from *Belgravia*, 5 (June 1868: 66), a magazine which serial-ized novels by Dickens and Hardy among others, shows one of the side-effects of reading: this woman has fallen into a trance imagining the happy day of her own wedding.

'It is a general phenomenon of our nature that the mournful, the shocking, the shudder-inducing attracts us with irresistible magic, that we feel ourselves repelled and attracted with equal force when lamentation and fright come upon us.' These words by Friedrich Schiller, from his essay 'On Tragic Art' (1970 [1792]: 30; my translation), emphasize the powerful effects of art, and are as applicable to the concept of catharsis in antiquity as to the eighteenth-century sublime; as relevant to the tender emotions promised by the sentimental novel as to the blood-curdles of the Gothic or the nerve-tinglings of sensation fiction; are still as germane to the shock tactics of the twentieth-century avant-garde as to the thrills of the Hollywood blockbuster in our own time; and will be pertinent when it comes to the multisensory stimulations of virtual reality. It is one thing, of course, to concede that a work of imaginative art can move us to compassion and force tears to our eyes, or strike such fear into its readers so as to make their hair stand on end, or that an erotic work might tease us sufficiently to inflame our passions; it is another thing, particularly in our present age, to fathom the idea that absorbing ourselves in fiction might kill.

Such a view was not without its supporters in the eighteenth and nineteenth century. Johann Adam Bergk's comment in 1799 that excessive reading leads to 'world-weariness and an early death' (1966: 411), a condemnation also shared in 1867 by a reviewer for *Sharpe's London Magazine,* who warned that reading used for 'killing time' was in effect a way for readers to 'commit suicide' (Anon. 1867: 316). When Samuel Taylor Coleridge spells out the dangers of reading in his 1811-12 lecture series, it is clear that it is the novel, and its readers' addiction to it, that is to blame: for 'where the reading of novels prevails as a habit, it occasions in time the entire destruction of the powers of the mind; it is such an utter loss to the reader, that it is not so much to be called pass-time as kill-time' (1987: 463). These remarks do not say merely that readers, instead of living, preferred their books, but that novels can seriously damage your health, and as such they must be understood literally rather than be taken metaphorically. The reception even of worthy novels by reputable literary figures such as Johann Wolfgang von Goethe indicates how deadly fiction could be or, as Goethe himself put it, how 'highly dangerous' his first novel, *The Sufferings of Young Werther,* had become (1949: 192). The worry that impressionable readers would over-identify with Werther's woes and, like their hero, take the decision to end their own lives was 'at first the case among a few people', Goethe remembers, and 'later on became general among a larger public' (ibid.). What suicide demonstrates here is 'a shocking acknowledgment that some feel too much to go on living' (Mullan 1996: 250).

Dangers of reading

But why was the novel especially blamed for endangering a reader's health, even society's health? Why should the healing properties, which Aristotle attributed to tragedy, the most revered of ancient literary genres, not also be applicable to the modern genre of the novel? Why should those reading about Werther's tragic death not be 'restored to health and attain' what Aristotle in the *Politics* called 'pleasurable relief' (1342a4-15), but have produced more tragedy by committing suicide themselves? Is this because the novel, as an essentially private form of entertainment, is almost by definition therefore a genre that provides an escape from the world, figuratively and literally, as opposed to theatre, which is always public and which draws us out into it? Is a response that is private, and thus removed from public scrutiny, more sub-versive and therefore also more dangerous to the state than a publicly obser-vable outpouring of emotion? Or are the reasons for the novel's potentially harmful effects to be found in 'its introduction of the "fourth wall"' (Habermas 1989: 50), and thus a structural feature of its very form?

In *The Progress of Romance* (1785), one of the earliest comparative studies of the novel and of its predecessor, the romance, Clara Reeve gives us this clue:

> The Romance is an heroic fable, which treats of fabulous persons and things. – The Novel is a picture of real life and manners, and of the times in which it is written. The Romance in lofty and elevated language, describes what never happened nor is likely to happen. – The Novel gives a familiar relation of such things, as pass every day before our eyes, such as may happen to our friend, or to ourselves; and the perfection of it, is to represent every scene, in so easy and natural a manner, and to make them appear so probable as to deceive us into a persuasion (at least while we are reading) that all is real, until we are affected by the joys or distresses, of the person in the story, as if they were our own.
>
> (2001 [1785]: 14)

What differentiates the novel from earlier forms of narrative is that it depicts scenes from everyday life with a realism that readers had hitherto never encoun-tered, nor ever felt to have been so directly addressed to them. Unlike the epic tradition, which told of powerful gods, great kings and brave warriors, or the romance tradition, with its narratives about heroic knights and courtly love, the novel reflected particular concerns to which the newly emerging middle classes could directly relate. Not only could it 'speak in extraordinarily detailed fashion about the pains and deaths of ordinary people' (Thomas Laqueur 1989, qtd. Porter 2000: 288) but, like no other literary form before, it also encouraged a close bond between characters and readers, thereby creating new possibilities for identification. The fear that readers would over-identify with what they read, as Don Quixote famously did (Cervantes 1992: 22-3), and form false expectations about life is a widespread concern during the period of the rise of the novel. The distinction that Reeve therefore makes between the novel and romance is cru-cial: since the novel makes everything appear 'natural' and 'probable', it manages 'to deceive us' into thinking fiction is fact. It is precisely this which troubled eighteenth-century critics, who thought, as Samuel Johnson did in 1750, that the romance's 'incredibilities' were far less dangerous to the reader than the novel's 'accurate observation' (1969 [1750]: 20). For if a reader, say Don Quixote, who is an avid devourer of romances can believe in the *improbable*, a reader as gullible as he, reading narratives that are *probable*, is perhaps all the more likely to mistake illusion for reality. This is to say, the novel is potentially more dangerous than the romance, because 'there is a doubling of the novel's mimetic operations: the novel imitates life; the reader imitates the novel' (Brantlinger 1998: 28).

The fear that large swathes of the population, because they were avid novel readers, would succumb to what Matei Calinescu in describing Don Quixote calls a 'mimetic disease' (1993: 68) was by no means a concern expressed just in the periodical press, which took upon itself to police the rapidly expanding literary marketplace from the eighteenth century onwards. Nor was it just of concern to poets seeking to defend an old art against a newcomer, verse against prose, as is the case with Coleridge in the *Seven Lectures on Shakespeare and Milton* (1811-12), or with Wordsworth in the Preface to *Lyrical Ballads* (1800). It is also in well-known works of fiction that debates about the dangers of reading resurface again and again. During the novel's heyday there are countless depictions of fictional readers,[1] and although reading is a positive educational project for some, for others it is the opposite. While reading teaches Jude Fawley that more is to be learned from life than from books, it helps Jane Eyre to define herself as a woman. While reading teaches some how to become criminals (Oliver Twist) or to become human (the Monster in *Frankenstein*), for others too much exposure to fiction makes them lose touch with reality (Arabella) or drives them insane (Don Quixote). Whether reduced to uncontrollable weeping (Lotte and Werther), tormented by irrational fears (Catherine Morland) or inflamed by illicit passions (Emma Bovary), reading novels – these novelists paradoxically show us – can make nervous wrecks of us. Is the danger of reading therefore a question of *what* we read, or is it also connected with *how* we read? (As we saw in chapter 2, it was also a question to do with *how much* readers consumed in the age of print.)

What I want to do in this chapter is to look at several European novels, each of which poses the dangers of reading from a different perspective. In particular, I want to examine how this danger is associated with the loss of control over the body, as if a translation of the body of the text takes place into the body of the reader.[2] This is to say, reading fiction is dangerous, these novels suggest, not just because a reader might over-identify with what he or she reads, but because unlike serious reading, which 'lifts the reader from sensation to intellect', as Hannah More argued, the novel actually does the opposite (1799, qtd. de Bolla 1989: 269). Similarly, Coleridge found that a novel 'produces no improvement of the intellect, but fills the mind with a mawkish and morbid sensibility, which is directly hostile to the cultivation, invigoration and enlargement of the nobler faculties of understanding' (1987: 463). What comes across from such critiques is the fear that the novel appeals neither to common sense nor to our faculty for sense-making, but to a reader's sensations. If novel reading is processed sensually, through the body, the danger is that readers might switch off their minds, allow themselves to be absorbed so utterly in the fiction, and identify so closely with what they read that they might well succumb, animally, to its pleasures, and therefore forego becoming, to use Mary Wollstonecraft's turn of phrase, 'rational creatures' and remain 'creatures of sensation' (1994 [1790, 1792]: 101, 131).

The tearful reader

Goethe's *The Sufferings of Young Werther* (first edn 1774; rev. edn 1786) must be understood in the context of a backlash against the sober rationalism of the age of Enlightenment, since, for Goethe, it is sensation through

which takes place the experience of the self as self. It is also through sentiment that we can feel sympathy for someone else, or that readers can share
'the joys and distresses, of the persons in the story, as if they were our own'
(Reeve 2001 [1785]: 14). Since tears are the outward physical manifestations that display not just one's own suffering but also one's identification
with someone else's, it is through tears that characters bond with characters, readers with characters and, as we shall also see, readers with readers.
Like the readers of Rousseau's novels (see chapter 3), Goethe's readers cried
oceans of tears in sympathy with Werther. Lamenting Werther's love-sickness
for a woman betrothed to another which eventually drives him to his death,
this comment by Wilhelm Heinse from 1774 is not atypical of readers' reactions at the time:

> Whosoever has felt, or feels, what Werther felt; in such a person thoughts disappear like
> light mists in the burning sun, should he but show it. One's heart fills up, and one's whole
> head feels full with tears.
>
> (qtd. Rothmann 2000; 131; my translation)

This response feels and reads like Werther's own words, not least because
Heinse too belonged to the *Sturm und Drang* (Storm and Stress) generation.
Like the heroes and heroines of other novels that were part of the culture of
sensibility (*Empfindsamkeit*), and like the readers who identified with them,
Goethe's Werther is deeply sentimental. More often than not, he tells us, 'I was
no longer in control of my emotions' (1970 [1786]: 53). Not ruled by his
head but by his heart, Werther is a true man of feeling who, in a quasi-
Nietzschean gesture, seeks the dissolution of his 'I', yearning as he does 'to
surrender' his whole being (ibid.: 19). No wonder that oblivion finally comes
when he points a gun to his head and pulls the trigger.

Heinse was the kind of reader which a reviewer in the *Lady's Magazine*
would have singled out for being too 'swallowed up in those sympathetic
emotions which the sorrows of a Werter [*sic*] inspire' (Anon. 1812: 222). The
reviewer lays the blame for this with Goethe for creating a 'hero and heroine
[who] are so truly amiable' that 'the immoral tendency of the work excites
no sentiment of abhorrence' (ibid.). The literary form most appropriate in
terms of activating sympathy, which this reviewer finds so objectionable, is the
epistolary novel. Since in 'the age of sentimentality', Jürgen Habermas points
out, 'letters were containers for the "outpourings of the heart"', and as such
'practically were to be wept' (1989: 49), it is this literary form, like none
before it, which allows for the closest possible intimacy between those who
write them and those who receive them. Like Richardson's *Pamela* (1740) or
Rousseau's *La Nouvelle Héloise* (1759), which were still, by the time *Werther*
was written, influential examples of this practice, Goethe's novel uses this
literary form because it allows the reader to share a character's innermost
thoughts and feelings. If the aim then is to make the reader feel the same as,
or at least feel with (*Mitgefühl*), a given character, this is precisely what happens at the climactic moment of the forbidden love scene between Lotte and

Werther when 'sympathetic emotions' turn into amorous passions. Crucially, like the affair between Francesca and Paolo in Dante Alighieri's *The Divine Comedy* (written ca. 1314, printed 1502), their moment of passion is prompted by a literary work – here, Werther reading out aloud passages that he has translated from the songs of Ossian.

> A flood of tears that streamed from Lotte's eyes and relieved her burdened heart checked Werther's recitation. He threw the papers down, grasped her hand and wept the bitterest tears. Lotte supported herself on the other hand and covered her eyes with her handkerchief. Both manifested a fearful agitation. They felt their own misery in the destiny of the heroes, felt it together and were united in their tears. Werther's lips and eyes burned on Lotte's arms; a shudder possessed her [...] The world ceased to exist for them.
>
> (Goethe 1970 [1786]: 88)

Just as Dante's lovers 'read no more that day' (V, 138), so Werther and Lotte lose themselves in each other, if only for a short while. As we know from the heartfelt responses with which the novel was first received, Werther's and Lotte's empathetic reading in effect anticipates this reaction. They share the protagonists' sufferings recounted in the poems of Ossian, and readers of *Werther*, by extension, share theirs.[3]

In retrospect, it might seem ironic that Werther and Lotte were moved to passion by what, although regarded as 'the poetry of the heart' (Blair 1996 [1763]: 209) and unbeknownst to Goethe at the time, turned out to be a forgery. Famously, these poems were not a lost folk ballad; rather than having been found, edited and then translated by James Macpherson from the Gaelic, he had actually scripted them himself. Their being fakes rather than 'originals' does not in any way dampen, as Martin Swales has argued, the fire of the emotions that these songs sparked in the couple (1987: 42); if anything this makes the case as regards the powerful hold of literature over the imagination of its readers during this era even stronger. Similarly, *Werther*'s appeal to readers cannot be explained by the fact that Goethe had drawn on instances from his own life for his work (cf. Goethe 1949: 189-91); nor can the fact that 'Werther was not only felt, but known, to be true to life' (Swales 1987: 108) account for the intensity of contemporaneous audiences' responses to the novel. In the end it matters little whether something we read is a fake or an original or, indeed, whether it is based on fact or fiction: readers' disposition when it comes to literature must be such that they are not only willing to suspend disbelief, but that they also allow themselves to be affected by what they read. In the eighteenth century the receptivity towards affect was rife, and even cultivated.

That readers of *Werther* necessarily shared the same emotions as the characters they read about, or recognized their own lives in theirs, is not so. This is evident in the response the German writer Ludwig Tieck says he had when he read *Werther* as a young man. Looking back at his response, 'bathed in tears' as he was for 'four weeks', he writes in 1828, this was not the result of sharing Werther's suffering or eventual fate, that is, of identifying too much with him, but the opposite: by lacking Werther's disposition, he deplores that he could not be sufficiently 'like this man' (qtd. Swales 1987: 58). By not feeling the same as Werther, Tieck illustrates in his reaction that a reader's emotional response need not necessarily be based on proximity of feeling; it can also be produced if a reader experiences distance to a given character. In which case, an emotional response need not be the result of over-identification, that is, of identifying too closely, but can also be based on a conative identification, i.e., a desire to be like a character.

While Tieck did not feel the same as Werther, even if he felt *for* him, he also had feelings *about* Werther's particular sentiments. These latter feelings are not of the order of a spontaneous unleashing of emotions, but require the distance of judgement based on his comparison with Werther. Whatever feelings he had *about* Werther, the point is that he expressed these *through* feeling: he cried, which means that his response neither disconnects the head from the heart nor places reading solely on the side of the emotions outside of the realm of reason. Obviously Tieck's reading experience is not the same as that of other readers, such as Heinse for instance (who identifies closely with Werther), which is to say that *Werther* did not elicit the *same* responses from *different* readers; and yet, the response still is the *same* insofar as Tieck too is moved to tears. Therefore, even if Tieck did not identify with Werther, he might well have identified with the reaction of other readers, who cried because this is what readers did in the age of sentimentalism. To read tearfully, then, was clearly an expectation one brought to a sentimental text, and indeed finds confirmed in it, when learning, for example, that Werther's and Lotte's reading made the two of them 'united in tears' (Goethe 1970 [1789]: 88). If Tieck recognizes himself not in Werther but, as I am suggesting here, in the responses of other sentimental readers, and is just as 'united' with them in tears as the novel tells us Lotte and Werther were, this would seem to indicate a continuum between actual and textual readers. As this analysis shows, it is pointless to try to separate actual readers from textual readers at a theoretical level, to argue that authenticity of response is to be found only in one and not in the other, in self-representations by real readers rather than constructed representations of fictional readers, since both these representations blur seamlessly into each other at an affective level. Whether outside of or within the fiction, reading in the age of sentimentalism meant reading sensitively, both at an emotional and at a physiological level.

Famously, Werther wore a yellow waistcoat, as did his admirers to express, and display to others, their bond of sympathy with their literary hero. So concerned were the authorities in Leipzig by these manifestations of Werther-fever that the city council made it a punishable offence not only to sell the novel but also to dress up in Werther's garb, a ban first enforced in 1775 and only lifted half a century later (cf. Swales 1987: 97). What Werther's fellow yellow-waistcoat-wearers demonstrate is the becoming public of what, in rational, civil society, ought at worst to remain private, or at best to be entirely eradicated: the unruly passions. By forcibly removing from the public sphere affective demonstration such as Werther aroused, the authorities in Leipzig in effect granted this demonstration the role of a challenge to the social order. By trying to contain affect in the private sphere, the authorities also gave affect particularity in that they allotted it a body and, because private, a female body. In which case, novel reading, especially in public, and especially if read with tears in one's eyes, is manifestly effeminate.

There is little doubt that novel reading was a favourite pastime among women. Indeed, from its very beginnings the novel was associated more with a woman's domain than a man's. When the novelist Friedrich Schlegel declared in 1794 that '[t]he novel as a whole is feminine' (1997: 399), this gendering of the genre, together with the fact that novels, because closely linked to the private, domestic sphere, were an ideal medium for the budding female writer, meant that this new form of writing was doubly suspect: a second-rate litera-ture, aimed at mindless escapism, often produced by and for the second sex, apparently incapable of serious rational thought. In addition, the widespread assumption that '[r]eason is in man, feeling in woman' (Novalis 1997 [1795-6]: 382) fed the fear that woman's supposed emotionalism would lead her to over-react to what she reads. As Alexander Walker explained the issue at stake: 'the *sensibility* of a woman is excessive', because 'she is strongly affected by many sensations, which in men are so feeble as scarcely to attract attention' (1840, qtd. Flint 1993: 54). That critiques of reading should therefore have directed themselves towards a female readership, in particular, is not unexpected given such assumptions. Henceforth, the threat of over-identification, of over-wroughtness or oversensitivity, will in part be articulated in the form of tracts advising women how to read properly.

The frightened reader

One such tract, not in the shape of advice literature but in the shape of a novel, is Jane Austen's *Northanger Abbey*, published a year after her death in 1817, but written between 1798 and 1799. The novel is a reworking of Charlotte Lennox's *The Female Quixote* (1752), which satirizes romance reading, itself a reworking of Cervantes' *Don Quixote*. Like Lennox's protagonist Arabella, Austen's protagonist Catherine Morland is a perpetual misreader who must undergo a learning process, albeit by gentle self-realization rather than brutal brainwashing (which removes from Austen's writing the overly didactic tone that Lennox adopts). Like Arabella, Catherine reads too much, although she prefers Gothic fiction to romances. This is because, when Austen began to write the novel, Gothic fiction, which had first bubbled to the surface in the 1760s, had become the rage. Its tales, featuring superstition, delusion, corrup-tion, immorality, transgression, and all things evil, were like the dark underside of everything associated with the enlightened values of this era, such as knowl-edge, reason, morality, convention and civilized behaviour (cf. Botting 1996: 1-2). A product of the Enlightenment, insofar as the Gothic tends to resolve and explain its mysteries at the end of each narrative, it is also a reaction to it, insofar as it suspends our faculties for rational thinking by activating irrational feelings of terror. In other words, it can 'produce effects almost without the intervention of the will' (Johnson 1969 [1750]: 22). Although Samuel Johnson made these remarks about the novel in general, they are 'prophetic' in Patrick Brantlinger's view when it comes to Gothic fiction (1998: 28). Since the Gothic is designed to strike terror into our hearts, our responses to it are immediate, involuntary and visceral. The reader cannot help but shudder and tremble.

It is in this sense that the Gothic tapped into, as we know Wordsworth once feared, his age's 'thirst after outrageous stimulation' (1974 [1800]: 130). What its popularity among so many readers also highlights, worryingly for some, is, as Fred Botting argues, 'that the control of literary production was shifting away from the guardians of taste and towards the reading public itself' (1996: 47). This literate middle class, enabled by the growth of the circulating libraries to borrow books cheaply, could now seek their stimulation not just in sentimental literature but also in tales of terror. Whereas *Werther* had invited empathetic identification between readers and characters, based on sorrow and suffering, in Gothic fiction the form this takes is that of empathizing with the 'perils and plight' that its characters have to endure.[4] This switch of atmosphere from pathos to terror thus extends the range of sensations of what can, both emotionally and physically, be experienced when reading; 'the only difference' for the reader being that 'the gasp replaces the tear as the measurable unit of response' (Mudrick 1976: 75). This is not to say that Gothic fiction was replacing sentimental fiction, for the two largely overlapped, but the range of responses to be had from fiction diversified and, despite warnings in the periodical press, intensified in the course of the nineteenth century, with powerful stimulation in the form of shocks and thrills aimed at readers' nerves, amply administered by the sensation fiction which was to emerge in the 1860s (cf. Cvetkovich 1992; Brantlinger 1998: 142-65; Flint 1993: 274-93).

This said, *Northanger Abbey* is not a Gothic novel. It is a parody of how the Gothic works and, especially, how it works on the reader, exposing what Edmund Burke saw as the delightful sensations of fear and terror.[5] To this end, Catherine's response to Mrs Radcliffe's *The Mysteries of Udolpho* (1794), a novel she reads with as much eagerness as terror, exemplifies the reading experience of the Gothic, resulting, as it does, in 'a raised, restless, and frightened imagination' (Austen 1995 [1818]: 47). The immediate effects of the Gothic on Catherine are somatic; its 'after-effects', which the novel also explores, are quixotic, insofar as she begins to respond to the world around her in the manner of a Gothic heroine. When Catherine is invited to stay at Northanger Abbey, the creaky ancestral home of the Tilneys and the kind of place Catherine suspects is 'just like one reads about', she does, despite having been teasingly forewarned that to stay there requires '[n]erves fit for sliding pannels and tapestry' (ibid.: 138), react to the house once she arrives, not as if it were a building marked by the traces of history, but as if it were haunted by the ghosts of fiction. Her first night there becomes a Gothic adventure when, during a violent storm, she discovers a carefully hidden 'precious manuscript'. All the while, of course, her 'heart fluttered, her knees trembled, and her cheeks grew pale' (ibid.: 148). It is only in the cold light of the morning after, when her 'greedy eyes glanced rapidly' at the document she had found that she realizes, to her horror, she was in fact holding 'a washing bill in her hand' (ibid.: 150). This incident, together with her suspicion that General Tilney, the master of the house, is guilty of a heinous crime, of having either murdered his wife or made her his secret prisoner, marks a turning point for her. Only after Henry Tilney, the son of the general, and her love-interest, urges her to consult her 'own sense of the probable' (ibid.: 171) against her unfounded suspicions does she begin to reassess her actions and reactions. The realization that her delusions were 'self-created', because even 'before she entered the Abbey, [she] had been craving to be frightened' (ibid.: 173), leads her to admit to herself that these very expectations could 'be traced to the influence of that sort of reading which she had there indulged' (ibid.:174).

The novel does not suggest that *what* Catherine reads is at fault, but rather that *how* she reads is problematic. Nor does it suggest that reading novels is something only women do (Henry tells Catherine that she is mistaken in believing that he has no interest in, or has not read, Radcliffe's novels). Nor for that matter does Austen suggest that novel reading *per se* is bad. At the end of chapter 5, for instance, a first-person authorial voice intrudes into the narrative and staunchly defends the novel from the perspective of the novelist. Novel reading need not be harmful, then, provided that it teaches us something, which is precisely what *Northanger Abbey* does. As a *Bildungsroman* it traces Catherine's education. It also educates us along the way: readers have to assess carefully whether certain characters' actions and motivations can or cannot be trusted, in the course of which we have to adjust and reassess our own feelings about them. Right from the start the novel keeps us at arm's length from its main protagonist. When Catherine is first introduced, she is presented not as a heroine, as conventions of the novel would lead us to expect, but as an anti-heroine, neither very bright nor pretty, we are told (Austen 1995 [1818]: 13). Thus, rather than creating a bond of sympathy between Catherine and her reader, the narrative voice creates an ironic distance to Catherine, deliberately opening up a space for readers to judge her rather than identify with her. Indeed, the whole tone of *Northanger Abbey*, whether ironic, parodic or intrusive, is designed to give us the kind of distance to the novel that Catherine herself lacks when she is reading. It is not only through the contents, then, but also through its form, that *Northanger Abbey* sets out to teach the female reader a lesson in reading. As a work which self-consciously foregrounds the conventions of fiction writing and just as self-consciously interrogates readers' responses to fiction, it makes us as readers conscious of the novel as an artifice as well as of our own reading practices. *Northanger Abbey*, like other novels featuring female reader-protagonists, 'alerts the reader to pay attention to the implications of her own practice and to be aware of her own expectations of a novel' (Flint 1993: 256).

The passionate reader

One reader who does not learn from her mistakes is the main protagonist of *Madame Bovary* (1857), penned by Gustave Flaubert half a century later. Unlike Catherine, whose education sanctions her entry into the safe harbour of marriage, where she will, we can assume, lead a happy life, Emma Bovary learns just how empty and passionless married life can be. Unlike Isabel Gilbert,[6] who merely flirts with the idea of an extra-marital affair, but learns to love her husband, Emma ends up an adulteress. Emma's reading plays a crucial role in that. She is unhappy not because, like Werther, she cannot be with a loved one, but because she cannot find true romantic love: her life never did measure up to her books, the book heroes never to the lovers in her life. When Mary Ann Evans (alias George Eliot) wrote in a letter in 1839 that 'I shall carry to my grave the mental diseases with which [novels] have contaminated me' (qtd. Flint 1993: 219), this is precisely the fate that awaits Emma. Despite attempts to prevent her from obtaining books from the lending library, which her mother-in-law regarded as nothing less than a 'poisonous trade' (Flaubert 1992 [1857]: 101), Emma continues to be '[b]usy reading novels, wicked books' (ibid.). This reading addiction contributes to the many nervous disorders she suffers, but also slowly poisons her, a death only hastened when she takes arsenic at the end of the novel.

Emma not only reads novels and has no particular preference for any specific genre, as Catherine did, her reading hunger is so ferocious and uncontrolled that she seemingly reads everything in print, from the Bible, advertisements, reviews of dinner parties and 'bizarre books, full of orgiastic set-pieces,' to 'bloodthirsty adventures' (Flaubert 1992 [1857]: 45, 235). Emma is a true product of print culture, as well as its prototypical mass consumer. Less interested in quality than quantity, or in style than plot, she reads only for immediate pleasurable gratification: '[f]rom everything she had to extract some kind of personal profit; and she discarded as useless anything that did not lend itself to her heart's immediate satisfaction' (ibid.: 28). It is not just that she 'would forge connections' between real life and fictional lovers (ibid.: 45), but so intensive is her reading, and so absorbed is she by it, that '[s]he was the lover in every novel, the heroine in every play, the vague *she* in every volume of poetry' (ibid.: 215). As the episode in the opera makes clear, her identificatory impulse goes deeper even than that. Not only does she recognize in the voice of the heroine on stage 'the echo of her own consciousness' (ibid.: 181), but she so utterly lacks distance to what she sees that she falls in love with the opera's hero, before being overcome by the 'mad idea' that it was he himself who kept 'looking at her' (ibid.: 182). It is not just that Emma reads her own life into the fiction she sees unfolding on stage, she also wants her life to be like the life represented in the fiction. Moreover, reading introduces drama into her existence, illustrative of her willingness to live her life as if it were a fiction.

On the one hand, then, Emma is an intensive and absorbed reader. On the other, she reads so extensively that her reading practice cannot but be disparate. Thus, 'her reading went the same way as her needlework, cluttering the cupboard, half finished; she picked it up, put it down, went on to something else' (Flaubert 1992 [1857]: 100). This makes her the paradigmatically modern reader, already encountered in chapter 3: both addicted to books and with a nervous disposition, she reads distractedly and fleetingly. Perpetually on the lookout for stimulation and excitement, she hurries from one page, or book, to another, using fiction 'to kindle her passions' (ibid.: 30) and to feed her 'impure longings' (ibid.: 76). She yearns for the kind of life that 'brings the senses into bloom' (ibid.: 34). And whether she would fall into a trance (ibid.: 47) over a book, or scream in terror (ibid.: 235), or whether she would be 'trembling all over', which she does at the opera 'as though the bows of the violins were being drawn across her nerves' (ibid.: 180), or be 'sinking her fingernails into the velvet on her box' in the theatre (ibid.: 181), or nearly faint with the pressure of 'suffocating palpitations' (ibid.: 183), her enjoyment in all these instances is bodily. Her interest in fiction is therefore 'rooted in sensual rather than cognitive interests' (Felski 1995: 84). Even her engagement with religion, and its ostensively instructive texts, she turns into extensions of her own romantic and sensuous fantasies (ibid.: 27).

But how do we as readers read Flaubert's novel? Flaubert's narrative style of writing oscillates between 'sympathy' and 'irony' (cf. Crosman Wimmers 1988: 58), thus positioning the reader sometimes with, and sometimes against, Emma. The novel introduces the narrative device of 'a subjective consciousness without "point-of-view" that freely espouses the reveries' of Emma; it also, however, features 'an objective narrator who can stand back and observe while maintaining an ironic distance' (de Man 1965: xii). Her death, for instance, is observed from the uninvolved perspective of a detached observer, and we share little of Emma's suffering with her. On other occasions, the narrative voice allows us 'unmediated' access to Emma's innermost emotions, even her more sensuous, carnal sensations, without judging her. At times, therefore, '[w]e feel that we are inside her head, under her skin, as we read', so much so, according to Geoffrey Wall, that as readers we are even aroused sexually (1992: xiv). On such occasions, the reader melts with Emma's point of view, merges with her identity, as she in turn melts into the characters she reads about. Conversely, by providing a detached narrative perspective, in contrast to Emma's subjective voice, Flaubert introduces a corrective to such indulgence. In this respect the ironic tone of the narrator returns to the reader the autonomy momentarily lost on those occasions when the narrative melts us with Emma.

Since Flaubert's free indirect style never makes it entirely clear who is speaking the narrative, whether Emma, another character, a narrator or

Flaubert himself, the novel creates an ambiguity which, as James Smith Allen has shown, leaves the reader without moral guidance. Never quite sure whether the text positions the reader with or against Emma, for some contemporaneous critics this ambiguity made it the most immoral text ever printed; for others it signalled one of novel writings' greatest achievements (Allen 2001: 185-9). Unlike Jane Austen's reader, who is left in little doubt as to how to judge her heroine, Flaubert's reader remains in a state of limbo as to how its author intended his text to be read, making it impossible to derive a definitive lesson from *Madame Bovary*. As Baudelaire recognized in 1857, 'it is the reader's task to draw the right conclusions from its outcome' (1965: 340).

In this respect, *Madame Bovary* is both a readerly and a writerly text. Emma is a passive, absorbed reader who reads herself into the literature as if she could inhabit these fictions as its heroine; the reader when he or she shares Emma's consciousness is similarly drawn into the world of fiction. At those junctures in the text we read like her, forget ourselves momentarily (as Geoffrey Wall's comment indicates). We read passively then, allowing sensations to act upon us. At other junctures, when we are distanced from her, we become active readers because the text demands that we stand back to try to make sense of exactly *who is speaking*:[7] is it Emma's, Flaubert's or someone else's voice we are hearing? It is then that we must interpret what we read, which makes reading no longer about a 'pleasuring of the body' (Ferris 1991: 40) but about the 'pleasure of the text' in the Barthesian sense. This is to say, our pleasure in reading is no longer derived from sensations, the way in which Emma reads, but is intellectual because it comes from teasing out the multiple senses of the text.

Emma never reads between the lines; rather, the novel suggests, her mode of reading is akin to 'dreaming between the lines' (Flaubert 1992 [1857]: 47). As Rita Felski explains, the reason why Emma reads too 'literally', and consequently blurs the distinction between 'life and art' (1995: 87), is because she fails to recognize 'the mediating authority of literary form' (ibid.: 83). This implies that Emma's literality in reading is a sign of her literary illiteracy, which makes her *de facto* an uneducated reader. As Felski puts it: Emma's 'uncritical devouring of fiction is a disturbing and threatening phenomenon, because it negates the autonomy of the literary artifact' (ibid.: 86). True, Emma has lost consciousness of the form which shapes the contents of a story, because it is transparent to her, but she has also lost consciousness of self. What is disturbing and threatening about Emma's self-absorbing mode of reading is therefore not, as Felski suggests, that it negates the *autonomy of the literary artefact* but that it negates the *autonomy of the subject*, that is, this subject's – here the reader's – agency.

Pathology of reading

If a novel, to come back once more to Samuel Johnson's point, can 'produce effects almost without the intervention of the will', this suggests that readers are powerless because a work of art has the capacity to cast 'a spell on us' by 'winning a complete mastery over our minds' (Longinus XXXIX). What this undermines is our mental mastery over a text, and therefore our agency as rational beings in control of ourselves and everything we come into contact with. It is true, of course, that as rational thinking beings we must know the difference between fiction and reality (and Emma manifestly does not), but this does not mean that, whenever we pick up a novel, we read between the lines and look out for the 'mediating authority of literary form'. It is a precondition of reading to suspend disbelief. How else would fiction allow us the pleasures of sympathy, empathy, passion or terror? To get carried away by affect is a dissolution of the 'I' as an autonomous subject, because it 'lifts us beyond ourselves'; and since we are therefore 'no longer masters of ourselves', as Heidegger (1991: 1. 45-6) explains Friedrich Nietzsche's notion of 'Kunst als Rausch' [art as rapture or intoxication] (1967– [1888]: 328), this is a threat to a humanism which puts this rational 'I' at its centre. Being lifted beyond ourselves is what happens to Emma: it is not a lifting above ourselves, deploying contemplative distance, but a seizure of ecstasy.[8]

This distinction can also be explained with regard to the difference between a Nietzschean aesthetics-as-physiology and a Kantian aesthetics.[9] Whereas Kant had insisted that our pleasure in that which threatens to overawe us in art and in nature is based on our mental mastery, precisely because we are able to resist its affective power over us (see chapter 5), the Nietzschean take is the opposite. Affective charge sets us free from rational and therefore moral constraints. It is in this sense that we must understand Nietzsche's claim that 'aesthetic delights are biological delights' (1905–: XIV. 165, qtd. Heidegger 1991: 1. 114), which stands in counterdistinction to Kant, for whom those delights are purely intellectual ones. If our hearts are unruly, and can rule our heads, then this is also a threat to Descartes' notion that *I think and therefore I am*, because it says instead that I feel first and then I think and therefore I am two: a *creature of sensation* and a *rational creature*.

The danger of reading, which manifests itself in terms of an excess of passions, is associated with what Nietzsche calls 'the pathological element in rapture' (1967– [1888]: 327). It is this pathological element which constitutes 'the physiological danger of art'. Reading then is dangerous because it is ingested by the body before it is chewed over by the mind, a danger which is linked to passive consumption, namely, over-identification, and the concomitant loss of self. Or, to put this slightly differently, since passivity draws on the root of the word – *pathe* – which it shares with 'pathology', 'sym-pathy', 'pathos', 'patient', the etymological connection suggests that to read with pathos (being acted upon) is to read passively, and therefore to read pathologically. Werther and Lotte read with too much sympathy, which turns into passion; readers of *Werther* had too much sympathy for Werther, which led to uncontrollable tears, or even suicide. In this sense, suicide is the passional consummation of all action. All these readers are pathological to a greater or lesser extent: reading acts on the body and is acted out in terms of bodily responses. Similarly,

Catherine identifies too much, and so does Emma. As a result they are drawn into a given novel and *dream* rather than *read* between the lines. Not to be able to tell the difference between life and fiction is a pathological condition.

But why is it that the quixotic reader-protagonists who so frequently appeared during the rise of the novel, and until the genre's middle years in the nineteenth century, no longer figure in literature by the early twentieth century? Based on the argument so far, the hypothesis which suggests itself is this.

Reading games

The modern novel, already with Flaubert, and most self-professedly with Henry James, is based in aestheticism, and the modernist novel, especially, is directed towards bold stylistic experimentation. No longer just escapist litera-ture, the novel had come of age as an art form. Its status as a genre was assured, and it had become serious reading. By the early twentieth century the novelist is concerned far more with portraits of the artist than with the figure of the reader, and if anybody is shown to be deluded in these novels then it is the aspiring writer and not the over-identifying reader. As a literary form the novel has been associated with realism since Cervantes, and whether during its infan-cy, when distinguishing itself from the improbabilities of romance, or during its classic realist period, the novel tended to encourage identification (because of the kind of life it presented as well as the way in which it presented it). What Matei Calinescu calls 'mimetic disease' is therefore a product of the novel's real-ism, and comes to an end with the formally experimental novel of modernism which discourages identification.

A modernist text does not allow the reader to forget that he or she is read-ing, because its innovative stylistic devices are designed to disrupt the illusion, and with it any possibility for identification. Reality in the modernist text is continuously foregrounded as constructed; reality in the realist text is so care-fully constructed that it hides the nuts and bolts of its construction. Realism introduced the 'fourth wall'; modernism dismantled it to lay the stage bare. When Barthes allied classic realism with the 'readerly' text and modernism with the 'writerly' text, it was to distinguish between two modes of writing and reading: the readerly offers itself to the reader to be passively consumed, and the writerly demands active, critical participation of the reader in con-structing meaning (1974: 4). If the danger of reading, as we have seen in this and the previous chapter, has to do with the physiology of consumption, then it is hardly surprising that this should no longer be an issue for modernist writers. The modernist text, because it engages its reader *actively* in the process of sense-making, dispels the fears that the reader, *passively* and animally, might give him- or herself over to sensual stimulation such as tears, fear or passion.[10] We can rest reassured then that a literature as concerned with formalist innovation as modernism is a literature which taxes its audience by involving them in endless plays of signification. As an illusion-breaking literature, as opposed to an illusion-making one, it provides the kind of serious reading of which Hannah More said that it 'lifts the reader from sensation to intellect'. In short, over-identification begins to give way to 'overinterpretation'.[11]

Even postmodern literature which parodies and pokes fun at the literary conventions of the past suffers from the strain of 'overinterpretation'. When John Barth referred to postmodernist literature in 1967 as a 'literature of exhaustion' (1981: 19), what he is describing is a 'used-upness' which occurs when fiction seemingly has explored all there is to be explored as regards the conventions of fiction writing. This theme is central to postmodern writers who tend to write fictions about fiction writing. What this kind of writing demands of the reader is a literacy which recognizes the range of reference, and therefore relies on the reader's activity of *comprendre* (literally bringing together): to comprehend a text is to assemble its meaning, as if it were a puzzle. Although literary 'exhaustion' and literary 'playgiarism' (Federman 1975/6: 565) might be taken, as some critics did, as signs that 'the novel is dead' (Federman 1981: 5), there are other reasons why this might have been thought to be the case. The opening paragraph of Italo Calvino's *If on a Winter's Night a Traveller* (1979) gives a clue not just why the novel, but indeed why the medium of the book itself, might be dead.

> You are about to begin reading Italo Calvino's new novel, *If on a winter's night a traveller*. Relax. Concentrate. Dispel every other thought. Let the world around you fade. Best close the door; the TV is always on in the next room. Tell the others straight away, 'No, I don't want to watch TV!' Raise your voice – they don't hear you otherwise – 'I'm reading! I don't want to be disturbed!'
>
> (1982 [1979]: 9)

This passage is typical of the self-reflexive and playful writing that characterizes postmodern fiction. Right from the start this novel breaks the illusion by doing away with the 'fourth wall', keeping the reader alert to the fact that he or she is about to enter the artificially constructed world of fiction. By pitching print culture against screen culture, reading against watching, this passage addresses head on the new challenge faced by the novel. The real threat to the novel is not from the novel of the circulating library, not from genre fiction, but from another evil which besets culture: TV. It also gives a clue where the passive reader, who has disappeared as a character in the modernist and postmodern novel, might have gone. While reading Calvino's novel requires concentration, as this passage insists, TV with all its noise produces distraction. It is here that mindless consumption is now to be found.

The danger of a future without books

Passive consumption and all it entails, such as sensation, addiction and poisonous contamination, dies with the experimental fictions of the twentieth century. Although it lives on in genre fiction, bracketed off from canonical literature into the shelves of popular fiction, or is appropriated and intellectualized by the metafictional works of postmodernism, consumption is reserved predominantly for the seats in the cinema. When the danger of reading crops up once more it is not to do with reading too much, but with the fear that a post-cinema generation reads too little. In the science fiction novels *Brave New World* (1932) by Aldous Huxley and *Fahrenheit 451* (1954) by Ray Bradbury, books are too subversive to be tolerated by the totalitarian regimes that rule our future, and are either forbidden or burnt. The authorities represented in both novels pacify (or 'passify') their citizens by encouraging them to indulge in entertainments presented on screen for mass consumption, but discourage them 'to indulge in any solitary amusement' such as those offered by imaginative literature (Huxley 1994: 147). Book culture has been usurped in *Fahrenheit 451* with the 'televisors' as a new form of entertainment, and in Huxley's dystopian new world with the 'feelies'. Families in Bradbury's novel want to install televisors on all four walls of their living parlours, so as to give them maximum immersion in the worlds presented on screen; in Huxley's novel, the feelies transmit the sensations and emotions screen actors experience to film viewers. Both these technologies are forerunners of virtual reality, because they fulfil a spectator's desires to experience what they see as realistically or as viscerally as possible.

The subtext of these novels is not that reading is bad for you, but that watching moving images is bad; and watching is bad because it has a more immediate (or cruder) impact on its recipient than reading does. This is illustrated by the following exchange between Faber (who refuses to have televisors in his parlour) and Montag (whose wife aspires to plaster all four walls of their parlour with screens):

[FABER:] The televisor is 'real'. It is immediate, it has dimension. It tells you what to think and blasts it in. It *must* be right. It seems so right. It rushes you on so quickly to its own conclusions your mind hasn't got time to protest, 'What nonsense!' [...]
[MONTAG:] My wife says books aren't 'real'.
[FABER:] Thank God for that. You can shut them, say, 'Hold on a moment.' You play God to it. But who has ever torn himself from the claw that encloses you when you drop a seed in a TV parlour? It grows you any shape it wishes! It is an environment as real as the world. It *becomes* and *is* the truth.

(Bradbury 1976: 84)

The TV parlour, like the cinema, 'assaults every one of the senses using every possible means' (Kracauer 1987 [1926]: 92), and does not therefore allow sufficient time for reflection. The quick succession of images is harmful to the spectator, because it privileges distraction over contemplation, feeding an eye-hunger, as we saw in our discussion of the cinema previously, which 'does not seek the leisure of tarrying observantly, but rather seeks restlessness and the excitement of continual novelty and changing encounters' (Heidegger 1962: 216).[12] The message of Bradbury's novel is that leisure pursuits such as these involve the impoverishment of our senses, a critique directly linked to the emergence of mass culture. This comes across most clearly in a description Montag gives of a televisor show. What the viewer sees are fragmented images – of swallowing and seeing the inside of a body, of bodies in pieces, and bashes turning into crashes – images which do not add up to a larger picture but are meant to cater to the hunger for sensations (Bradbury 1976: 93). Inchoate these images may be, but we cannot take our eyes off them, the novel suggests. Similarly, Huxley's feelies appeal to the raw sensations. They do not evoke fine sentiments as literature does, but provide 'electric titillation':

'Aa-aah.' 'Ooh-ah! Ooh-ah!' the stereoscopic lips came together again, and once more the facial erogenous zones of the six thousand spectators in the Alhambra tingled with almost intolerable galvanic pleasure. 'Ooh ...'

(Huxley 1994 [1932]: 152)

Characters such as Mildred Montag in Bradbury's novel and Lenina Crowne in Huxley's are modern incarnations of Emma Bovary. The only difference is that they are addicted to a different medium.

Multisensory media

From a modern perspective it is not easy to appreciate quite the degree of intensity that early novel readers experienced with regard to the written word. Then, of course, the novel was a relatively new medium. As is the case with any new medium, once we are familiar with its conventions, we also to a certain extent become desensitized to its effects. With the emergence of the cinema, fiction film promised to reinvent, even amplify, the kind of absorption which had first attracted audiences to the novel. By the time Huxley was writing, he already imagined a representational technology far more powerful than the novel once was, and than film could ever be. The spectators of the feelies are already in tune with what virtual reality might one day be able to offer, that is, allowing users unmediated access to the experiences and feelings of fictional characters, sharing their 'joys and distresses', to recall Clara Reeve's words, 'as if they were our own'; or, as is the case in *Brave New World*, feeling the same erotic titillations as the actors in the feelies. The worry in predictions about virtual reality entertainments is, as they once were for the novel, that those who immerse themselves in fiction might not only get addicted to this form of escapism, but will become incapable of distinguishing art from life. But there is a crucial difference between the novel and VR. If the novel is a 'machine for producing possible worlds' (Eco 1979: 246, qtd. McHale 1987: 194), virtual reality is literally the machine to make this a reality: it is the novel realized.

The group of artists and scientists that had so far done least was the one that had attracted the *greatest interest* and the *greatest alarm*. This was the team working on '*total identification*'. The history of the cinema gave the clue to their actions. First sound, then colour, then stereoscopy, then Cinerama, had made the old 'moving pictures' more and more like reality itself. Where was the end of the story? Surely, the final stage would be reached when *the audience forgot it was an audience*, and became part of the action. To achieve this would involve *stimulation of all the senses*, and perhaps hypnosis as well, but many believed it to be practical. When the goal was attained, there would be an enormous enrichment of human experience. A man could become – for a while, at least – any other person, and could take part in any conceivable adventure, real or imaginary. He could even be plant or animal, if it proved possible to capture and record the sense impressions of other living creatures. And when the programme was over, he would have acquired a memory as vivid as any experience in his actual life – indeed, *indistinguishable from reality itself.*

The prospect was dazzling. *Many found it terrifying* and hoped the enterprise would fail.
(Clarke 2001: 42-3; emphases mine)

This passage, from Arthur C. Clarke's novel *Childhood's End* (1954), is illustrative of the dangers associated with the new representational technologies. For whether already in existence, such as the cinema, the cinerama or the sensorama,[13] or whether merely imagined, such as Huxley's feelies, Bradbury's televisors or William Gibson's 'simstim', these technologies have one thing in common: they are dangerous because they are multisensory media. The reason why, for Huxley and Bradbury, books are less dangerous then is, as Janet Murray explains: '[b]ooks are praised as a better representational technology by virtue of their limitations; their meagre sensory input makes their illusion easier to resist. You can shut them and say, "hold on a moment"' (1997: 21). Had Emma Bovary lived in Huxley's brave new world, there is little doubt she would have been addicted to the feelies; in Bradbury's world she would have spent her last pennies on the fourth televisor; and in Gibson's *Count Zero* she would have been Bobby Newmark's mother. But even an addict as great as Emma was able to let the book 'fall into her lap' (Flaubert 1992 [1857]: 47), though only to dream between the lines rather than shut it. Catherine also puts her books aside, in effect saying to herself 'hold on for a moment', but only after Henry has told her to. Werther and Lotte too put the book down, and like Dante's Francesca and Paolo 'read no more that day'.

The novel absorbs its readers and creates possibilities for identification, but by virtue of being a printed medium it also enables the reader to pause. In a virtual reality environment identification is all absorbing, since that final stage has been reached: 'total identification' means, as Arthur C. Clarke suggests, that 'the audience forgot it was an audience, and became part of the action.' The distinction drawn out here between these different representational technologies can be mapped onto a distinction between cognition and sensation. As Leo Charney explains,[14] since 'sensation [...] feels the moment in the moment, and cognition [...] recognizes the moment only after the moment' (1995: 279), this means that sensation and cognition 'can never inhabit the same moment' (ibid.: 281). We can reflect on the moment only after it has already passed, which is why the moment itself, by necessity, is experienced 'not in the realm of the rational catalogue but in the realm of the bodily sensation' (ibid.). Since identification in VR is unmediated, it is immediate: '[i]nside the immediate presence of the moment, what we can do – the only thing we can do – is feel it. The present presence of the moment can occur only in and as sensation' (ibid.: 285). Over-identification comes close to VR's total absorption, but not close enough. In the print medium, identification entails that the reader recognizes him- or herself in the other, a distancing which cannot occur without a moment's pause. Put differently, VR is more dangerous than print or the moving pictures, because it annihilates the distance necessary for cognition or reflection to take place: it is designed to stimulate all of the senses all of the time. 'All the representational arts can be considered dangerously delusional', and have been since the parable of Plato's Cave, but 'the more entrancing they are', Murray argues, 'the more disturbing' they become (1997: 18). With the invention of the cinema these fears deepened, which is why the danger of reading is displaced in Huxley and Bradbury by the danger of watching images.

Huxley's fear about 'the Age of Television Addiction' (1983: 129) is especially revealing here. Since '[p]eople like to feel strong emotions and therefore enjoy tragedies, thrillers, murder mysteries and tales of passion' (ibid.: 135), he worries that those feelings might be manipulated, and intensified, without people even knowing it, if techniques culled from subliminal advertising were to be used for TV and cinema. That this was indeed the case, before being declared illegal, goes some way towards explaining why passive, or passional, consumption is synonymous with mindless consumption, since it quite literally bypasses the conscious mind by acting on our 'subconscious perception' (ibid.: 130). Although Huxley's fears are entirely justified here, they can also be taken as expressive of a larger cultural anxiety, namely, that the body, because it is the other of mind, spirit and soul, and because it reacts immediately – whether engineered subliminally, induced chemically or manipulated perceptually – evades the disciplining strictures of reason, dragging us down the evolutionary ladder rather than up it. It is the legacy of the Enlightenment to awake our critical faculties, and therefore everything which puts us into rapture, whether in terms of being overcome by pity, fear or passion, must be resisted.

Between the writing of Werther, the writing of Emma, and the writing of Huxley's, Bradbury's and Clarke's scenarios, several shifts have occurred which characterize modern culture in more general terms. It could be argued that there was a shift from sentiment, as the experience of refined feeling which might be recollected later in tranquility to evoke Wordsworth's words (1974 [1800]: 148), to sensation, as the experience of raw sensuality which makes itself felt in the immediacy of the present. Finally, sense-making is what is foregrounded in formalist experimentations in literature, art for art's sake, aestheticism and modernism. Much of this has to do with Kant's notion of the autonomous artwork, as explained in the next chapter. To borrow Kant's terminology, modernist novelists do not '*break your heart*', 'as sentimentalist novelists do', but they '*break your head*' (1902–:V.334; 1987: 205). Clarissa Harlowe broke our hearts, Clarissa Dalloway does not. Modernist texts demand that readers be critically alert and active contributors in making meaning. Although written in a different context, Geoffrey Hartman's insight is nevertheless entirely pertinent here: it is as if 'interpretation *interrupts* a spell which has made us too enjoyably passive' (1975: 12). Once literature becomes an occasion for hermeneutics, and not aesthesis, then it is clearly concerned more with how and what a text means than with what effect or affect it has on a reader: sense-making rather than sensation. This shift from aesthesis to hermeneutics is one that we can see not just in literature, but also in the histrory of literary criticism, the topic to which we shall now turn.

5 The Role of Affect in Literary Criticism

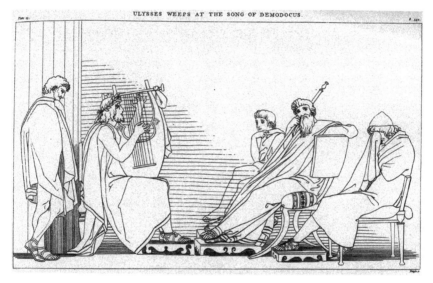

ULYSSES WEEPS AT THE SONG OF DEMODOCUS.

Figure 6 John Flaxman's depiction of ca. 1800 of the scene in Homer when Odysseus is moved to tears by Demodocus' song.

Consider the following line from a poem: 'Nymphs and shepherds, dance no more'. What kinds of reaction do you as a reader have to these words? Do these words evoke an intense emotional response in you? Compare your own reaction with that described by the poet and critic A. E. Housman:

But in these six simple words of Milton – Nymphs and shepherds, dance no more – what is it that can draw tears, as I know it can, to the eyes of more readers than one? What in the world is there to cry about? Why have the mere words the physical effect of pathos when the sense of the passage is blithe and gay?

(1933: 45)

What is strange about Housman's reaction is not that his eyes fill with tears when reading those words, but that this should happen to a man in the twentieth century. Had Housman lived two millennia earlier, even just two centuries earlier, his reaction would not have seemed strange at all.

Take Odysseus, who, during a feast in his honour, listens to the poet Demodocus' recital of his and his warriors' deeds in the Trojan war, and is so stirred that he 'melted into tears, running down his eyes to wet his cheeks' (Book 8, ll. 586-7). Only Alcinous, who was sitting close to Odysseus, had noticed his tears, and had 'heard the groan in the man's labored breathing' (ll. 601), and recommends that Demodocus should stop his moving song so as to give Odysseus relief from the 'grief that has overpowered his heart' (ll. 609). We would be mistaken to believe, however, that Odysseus' 'tears and throbbing sorrow' (ll. 608) are solely a consequence of his having to relive painful memories, and that the emotions unleashed are therefore based exclusively on an identification with his earlier self. While identifying with the fate of a character is a recurring motif within literature and criticism, we should not ignore that it is also the power of the poet's words themselves which move an audience. As Odysseus himself remarks, 'what a fine thing it is to listen to such a bard as we have here – the man sings like a god' (Book 9, ll. 3-4). That poetic expression can leave an audience 'enthralled' (l. 8) in 750 BC, as the *Odyssey* tells us, or that 'words' can have 'the physical effect of pathos' in the twentieth century is a testament to the powerful effect of artistic expression, whether this is represented in a work of fiction (Homer) or in a work of criticism (Housman). In our own times, though, it is rare for poetic expression to unleash such heartfelt emotion.

So, what happened to alter the ways in which we conceive of and are willing to receive literature in more recent times? Why is Housman's claim that '[p]oetry indeed seems to me more physical than intellectual' (1933: 45) so at odds with the current sense of what literature is?[1] My contention is that we respond to literature differently than used to be the case, at least as far as our reactions to it, and our actions upon reading it, are concerned. While there was little doubt among critics once that literature was meant not only to please (*delectare*) and instruct (*docere*) its readers, but also to move (*movere*) them, such a trichotomy holds little value in the twenty-first century among those who write, read or comment on literature. Very few of us now would be inclined to define what literature is, or to recognize it, as Housman did, 'by the symptoms which it provokes in us' (ibid.: 46).

Reading with/without pathos

Responding to a poem is for Housman by no means a response to its intellectual qualities, or its meanings (1933: 36-7), but a response to the sensations that poetry can evoke, how a poetic line can make the skin 'bristle', send 'a shiver down the spine' and cause 'a constriction of the throat and a precipitation of water to the eyes' (ibid.: 46). His stance here is reminiscent of those recounted by many eighteenth-century readers, who seemed only too willing to swim in a flood of sensations (see chapter 3), but far away from the sensibilities of his contemporaries. A case in point is Q. D. Leavis, whose *Fiction and the Reading Public* (1932) was published a year before Housman's *The Name and Nature of Poetry*. Leavis champions an 'intellectual stimulus' (1965 [1932]: 154) to literature rather than an affective one and, unlike Housman, sees 'tears, pity, shudders, and so forth' (ibid.: 134) as a 'form of emotional self-indulgence' (ibid.: 135). In her view impulses such as tears must be resisted, and can be, provided that the reader has 'an alert critical mind' and is therefore able to 'cut them off at the source in a revulsion to disgust' (ibid.: 156). Indeed, when she writes that the tears which readers wept when reading Samuel Richardson[2] were not involuntary responses to his fiction, that is, were not outpourings of emotional intensity but the result of a conscious and calculated decision, her take betrays a modernist concern that is far removed from the rhetorical traditions derived from antiquity, which tended to praise and prize a work for its effects.

No one made the mistake of confusing the subject-matter of this kind of art with 'life'; the emotions aroused by it (we know they were aroused from Richardson's correspondence and Sterne's imitators) might be called intellectual since they required an intellectual stimulus. The reader wept because she knew she ought to weep [...].

(1965 [1932]: 154)

Leavis's translation of an ostensively affective response into an 'intellectual stimulus' constitutes the kind of mentalist bias which not only draws stringent lines of demarcation between high and popular literature, but seeks to exclude that which addresses itself to our bodies, in this case, the inner workings of the heart.

Of course, Leavis is talking about the novel, less established or esteemed than poetry ever was. But the general point still holds: what she advocates is a literature that makes purely intellectual demands. Worried that the Philistine mass culture that ours has become is too unthinking, dumb or 'naïve' (1965 [1932]: 156) to appreciate the more refined literatures which appeal to our senses rather than our sensations, she calls upon, in the words of her husband, a 'small minority that the discerning appreciation of art and literature depends: it is [...] only a few who are capable of unprompted, first-hand judgment' (F. R. Leavis 1930: 3-4, qtd. Q. D. Leavis (1965 [1932]: 202). By endorsing reading as a 'bracing mental exercise' (1965 [1932]: 135), and by rejecting therefore that which touches its audience physically or emotionally, she removes from the rhetorical trichotomy – *docere–delectare–movere* – its third component, that literature is also pleasurable, and as such worthy, because it *moves* its audience, a dictum which had 'served for centuries to collect under three heads the sum of aesthetic effects on readers' (Abrams 1953: 16) and 'justified all aesthetic practice from antiquity to the later modern period' (Jauss 1982a: 30).

The consumption and critical reception of literature is not exclusively about learning, discerning and the improvement of minds, those qualities associated with reason, thought and interpretive acuity, which the Leavises, Leavisites and other twentieth-century 'textualists' defend above all else, but also about affects, those qualities associated with sentiment and sensation. As I will show in this chapter, the reader, just like the literary critic as a kind of expert reader, evolves in the course of literary-critical history from a sensuous being into a phenomenological[3] one, whose engagement with literature is confined to acts of contemplation, understanding, sense-making. I take my cue here from Jane Tompkins's argument that the shift from a conception of literature as a 'unit of force' which acts upon the reader, even spurs him or her to certain actions (doing), to a conception of the literary work as an 'object' to be interpreted for its meaning (being), marks the difference between a theory of literature that adheres to a long rhetorical tradition and a literary theory that has adopted the relatively recent doctrine of formalism (1980: 201-32). Thus, the bulk of literary theories in the twentieth century, including those that profess to be concerned with readers' responses, are predominantly about the readers' mental activities, how a reader makes sense of a text, whereas theories of literature before that were very much working within what might be called a tradition of 'affective criticism'. That affect has been ignored in modern critical practices, which tend to seize on a text as a signifying effect (i.e., for its meaning, or its limits to intelligibility) to the exclusion of any other effects, represents therefore a relatively tiny instance of a much longer history of criticism, one which we are likely to forget, or relegate, if we focus too intently on criticism produced in the last eighty years or so.

Docere–delectare–movere

If we cast our eye back to criticism from classical antiquity, we can see that Plato is ambivalent about the effect that poetry can have on its audience, and argued that it 'ought to be controlled' because of the passions it 'feeds and waters' in us (*Republic* ca. 373 BC, 607). Implicit in this very critique is his acknowledgment of the affective powers of literature, an issue which he debates in *Ion* (ca. 390 BC, 535):

ION: I will tell you frankly that whenever I recite a tale of pity, my eyes are filled with tears, and when it is one of horror or dismay, my hair stands up on end with fear, and my heart goes leaping.
SOCRATES: Well now, Ion, what are we to say of a man like that? [...] Shall we say that the man is in his senses?

Literature's ability to stir the emotions, and ability to engender make-believe, is what renders it potentially dangerous, a conception which leads Plato not only to favour philosophy over poetry but to banish the latter from the Republic. Aristotle, on the other hand, has a much more positive view of the poetic, and sees in tragedy especially, since it articulates and arouses emotions such as pity and fear, a potentially purgative effect. By feeling with, or feeling oneself into, the action presented, the spectator undergoes a catharsis because the performance provokes a 'calm of mind, all passions spent' (Aristotle, qtd. Daiches 1956: 39). For Aristotle then the pleasure of the poetic lies in the way an audience is *moved* by it, which is why catharsis, alongside poiesis and aesthesis, constitutes a crucial category of aesthetic experience. In this respect it is not surprising that a modernist playwright such as Bertolt Brecht (cf. 1978: 71), who lays great emphasis on educating the spectator, should have rejected Aristotle's notion of catharsis on the grounds that the emotions the tragic engages in the audience lull them into a passive submission to the action presented on stage, rather than enhancing their critical faculties in the process of viewing. Whereas Brecht argued that theatre ought to wake up the spectator from potential reverie and disrupt the process of empathy between spectator and character, or for that matter that between character and actor, for Aristotle the point is to imitate or put oneself through the array of sensory emotions played out in the play. The point for Brecht is not to imitate the gestures of those on stage but to question, criticize and counteract them: the audience must step back from the action so as to judge it, and ultimately act differently. Neither empathy nor persuasion therefore have a place in the Brechtian conception of theatre, since the impetus for action comes from the disjunction between that which is shown and that which the audience must see for itself; whereas, for Aristotle, in common with the rhetorical tradition, emotion – because it *moves* the audience – is part of the art of persuasion, and it is not by intellectual disengagement from but by engagement with the emotions that a better citizen is produced.

It is Longinus (probably first century AD), however, whose influence has made itself felt most among those who have considered literature's effects from the perspective of its affective impact on its audience. In his treatise *On the Sublime*, rediscovered in the Renaissance through Niccolo da Falgano's translation into Italian (1560), and made popular in eighteenth-century Europe through Nicolas Boileau's rendition into French (1674), Longinus grants particular importance to the emotions when he says that 'nothing makes so much for grandeur as genuine emotion in the right place. It inspires the words as it were with a fine frenzy and fills them with divine afflatus' (VIII). Unlike the emotions associated with Aristotelian catharsis, which are experienced as therapeutic, in Longinus' assessment the emotions triggered by the sublimity of composition have an immediate and striking impact, transporting the recipient to 'new heights of passionate experience' (Daiches 1956: 46). Emotions are not merely an index of the persuasive power of literature, a means by which we experience delight and gain greater understanding (*delectare–docere*), but the hallmark of poetic greatness insofar as *moving* the audience to rapture is a valuable end in itself.

For the sublime not only persuades, but even throws an audience into transport. The marvellous always works with more surprising force, than that which barely persuades or delights. In most cases, it is wholly in our power, either to resist or yield to persuasion. But the Sublime, endued with strength irresistible, strikes home, and triumphs over every hearer. (I)

In this scenario of audience response, it is apparent that the hearer/reader, when faced with the sublime as the very height of poetic achievement, is powerless against its 'irresistible' effects. Critical detachment is of no relevance here, since this is an appreciation of literature focused entirely on affect, that which sublime composition, itself the result of a passion unleashed, is capable of unleashing in us: we experience rapture or ecstasy because it 'casts a spell on us' by 'winning a complete mastery over our minds' (XXXIX). *On the Sublime* not only gives us a glimpse of Longinus' theory of literature, but it also reveals a key aspect of the function of criticism in antiquity. As Tompkins explains, the critic's task then was not to analyse a work for what it meant, but to identify, describe and, crucially, also prescribe the means by which the poetic moves its audience, since 'the ultimate goal in studying literature is to become master of a technique' (1980: 203), the kind of 'eloquence' of which Cicero once said that it 'thunders like a mighty torrent, which all look up to and admire, but despair of emulating' (*Orator*, rpt. Selden 1988: 326).

   Ideas about the poetic which had been debated in antiquity still domi-nated thinking in the early modern period, with many of the ancient texts being rediscovered, the Greeks translated into Latin and, later, Latin texts translated into the vernacular. Following the ancients' advice on how rhet-oric might equip a work for effect, critics continued the debate on how a work might best instruct, delight and move an audience, albeit not always ascribing equal weight to these categories (cf. Abrams 1953: 16). One of the most important neo-classical treatises was undoubtedly Sir Philip Sidney's *An Apology for Poetry* (1595). In this essay he puts forward the doctrine that the poet's aim is 'both to delight and teach: and delight to move men to take that goodness in hand' (1973: 103). Sidney makes it clear that *moving* the audience entails not just that 'their hearts [be] moved' (ibid.: 114), but that the poet also 'moveth to virtue' (ibid.: 123). Literature in this conception has an effect on an audience, in the sense of moving them to affect; it is also, however, imbued with a moral dimension. The poet, just like the philoso-pher, is capable of 'instructing' his reader, says Sidney, but, when it comes to 'moving', the poet 'leaves [the philosopher] behind him' (ibid.: 120), because it is the poet, and not the philosopher, who 'most inflameth the mind with desire to be worthy' (ibid.: 119). Poetry can teach us more than philosophy, but only because it moves us more, which is why, for Sidney, 'moving is of a higher degree than teaching' (ibid.: 112). Since moving the audience must also be a 'moving to well-doing', it follows that what Sidney puts forward is a 'moral doctrine' (ibid.) which gives poetry its *raison d'être*, but which makes this *raison d'être* entirely dependent on literature's power to affect readers.

Sidney's claim that poetry, because it moves us more, also teaches us more deliberately undermines Plato's utility claim for philosophy that it alone can transform and reform us. According to his reasoning in the *Republic*, the poet by contrast to the philosopher is a peddler of artifice and lies, which make his art – indeed, art *per se* – dangerous to the well-being of society. If for Plato poetry failed to have moral purchase because, rather than teaching us something useful, it incites our passions, for Sidney the opposite is true. It is the specific virtue of poetry that, by exciting the passions, it can inculcate virtue. Sidney's conception of the function of poetry is therefore very much of its time, given that literature in the Renaissance was primarily 'defined as a shaper of public morals' (Tompkins 1980: 207).

Literature affects us, insofar as it excites the passions; it also has certain effects on us, namely our reform or betterment. What come together here are two poles, one to do with aesthetics, the other with ethics. Passion as a category of aesthetic experience induces a reaction within the reader, thus poetry acts upon the reader; equally, however, passion moves the reader beyond the poetic, either to action or to virtue. Since the passions are sentiments experienced within, they are affective responses by which literature moves the reader internally. To say that literature affects, and that reading is an affective experience, is very different from saying that literature has certain effects on our behaviour, can move or persuade a reader to take certain actions. In the broadest sense, one has to do with feeling and physical reaction, the other with persuasion and social action. One moves inward, the other outward. One is played out in the realm of private sensations; the other manifests itself in public actions. While affect and effect worked in tandem in the rhetorical tradition of criticism, because both terms describe literature's ability to *move* its audience, a certain rift makes itself felt from the eighteenth century onwards between that which *affects* and that which has *effects*.

In the Enlightenment period, the tendency to affirm the aesthetic in its own right becomes increasingly apparent. Critics seize on aesthetics to explain the whole spectrum of our sensate experience of the world, including art and literature, while turning away from rhetoric as the ancient art of persuasion by which discursive disciplines such as literature, philosophy and history exert certain influences in the world. The greater emphasis on affect, as opposed to effect, signals a retreat from a public into a more intimate sphere: the private world of emotions and sensations. What emerges is '[a] new kind of human subject – sensitive, passionate, individualist' (Eagleton 1990: 27). Although the Renaissance had put the human subject at the very centre of its activity, the passage to the eighteenth century witnessed a transition from a humanism still deeply steeped in religious culture to the more secular society of the Enlightenment, where theological certainties had receded so much that man was now thrown back upon himself, and had to look within to find the sources and forces which moved him. This is also why questions about affect, once closely tied to effect, are posed less and less in relation to civic behaviour and ethical action, as Sidney certainly had done, but probed more and more from the perspective of aesthetics, and later also from that of psychology.

The reception of Longinus' *On the Sublime* is illustrative of this rift between affect and effect, especially as presented by Boileau, who apart from the translation itself wrote several prefaces and commentaries on the work between 1674 and 1710 (cf. Lyotard 1991: 95). Longinus, like other critics belonging to the rhetorical tradition, assumes that writers can be taught the art of persuasion. Accordingly, poetic intensities which evoke pleasures seemingly beyond the audience's control are based on *techne,* with rules of composition that can be learned and deployed so as to transport audiences to rapture and ecstasy, or in Sidney's sense, to 'well-doing'. However, when Boileau insists that what makes the sublime sublime cannot be taught because 'it is not linked to rules that can be determined through poetics', he introduces a decidedly modern take on the sublime. As Jean-François Lyotard explains, the sublime 'requires a further "je ne sais quoi", also called *genius* or something "incomprehensible and inexplicable", a "gift from God", a fundamentally "hidden" phenomenon that can be recognised only by its effects on the addressee' (ibid.: 96).[4] The idea that the sublime is an uncertain 'je ne *sais* quoi', a non-knowledge, adumbrates a Kantian asthetics insofar as the latter regards the sublime as that which incapacitates the faculty of understanding. If the sublime is non-knowledge, it cannot be transmitted or acquired as something knowable. Fundamentally it is an experience and cannot be learned, because it bypasses understanding and goes staight to the senses. Two issues arise from this. Firstly, for Lyotard, this is 'how aesthetics, the analysis of the addressee's feelings, comes to supplant poetics and rhetoric, which are didactic forms, of and by the understanding, intended for the artist as sender' (ibid.: 97). Secondly, the sublime not only strikes the addressee with unforeseeable force, but also overcomes the artist with feelings he is unable to master. Boileau's insistence that didactics are powerless when it comes to the sublime recasts the role of the artist, who becomes, 'in so far as he is a genius, the involuntary addressee of an inspiration come to him from "I know not what"' (ibid.: 96). It is this emphasis on the artist as genius which, although already present in Longinus, becomes crucial for the Romantics, insofar as it feeds the idea that the feelings of the artist – and not those of the addressee – are of paramount importance for critical enquiry.

From reader to author to text

This marks one of the most significant shifts in the history of criticism, since a concern with what affects and moves the reader becomes slowly supplanted with a concern with what affects and moves the author. Concerned less with seizing on sentiment as a primary force of literary reception and consumption and more with seizing on sentiment as a primary force of literary production, critics of the Romantic era begin to look more to the figure of the author than the reader. As M. H. Abrams shows, in *The Mirror and the Lamp* (1953), judging a work of art by how much it moves its audience is no longer of primary importance for the Romantics; rather, the 'predominant cause and even the end and test of art' is to be found in the poet's 'own mental powers and emotional needs' (1953: 21). What begins to wane at this point in the history of criticism is a notion of literature intended to have an effect upon an audience, and what begins to emerge in an embryonic form instead is literature as an expression of authorial intention.

In Abrams's view, William Wordsworth was the first Romantic to have made 'the feelings of the poet the center of critical reference', which is why his writings 'mark a turning-point in English literary theory' (1953: 103). When Wordsworth states, in the revised edition of the Preface to *Lyrical Ballads* from 1850, that the poet is 'a man pleased with his own passions and volitions', and that he 'rejoices more than other men in the spirit of life that is in him' (1974: 138), it is clear that he still operates with the concept of *movere*. Crucially, though, the concept of *movere* affects the poet more than it does his fellow men. It is not just the poet's receptiveness to his environment that is more developed, but both his imaginative and his expressive powers are also superior to those of other men. If the feelings are stronger in the poet than in any of his fellow men, then they are also stronger than any feelings that the poet might evoke in any of his readers. It is here that the artist rises above his fellow men (he is a genius) and as a result is also set apart from them. Thus, when Percy Shelley claims, in 'A Defence of Poetry' (1821), that the poet 'is more delicately organized than other men, and sensible to pain and pleasure, his own and that of others, in a degree unknown to them' (1965: 139), not only does he echo Wordworth's assessment, but his statement epitomizes the Romantic notion of the lonely and suffering artist par excellence.

That this turn to the author should have occurred at the end of the eighteenth century is not without context. Not only was the old patronage system disappearing with commercial printing, but the whole literary marketplace was undergoing changes. With the reader increasingly distant, part of an ever more heterogeneous and unknowable audience, it is as if the author turns inwards and literature becomes the subjective expression of its author's personality, an introverted form of communication by a solitary artist to a reader, whose reaction this author can barely gauge. Indeed, the author becomes so removed from the world of his reader that, by the time John Stuart Mill debates what poetry is in 1833, he boldly asserts that '[p]oetry is feeling, confessing itself to itself in moments of solitude' (qtd. Abrams 1953: 25). For Abrams this claim is indicative of how '[t]he poet's audience is reduced to a single member, consisting of the poet himself', a further retreat therefore from a public into a private sphere, as well as the disappearance of the reader into the figure of the author. Mill's claim can also be taken as an instance of an emerging formalism, insofar as it allows a glimpse of what is to come: poetry 'confessing itself to itself' is surely poetry written for itself. It is worth dwelling on this difference further since it is suggestive of yet another shift that was occurring in the way in which criticism approached its subject of study at that time. For it might be argued that with the passage into the nineteenth century it is not just the case that the author turns away from the reader, and turns inward, but literary enquiry itself begins to turn inward.

A literary criticism less concerned with how the audience is moved by literature, what literature *does* to the reader, or what effects it has on the wider world, is a criticism that is ultimately more interested in what literature *is*, how it might be defined for the reader either by the author himself or by the critic as a spokesman for this author. What the turn from the reader towards the author, just as the turn from *doing* to *being*, would seem to initiate is a criticism that, by and large, is concerned more with questions about the nature of the literary itself than literature's wider utility, where literature does not fulfil certain ends but is an end in itself. Although we have to wait until the early part of the twentieth century for this transition to take full effect, we can already see the seeds of this thinking in Baudelaire's declaration of 1857 that it is not a poem's utility but its intrinsic aesthetic qualities that qualify it as a poem:

A whole crowd of people imagine that the aim of poetry is some sort of lesson, that its duty is to fortify conscience, or to perfect social behaviour, or even, finally, to demonstrate something or other that is useful. [...] *poetry will be seen to have no other aim but itself*; it can have no other, and no poem will be as great, as noble, so truly worthy of the name 'poem' as the one written for no purpose other than the pleasure of writing a poem.

(1983: 191-2; my emphasis)

Extricating a work from influences that might have fed into it or might emanate from it, i.e., everything that is strictly speaking external to the poem itself, signals an intrinsic approach to the literary object instead. This kind of formalism, which Mill's statement adumbrates and Baudelaire's spells out in the above quotation, is also, of course, what characterizes the literary practices of the 'Art for Art's Sake' movement and the practices of much twentieth-century literary criticism. More interested in the work itself than its impact on the receiver, this burgeoning 'text-centred' approach, which later even jettisons the author from its enquiry, brings to fruition the Kantian formulation that art is 'purposiveness without purpose' (1902–:V.226; 1987: 73).

Disinterested and contemplative reading

Much has been said so far about the importance that sentiment played in literary enquiry, be this the passions, feelings and emotions which poetry was said to incite in the reader or those that were subsequently held to guide the poetic process of creation. But little has been said about the dangers that were also perceived with regard to sensory experience. Kant is the figure whose work in the *Critique of Judgment* (1790) has been most influential with respect to this. Worried about the ways in which the poetic was hailed for its power to unleash passions in its readers, Kant in an attempt to curb such stimulation offered the remedy of 'disinterestedness' (1902–: V.203-11; 1987: 43-53). What he rejects is a conception of art which valorizes artworks for their affects and effects. To say that artworks have 'purposiveness without purpose', i.e., 'formal purposiveness', is to counter the idea that art has utility for social or moral ends; and to say that the reader or spectator must judge in a disinterested state is a means by which to counter the *false* idea that artworks affect their beholders in such a way as to demand their succumbing to sensuous pleasure and surrender of the self. Instead, Kant proposes that artworks be contemplated for their beauty disinterestedly, that is, dispassionately. The moment of contemplation requires that a distance be established between the self and its everyday interests and the object that might serve those interests. Aesthetic pleasure, according to this reasoning, is distinct from ordinary enjoyment, since it resists absorption, and creates critical distance instead. The point is to disconnect one's sensuous responses from that which, particularly with regard to the sublime, inspires awe, horror, terror or passion in us. Whereas Longinus' text on the sublime constitutes a manual for the production of affect, Kant's reconsideration of it turns the sublime into a means for the affects' suspension. Thus, contrary to Longinus, for whom the sublime is 'endured with strength irresistible' because it 'strikes home, and triumphs over every hearer' (I), for Kant, the recipient is never powerless before its 'irresistible' effects, provided we disengage our affective stimuli, such as emotion and passion, from the motives of our actions, in favour of our 'intellectual stimulus' (to use Q. D. Leavis's turn of phrase) to reflection and contemplation.

What the process of contemplation does is to separate the artwork from its more immediate effects on the beholder. The recipient must become as detached from the poem as the poem is from the world, and so the artwork stands by itself, an object we reflect upon and not an object which acts upon us. If literature should not be 'felt', but thought about, then it follows also that it is less its effects which are of importance to the critic than its value in itself, its definition and internal structure. With Kant then we can see the emergence of the kind of 'text-centred' approach which Baudelaire puts into practice in the nineteenth century, and which the New Criticism makes the dominant practice of the first half of the twentieth century. It is here also that literature begins to appeal less to our hearts than to our heads, less to our bodies than to our minds, less to our emotions than to our faculties for reasoning. Although Kant never denies either that artworks have effects or the reality of affect, i.e., that affect exists, he crucially shifts focus from these 'material' to the 'formal' elements of the artwork. Thus, while Kant seeks mechanisms by which to curb these harmful ('pathological') effects on the beholder, much of the criticism that is to come loses sight of affect altogether.

Only Nietzsche, as we saw in the last chapter, who insists in his notes 'Toward the Physiology of Art' (1888) on art as rapture, or intoxication (1967–: 327-8), strikes a bridge to the classical Longinian tradition, albeit from the perspective of the sense experience of modernity (see chapter 3). What

Nietzsche therefore still works with is an older conception of aesthetics, namely as sense experience which can bring about the dissolution of the autonomy of self by putting the 'I' into a rapture beyond itself, rather than the modern, post-Kantian conception of aesthetics, which lays claim to a reciprocal autonomy of self and artwork. Nietzsche dismissively counters his own aesthetics-as-physiology against a Kantian aesthetics: 'Since Kant, all talk of art, beauty, knowledge, and wisdom has been smudged and besmirched by the concept "devoid of interest"' (1905–: XIX.132). By embracing 'the pathological element in rapture' (1967– [1888]: 327), which Kant seeks to resist, Nietzsche in effect promotes the 'physiological danger of art', thus remaining a unique, if lonely, voice amid a new criticism which is otherwise disinterested in affect.

Debates on the harmful effects of literature live on, of course, in critiques of upstart genres such as the novel and later film (see chapters 3 and 4); but when it comes to that which is worthy of criticism, i.e., poetry, written for the few rather than the many, little consideration of affect survives. Instead, all that remains of the old rhetorical trichotomy of *docere–delectare–movere*, so crucial for literary enquiry since antiquity, is a sense that literature *moves* us not because it affects our sensations but because it provides a typology by which to improve our sensibility. *Movere* is directed more and more towards the improvement of our minds, and is largely irrelevant when it comes to somatic affect; *delectare* is neither enchantment, bewitchment nor sensory pleasure, but a sober delight in the beauty of the object, its form and internal unity; and only *docere* remains intact, albeit in an altered form. Literature's lesson, if it has one at all, is primarily moral rather than social or political. It makes us better human beings not because it moves us to virtue or leads us to action; it civilizes us because, in contemplating its perfection, it elevates our intellection.

That literature elevates our intellection is an assumption which Matthew Arnold makes throughout his treatise 'The Function of Criticism at the Present Time' (1865). The only proviso is that we read good literature, and here the critic can help, since the task at hand is 'to lead [man] towards perfection, by making his mind dwell upon what is excellent in itself' (1907 [1865]: 12). The trouble has been that criticism has 'so little kept in the pure intellectual sphere' (ibid.: 20), which is why Arnold is keen to institute a criticism that can make its reader 'remember that he has a mind' (ibid.: 17). What is gone from his writing are any references to affect. Neither Arnold nor the Arnoldian reader *remembers that he has a body*, that the literary once moved our hearts, transported us to new passionate heights, or enthralled and absorbed us so utterly that we forgot ourselves, even if it was for the merest of instants. All that is left is a moral efficacy, which demands our disinterestedness.

And how is criticism to show disinterestedness? By keeping aloof from what is called 'the practical view of things'; by resolutely following the law of its own nature, which is to be a free play of the mind on all subjects which it touches. By steadily refusing to lend itself to any of those ulterior, political, practical considerations of ideas, which plenty of people will be sure to attach to them, [...] but which criticism has really nothing to do with. Its business is, as I have said, simply to know the best that is known and thought in the world, and by in its turn making this known, to create a current of true and fresh ideas.

(Arnold 1907 [1865]: 18-19)

It is clear from this passage that, for poetry to have an effect on the world, it must withdraw from it, remain unsoiled by it, and be elevated above it. Text must be divorced from context, so that we can 'see the object as in itself it really is' (ibid.: 1), for only then, not as an end of or to something, but as an end in itself, can a poem claim eternal value for itself. However distasteful this propaganda for a canon might be in a contemporary light, the belief in the necessity of 'an infallible touchstone for detecting the presence or absence of high poetic quality' (Arnold 1906 [1880]: 17), so that we may know what is timeless and universal, is his way of not just making us better human beings, or civilizing us, but of attempting to save civilization as such. His humanism, as his concomitant elitism, like that of the Leavises, seems to be born of a fear that, without adequate guidance by the critic, the increasingly literate masses might read not what improves the mind, but what gives raw pleasure. Like T. S. Eliot later, and Wordsworth before, Arnold feels that his age is beset by rapid changes which have put his culture under assault. If for Wordsworth it had been sensory overload and overstimulation which 'blunt[ed] the discriminating powers of the mind' (1974 [1800]: 128), for Arnold it was the 'brutalising influence of our passionate material progress' (1907 [1865]: 17). It is clear from both their responses that the fast pace of modernity necessitated an antidote. Poetry, as this antidote, can presumably fulfil the function that religion once had; it can help, so Arnold says, 'to interpret life for us, to console us, to sustain us' (1906 [1880]: 2). The critical concerns of this period are perhaps best summed up in an observation by I. A. Richards: if confronted with 'a mental chaos such as man has never experienced', he explains, '[w]e shall then be thrown back, as Matthew Arnold foresaw, upon poetry. It is capable of saving us; it is a perfectly possible means of overcoming chaos' (1974 [1926]: 82-3).[5]

The point for Richards, in many respects an heir of Arnold's thinking, is neither to interpret nor to change the world, but – as with Arnold – to appreciate the best of it and provide a corrective for the worst of it. Since the world is anarchic, and poetry is not, poetry can save us from disorder by transferring on to the reader a state of order. Poetry is capable of organizing our minds, since through it, Richards says, we can attain 'a complete equilibrium' and rein in our manifold and 'disconnected impulses' (1974 [1926]: 29), that is, recalibrate them 'into a single ordered response' (1967 [1924]: 192). This is a complete reversal of the rhetorical tradition, for to put the mind in equilibrium is nothing other than an attempt at arresting *movere*. The reader is no longer *moved* by poetry, but poetry restores the reader's immobility in the face of the chaos which moves around us. True, poetry for Richards uses 'emotive language' which has a therapeutic effect on the reader, but emotion is not meant to be unleashed so as to cast 'a spell on us' by 'winning a complete mastery over our minds', as Longinus suggested. Instead, it is meant to be ordered within the reader's re-equilibrated, contemplative mind. Despite the accusation therefore by many of Richards's followers, namely proponents of the New Criticism, that what he practised was an affective criticism, Richards's largely psycho-physiological explanations of literary affect indicate – insofar as what he seeks is 'equilibrium' – that reading for him is not about affect but how to manage it. Whereas for Wordsworth poetry had been an author's expression of 'the spontaneous overflow of powerful feelings' (1974 [1800]: 148), and for Richards its management by the reader, Eliot goes much further: the aim or '[t]he end of the enjoyment of poetry is pure contemplation from which all the accidents of personal emotion are removed' – which is why good criticism is that which will 'aim to see the object as it really is' and 'bad criticism, on the other hand, is nothing but an expression of emotion' (1960 [1920]: 14-15). It seems that within the span of just over a hundred years affect has diminished from sublimity to fallacy. In that same timespan also the figure of the author, who was so central for Romantic theory, is ousted from literary enquiry, and it is the text itself which now takes centre stage.

Close reading

Eliot's famous declaration, in 'Tradition and Individual Talent' (1919), that 'poetry is not a turning loose of emotion, but an escape from emotion; it is not the expression of personality, but an escape from personality' (1960 [1920]: 58), thus becomes the guiding principle for two of the New Criticism's central tenets: what W. K. Wimsatt, and his co-author Monroe C. Beardsley, in the *Sewanee Review* called 'The Intentional Fallacy' (1946) and 'The Affective Fallacy' (1949). As is made clear in the following citation from *The Verbal Icon* (1954), in which both essays later appeared, neither the author's intention nor the reader's response are deemed desirable or necessary components of literary analysis.

> The Intentional Fallacy is a confusion between the poem and its origins [...]. It begins by trying to derive the standard of criticism from the psychological *causes* of the poem and ends in biography and relativism. The Affective Fallacy is a confusion between the poem and its *results* (what it *is* and what it *does*) [...]. It begins by trying to derive the standard of criticism from the psychological effects of the poem and ends in impressionism and relativism. The outcome of either Fallacy, the Intentional or the Affective, is that the poem itself, as an object of specifically critical judgment, tends to disappear.
>
> (1954: 21)

From this description it is obvious why the New Critics should have rejected much of Richards's work, since it falls into the trap of the affective fallacy. However, in another respect, Richards's approach to literature, not unlike Eliot's, is the crucial impetus behind (and the reason why he is also part of) the project of the New Criticism. In his book *Practical Criticism* (1929) Richards give an account of an experiment he conducted with his students, which entailed giving them unseen poems without titles or authors' names, and inviting them to 'comment freely' on those poems, responses which he then analyses. This empirical exercise, which for Richards showed up the shortcomings of his students' readings, more importantly, however, introduced a mode of study which has remained, certainly as concerns 'English students in England today', Eagleton says, 'whether they know it or not' (1983: 31), the dominant practice of doing literary analysis, namely practical criticism: the close reading of a text divorced from any context, and what F. R. Leavis would later call the close attention to the 'words on the page'. It is a text-centred approach par excellence, which, in the Arnoldian tradition, looks to 'the *object* as in itself it really is' and demands that the *subject*, be this the author or reader, vanish from literary enquiry. This is also why Wimsatt and Beardsley do not ask what the poem *does* (to the *subject* of the reader) but what it *is* (as an *object*).

Criticism here has truly turned inward. Not only does it make the text itself its primary focus, but, by asking for the definition of a poem by way of isolating those properties which make poetry poetic (as the Russian Formalists would say), the parameter is set for an enquiry into what the subject of literary study itself entails: it no longer requires that it be set in relation to wider issues or other disciplines (such as philosophy or history), but it truly focuses on itself. As such, neither the literary text nor literary study is any longer treated in relation to context.

As a self-enclosed entity, where textual elements operate with each other within their own 'context', the text itself is the place where all the tools of analyses lie. But unlike Richards, for whom the various elements are reconciled or harmonized within the reader, for his later disciples, a close attention to the poem itself will reveal that it is the text itself which has already undertaken this task. The assumption will be that unity adheres in the text, whatever contradictions, paradoxes, or ambiguity it might first appear to contain. As Wimsatt puts it, in *The Verbal Icon*: 'The kind of unity which we look for and find in poetry is attained only through a degree of complexity of design which itself involves maturity and richness' (1954: 81-2). Although the New Critics reject the Romantic emphasis on the author, they share a similar concern with organic unity. In line with their British counterparts Richards and Leavis, they look to poetry to find what John Crowe Ransom describes as 'an order of existence which in actual life is constantly crumbling beneath' (1938: 348). Once more, then, we have come back to the healing properties of poetry. It can save civilization because it provides a degree of order and harmony, through unity, which is missing from life, and in particular modern life with all its confusion and disorder. Only good poetry, however, is able to achieve this, its hallmark being its complexity, which, as Wimsatt states above, is defined in terms of a poem's unity of structure and meaning.

This the New Critics take to be an objectively observable fact by the kind of critic who pays close enough attention to what Ransom calls 'the technique of the art'. This entails an understanding of a text's language and structure and, with regard to the poetic more specifically, an understanding of its 'technical devices' and their 'systematic usage' – for instance, a poem's 'metric; its inversions, solecisms, lapses from the prose norm of language, and from close prose logic; its tropes; its fictions, or inventions, by which it secures "aesthetic distance" and removes itself from history' (1938: 347). The poem, in other words, is looked at from the perspective of that which qualifies it as poetry, isolating those properties of its language and structure which can be shown to differentiate it from prose. Such examinations, Ransom tells us, 'belong to criticism certainly', the task being that '[t]he critic has *to take* the poem *apart*, or *analyse* it, for the sake of uncovering these features' (ibid.: 349; my emphasis). Unlike the *prescriptive* criticism of the rhetorical tradition, which sought to 'dictate' how a poem might be written to best affect its reader, and unlike the Arnoldian tradition, whose *evaluative* criticism tried to determine the value of the literary by bracketing off good from bad literature, Ransom's approach epitomizes the New Critics' endeavour for a *descriptive* criticism that keeps its 'aesthetic distance', and is as coolly analytic as it is objective. The poetic work in this conception, to come back to Jane Tompkins's thesis, is not a 'unit of force' (1980: 204) which acts upon the reader, but an 'object' to be taken apart for analysis. As a consequence, '[l]iterary response', Tompkins says, 'becomes a meaningless category, since the chief object of critical concern is not the effects that poems have but their intrinsic nature' (ibid.: 221). Literature is no longer an object to be experienced (through our bodies), but an 'object of knowledge' (for our minds); and once defined in those terms, as signification not sensation, or 'as meaning not doing, interpretation becomes the supreme critical act' (ibid.: 222).

Reading for sense rather than sensation

Modern literary criticism, as instituted by the New Critics between the 1930s and the 1950s, still lives on in the day-to-day reading practices that so many of our students are asked to undertake in seminars. At best, texts are probed for the multitude of their signifying effects, at worst they are interpreted for their apparently correct meaning. What has got lost, then, and this we can attribute to the New Critics' fervour for a criticism that 'shall be objective, shall cite the nature of the object rather than its effects upon the subject' (Ransom 1938: 342), is any sense that literature is also about sensations, not just about sense-making. A criticism that is objective must therefore jettison the physiological from its enquiry, a point which Ransom makes emphatically when he states that

it is hardly criticism to assert that the proper literary work is one [...] that causes in us some remarkable physiological effect, such as oblivion of the outer world, the flowing of tears, visceral or laryngeal sensations, and such like; or one that induces perfect illusions, or brings us into spiritual ecstasy; or even one that produces a catharsis of our emotions.

(Ibid.: 342-3)

And yet, terms such as '*moving, exciting, entertaining, pitiful*', which Ransom declares as 'uncritical' (ibid.: 343),[6] circumscribed an audience's encounter with literature for over two thousand years, constituting therefore a 'long history of critical thought', as Tompkins points out, 'in which the specifica-tion of meaning [was] not a central concern' (1980: 201). While we can understand the distrust of emotion, particularly during a period of European history that saw emotionalism put in the service of fascist ideology (and a reason also of course why Bertolt Brecht continued to stress the importance of critical distance as a requisite for rational and analytic thinking), we can equally see our culture's insistence, as Susan Sontag does, 'to assimilate Art into Thought' (1987 [1967]: 13) as a decidedly historical gesture that hier-achizes sense-making, thinking and reason over a whole array of sensory experience, such as pleasure, feeling and passion. As Sontag argues, in *Against Interpretation*, '[i]n a culture whose classical dilemma is the hypertrophy of the intellect at the expense of energy and sensual capability, interpretation is the revenge of the intellect upon art' (ibid.: 7).

The revenge is not just of the 'intellect upon art', but of the intellect on a mass culture, where mass media such as the novel (at least in its earlier days, and certainly in the form of pulp fiction) and film threatened to undermine everything that the critic as a guardian of culture held dear. Just as F. R. Leavis felt prompted to turn the preservation of high culture into a 'moral and cul-tural crusade' (Eagleton 1983: 33) against the vulgar products of 'mass civi-lization', so Theodor Adorno – albeit coming from a different ideological position to that of Leavis – ventures an attack on art without thought, that is, art for consumption. Adorno's distaste for what he called the culture indus-try led him to formulate a concept of aesthetics which removes genuine art from the realm of sensory experience, now reserved for the 'lowly' forms of commodity art, and places it exclusively, as Hans Robert Jauss explains, in the realm of 'theoretical reflection' (1982a: 17). What Adorno called the 'aesthetics of negativity' (1970) not only insists on the autonomy of art (its removal from the social sphere as the only means by which art can remain oppositional to mainstrean culture, and therefore be political) but also adopts the Kantian principle of disinterestedness, which, by creating a distance between ourselves and the artwork, can procure the necessary critical moment in our relation to art and thereby resist the Philistine demand for immediate gratifi-cation that is the only form of aesthetic experience the culture industry knows. This is a reason why Adorno can accommodate Brecht's 'alienation-effect' within his thesis of negativity, a device by which the spectator gets distanced from the action on stage so as to allow a critical perspective on it, and why he must reject Aristotle's catharsis, given its emphasis on spectator identification as an emotional release valve. While the former is approved for making possible a political art that engages the reader/spectator to think, the latter is subject to disapproval, because, as is also the case in popular forms of entertainment, it aims at indulging in affect. The point is to prevent what Brecht called the 'culinary' consumption of art.

Hans Robert Jauss is one of the few recent voices, however, to have articulated a critique of those who privilege 'suprasensible cognition' over 'sensory experience' (1982a: 37), and who like Adorno, he protests, 'consider aesthetic experience genuine only when it has left all enjoyment behind and risen to the level of aesthetic reflection' (ibid.: 27). What such critics have done is to have relegated 'primary levels of aesthetic experience', such as 'astonishment, admiration, being shaken or touched, sympathetic tears and laughter, or estrangement' (ibid.: 153), even suppressed them, he says, 'in favour of the higher level of aesthetic reflection' (ibid.: 21). In his book *Aesthetic Experience and Literary Hermeneutics* (1982), which is very much also a revision of his earlier work (discussed in chapter 6), Jauss reminds us that pleasure in art consists of both: 'the direct sensuous surrender of the self to an object', which belongs to 'ordinary enjoyment' (1982a: 30), and 'the contemplative act of the viewer', which belongs to 'aesthetic satisfaction' and which, crucially, 'is always required to constitute the aesthetic object' (ibid.: 30-1). How literature therefore *acts* on the reader (affects him or her) and how the literary object is *actively* constituted as an object in the act of contemplation (how it comes into being through interpretation) are for Jauss the two modes by which aesthetic experience operates. Or, to put it into our vocabulary, sensation and sense-making are the two categories by which readers engage with literature. As the following passage reminds us, we must never underestimate

the communicative achievement of art at the level of primary identifications such as admiration, emotion, laughing, and crying with the hero which only aesthetic snobbery will consider vulgar. For it is in such identifications and only secondarily in the aesthetic reflection that detaches itself from them that aesthetic experience turns into symbolic or communicative action.

(Ibid.: 19)

What Jauss seeks to bring home to us then is a double articulation of aesthetic experience: that of 'understanding enjoyment and enjoying understanding', or what he also calls 'self-enjoyment in the enjoyment of something other' (1982a: 32). Interested not only in how pleasure might be analysed historically (through categories such as poiesis, aesthesis and catharsis), but also in a 'definition of pleasure', he puts forward the thesis that 'a completely sensuous and a highly intellectual affect thus come together in aesthetic enjoyment' (ibid.: 23). In turn of course this manages to bypass precisely what others, as different as Arnold and Adorno, sought to institute: the separation of lowly literature from high literature, and its concomitant, the cutting loose of lowly bodily functions, such as tears and fears, from the higher activities of the mind. Jauss's approach on the other hand serves to encompass both.

The twentieth century, as a culmination of all that the nineteenth century had already felt in terms of industrialization, the massification of society, cultural and sensory overload (see chapter 3), spawned the kinds of negativity theses that see what remains of our 'order of existence', to quote Ransom once more, in terms of something that is 'constantly crumbling beneath'. In literary-critical respects, it is as if the critic, and by extension the reader, must cope with disorder by elevating him- or herself above it; must either remain stoically unaffected by it or, by engagement, make order out of disorder. This requires that the intellect take control. One such way of seeking or imposing order is for the critic to adopt the mode of disinterestedness, that is, to create a distance between the art object and its beholder, and to contemplate a work so as to sever it from any potential somatic reactions in favour of directing political action; after all, that which flows through the body is both immediate and disorderly, provoking instantaneous and equally somatic reactions, therefore necessarily bypassing the conscious control of the mind.

The other way to maintain an orderly equilibrium is to make affective responses subservient to the production of meaning. And this is precisely what the only critic apart from Jauss who is notable for his work on affect, namely Norman Holland, has done. Unlike any of his contemporaries writing in the 1960s and 1970s, Holland does show a genuine interest in affect (1989: 281-307; 1975: 292-9), albeit not in the terms in which the Longinian tradition had focused, on sensation, but very much in tune with modern reader-oriented critics' emphases on sense-making. In his particular brand of psychoanalytic account of reading (matched only by David Bleich),[7] Holland argues that literature gives the reader an opportunity to transform fantasies not merely into pleasurable but also into socially acceptable forms. Having asked at the beginning of *The Dynamics of Literary Response* (1989) what is it in a literary work that invokes our 'emotional response' or 'arouses' us (ibid.: 3), in his chapter on 'Affect' he gives us a revealing glimpse of what happens when we read:

> The transformation of a central fantasy toward meaning creates a far more orderly mental process in us than we usually experience. There is also a kind of weakening of affect in the literary situation because we do not expect to act upon it.
>
> (Ibid.: 283)

It seems that the 'weakening of affect' is a consequence of the production of meaning, in which case – for all his talk about the subjective feelings readers experience – Holland exchanges affect for meaning, in effect subordinating sensation to sense-making. This shows how his concerns are very much part of modern reader-oriented criticism rather than rooted in the affective criticism practised by the ancients, insofar as what he advocates is not an unleashing of emotion but its containment into an intellectually recognizable order.

Whether this containment works by way of limiting meaning production in the figure of the author,[8] of keeping it firmly contained within (the unity of) the text (which is true of the New Critics), of making the reader responsible for harmonizing literary effects (as is the case for both Richards and Holland), or by making a strict distinction between a literature that is read for meaning, or *Bildung*, and a literature that is read for affect and entertainment (very much Q. D. Leavis's project), the point is to rule out pleasures and disturbances that cannot be explained rationally. So, when Wimsatt and Beardsley reject 'tears, prickles, or other physiological symptoms' (1954: 34) from literary enquiry, it is precisely because such responses are 'uncritical'; not in the sense, as Ransom has it, that they do not belong to criticism proper, but because they do not belong to our critical, mental faculties. The hypertrophy of the intellect, a sign of which is an increased activity of interpretation, is simultaneously then the deactivation of affect; but of what, in turn, this is a symptom is a desomaticized intellect and the dematerialized text.

This is true not only of criticism but also of reading within modern critical discourse. The dilemma of the reader has been that, with the hypertrophy of the intellect, the waning of affect and the transformation of the body into a critical trope, this figure has gradually disappeared from the coordinates of the critical map, signalled first by the appearance of the author and then by the text itself. And even when the figure of the reader gets resurrected in reader-oriented theories in the late 1960s and 1970s, all this reader can do, as we shall see in the next chapter, is to (mis)interpret.

6 The Reader in Theory

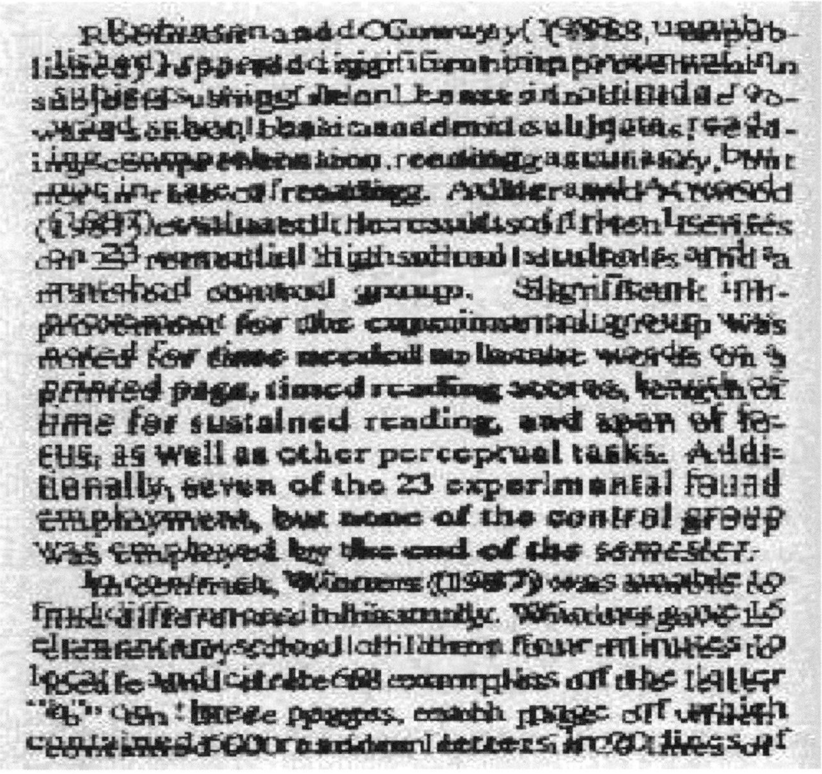

Figure 7 Is a text's readability dependent only on the material condition of the text? Or is readability a conceptual issue, namely, how we conceive of reading, textuality, interpretation, meaning, etc.?

In 1968 Roland Barthes announced that 'the birth of the reader must be at the cost of the death of the Author' (1977: 148). As a programmatic call to shift literary enquiry away from the figure of the author as both the originator and the creator of meaning towards the reader as the producer of meaning, Barthes not only advocated within literary theory a 'return of the reader' (Freund 1987: 13), but also promoted an empowerment of the reader hitherto unseen in literary discourse.[1] While audience response had been an indispensable condition of all literary activity until the eighteenth century, both for those writing and for those commenting on literature, the critical coordinates, as we saw in the previous chapter, began to shift, initially with Romanticism to the author, and subsequently with modernism to the text itself. When the reader re-emerges on the critical map, it is not, however, as a figure on which literature *acts*, or as a figure *moved* by literature, as had been the case in the classical rhetorical tradition, but as a figure who responds to literature as 'an occasion for interpretation' (Tompkins 1980: 206). The reader as a sense-maker, rather than as a sensuous figure, is what differentiates the work of contemporary literary theorists of reading, such as Iser, Jauss, Culler and Fish, from the Affective Criticism of their predecessors, who were more interested in the passions induced in the (therefore 'passive') reader than in the meanings produced by the (therefore 'active') reader. In this respect, post-Barthesian literary theory has turned the reader from a passive into an active figure, from someone *acted upon* to someone who 'intellectualizes' the literary work from the outset (Barthes 1974: 16): as Barthes says in *S/Z*, 'the goal of literary work (of literature as work) is to make the reader no longer a consumer, but a producer of text' (ibid.: 4).

Although Barthes goes much further here than some audience-oriented theorists are willing to do, his stance can in many crucial respects be aligned with that of the Yale critics, who equally mount an argument for the blurring of the categories of reading and writing.[2] Like that of Barthes, therefore, Miller's, de Man's, Bloom's and Hartman's extensive work on reading, deeply influenced by Derrida's deconstruction, 'refus[es] the subterfuge of a passive or restrictive role' for the reader, who, as Hartman tells us, 'becomes at once reader and writer [...] both an interpreter of texts and a self-interpreting producer of further texts' (1980: 162). Theoretically, then, the new coordinates of reading reposition the active reader, both against a being-acted-upon by literature (reading is producing) and, more pervasively, against the essentially passive role ascribed to the reader as a good or bad *receiver of meaning* from an 'Author-God' (Barthes 1977: 146).

However, the sheer welter of different approaches to the relations between text and reader makes 'audience-oriented criticism', as Suleiman put it, 'not one field but many' (1980: 6). Against these *ideal* and universal accounts of the reader, many theories of reading have turned to the various *actual* and *particularly embodied* readers, importing insights into literary theory from the study of gender, sexuality, race and ethnicity. The relatively recent theorizations of gay reading by Koestenbaum (1995) and the lesbian reader by Kennard (1986), or the many accounts of reading by feminist theorists (see chapter 7), including those on black women's responses such as Bobo's (1995), have multiplied a diversity which has made labelling in any other than the loosest terms difficult at best. Despite therefore the convenient umbrella term of 'reader-response criticism', not only would it be a mistake to assume a theoretical consistency among the theorists of the Konstanz School (Iser, Jauss) and the approaches of Culler and Fish in the US; it would be equally erroneous to assume any shared account of the 'reader' towards which such criticism is oriented.

Despite these many differences, the 'ingenuity of labeling' Robert Holub identifies (1984: xiii) in the term 'reader-response criticism' consists in its capacity to combine the South German and North American schools, alongside the Yale deconstructors and the more recent socio-political or cultural theorists, under a single heading precisely insofar as, following Barthes, they all make the reader a core locus of contemporary debate. Accordingly, whatever their internal differences, the conception of the active reader shared by post-Barthesian literary theorists and cultural analysts unites 'idealists' and 'actualists' alike in rejecting not only the reader as a passive receptor but also, however 'embodied' their analyses become, the reader as driven by sensation. Whatever portrait of the reader may emerge from each of these approaches, therefore, common to all will be the primacy of making sense. To this extent, therefore, 'idealists' and 'actualists' alike remain literary theorists insofar as they do not stop at asking how a particular reader reads a specific text, but ask instead after the protocols of reading in general, that is, how readers *make sense*.

(Un)readability

To the extent that meaning production becomes their focus, post-Barthesian theories of reading divide around one of the following contrary premises: 'the text must be readable' and '*all* texts narrate the allegory of the impossibility of reading'.[3] The issue of reading thus becomes that of readability, which becomes in turn a problem concerning the determinability of meaning. Theorists who adopt the first premise argue that meaning can and will be settled (even if a given text initially resists it), while proponents of the second premise reject the possibility of such closure. Underpinning these contrary orientations are two philosophical frameworks deriving from Hans-Georg Gadamer's hermeneutics and Jacques Derrida's deconstruction, respectively.[4] These two philosophies therefore focus the differences between those literary theorists who make *understanding* and *readability* a central tenet of text–reader relations and those who, conversely, stress *misunderstanding* and *unreadability*.

As 'the classic discipline concerned with the art of understanding texts', according to Gadamer's *Truth and Method* (1975: 146), hermeneutics proposes that the interpreter of a text acts as a 'go-between', mediating the distance between what a historically distant text said in the there and then and what can be heard of it in the here and now. In a 'similar' relationship to that between text and reader (Gadamer 1989: 41), the hermeneutic interpreter establishes a 'dialogue' between the horizons of text (or the past) and the reader (or the present) that eventually forges what Gadamer famously calls a *Horizontverschmelzung* (1975: 273), at which point alone an 'understanding' arises that is ideally so 'harmonious' that, as distinct particulars, both original parties 'disappear completely' in it (Gadamer 1989: 41). Just as, in any conversation, the views of each partner are modified and move beyond their original standpoints, so 'the consensus that emerges in understanding represents a new view' (Warnke 1987: 104).[5] Even past understandings, however, require to be thus 'synthesized' with present ones, so that Gadamer does not argue that such an act is completed once and for all in the here and now. Rather, 'the true meaning of a work of art is never finished; it is in fact an infinite process' (1975: 265).

This is not to suggest that, for Gadamer, meaning production is completely open-ended. Rather, interpretation is guided by a 'fore-conception of completion' or 'anticipation of completion' (*Vorgriff der Vollkommenheit*) as a 'formal condition of understanding', stating that 'only what really constitutes a unity of meaning is intelligible' (1975: 261). Insofar as this 'unity of meaning' is 'fore-conceived', it acts as an *a priori* for all interpretive acts that removes from the first the possibility of a failure to understand and constrains interpretation to the production of unitary meaning. As Gadamer puts it, '[n]ot only is an immanent unity of meaning guiding the reader assumed, but his understanding is likewise guided by the constant transcendental expectations of meaning' (ibid.: 261-2). Crucially, such an expectation is not the fruit of experience, but conditions interpretation even before it begins.[6]

If for Gadamer 'the goal of all communication and understanding is agreement' (1975: 260), for Derrida such a presupposition is problematic, because it is based on an 'absolute obligation to desire consensus in understanding' (Derrida 1989: 52, translation modified; cf. Rapaport 1989: 199). When, therefore, Derrida queries Gadamer on precisely this 'precondition for *Verstehen* [understanding]', suggesting that, instead of presupposing understanding, 'the continuity of *rapport* [...] is not rather the interruption of *rapport*, a certain *rapport* of interruption, the suspending of all mediation' (Derrida 1989: 53), he exposes Gadamer's blindness to anything other than a consensual understanding of understanding.[7] On this account, to submit to the rules of hermeneutics is to accept that all understanding must necessarily end in and with agreement. Derrida's concern with the limits of intelligibility, by contrast, repositions the possibility of communication breakdown as *a priori* ineliminable in any relation to another, or of text to reader. If the other is actually other rather than already 'fused into one', then the possibility of a 'relation of incomprehension' cannot be ruled out in advance, but must remain a necessary possibility in all relations. Insofar as it ignores this, hermeneutics achieves its 'fusion of horizons' by its failure to conceive of an otherness at the very heart of understanding, of the possibility of misunderstanding. Confronting it, by contrast, entails that the impossibility of understanding cannot be ruled out.

To read, therefore, according to the logic of deconstruction is always to risk misunderstanding and hence always potentially misreading. To deconstruction, misreading is not a failure of correct understanding, since the notion of a correct reading is a fallacy: precisely because misunderstanding is *necessarily possible*, it is just as much an *a priori* condition of communication as is understanding for Gadamer.

A priori conditions of reading

According to Richard Rorty, to ask: 'what are the conditions of possibility of ...?' is to engage in a 'specifically *transcendental* project' which seeks 'non-causal, non-empirical, non-historical condition[s]' (1989: 210, qtd. Mailloux 2001: 48) that hold true in general. That is, the *a priori*ty of (un)readability debate between Gadamer and Derrida is not conceived to hold only for a specific text and this text's particular reader, but is *transcendental* in the sense that it *necessarily* conditions each and every reading, regardless of *contingent* conditions of the time and place of the reading and the reader. Philosophy's transcendental questions are clearly the converse of those asked by history; for literary theory, however, whether the reader is or is not theoretically determinable in advance – that is, whether the ideal ('for all readers ...') or the actual ('this reader, here, now ...') has priority – remains a question.

The philosopher's procedures therefore differ from those of the literary theorist. Literary theorists also ask what makes reading (im)possible but, in answering it, turn to literature, using individual readings as an occasion from which to extrapolate a theory of reading, or thus deriving a general from a particular. In this respect the literary theorist is concerned not just with *a priori* conditions of reading, but also with *a posteriori* protocols of reading. Especially as formulated in the literary theories of the 1970s, the reader is very much a reader in theory: whether ideal (Culler), informed (Fish), implied (Iser) or textualized (Barthes), this entity is an abstraction who is neither an actual living reader, a flesh and blood being, nor a real historical person, but a transhistorical, transsubjective and transcendental receptor (cf. Machor 1993: viii-x). The continuing validity of these *a priori* conditions is evident in the two poles that govern reader-oriented criticism, with reader-response critics adopting readability as their premise and the Yale critics, by contrast, adopting that of unreadability.

Literary theorists have found much that is useful in Gadamer's and Derrida's thinking, especially since both have addressed how meaning comes to be produced, an issue core to the study of literature. Their different approaches to meaning can therefore be taken as markers of the dividing line between those literary theorists of reading who belong to a tradition of 'unitarian criticism' (de Man 1983: 28) and those who operate from the perspective of a difference criticism. What is at stake here has to do not only with whether we think meaning can or cannot be deciphered because intelligibility is or is not a given, but also with its *location*; the problem, as Gadamer succinctly characterizes it, is '[w]here [...] the multiplicity of meaning [is] really located' (1989: 115).

Reader-oriented theorists indebted to Gadamer's thinking, such as Jauss and Iser, insist that meaning emerges as a unitary phenomenon in the ongoing encounter between text and reading. Since interpretation is necessarily ongoing, consisting of successive readings, Gadamer's 'inexhaustibility' principle presents the multiplicity of meaning *within* the horizon of possible understanding, and 'anticipates' therefore that 'the whole truth' of a text (1975: 262) will eventually be revealed. For Gadamer, the truth of the text is 'whole', therefore, towards and within which the multiplicity of *interpretations* must be oriented insofar as these are interpretations *of* that text. For Derridean theorists such as the Yale deconstructionists, by contrast, meaning production is unstable and irreducibly plural, provoking and multiplying undecidability with every reading. Reading or interpretation does not so much superadd multiplicity to an inherently stable textual meaning, but amplifies the instability, the multiplicity of the 'warring forces of signification' (Johnson 1980: 5), within it. Accordingly, undecidabililty necessarily exceeds its conversion into a full, even if distant, meaning, so that the multiplicity of meanings remains uncontained. As Derrida therefore counters Gadamer, '[r]eading is freed from the horizon of meaning or truth' (1979: 107). With these contrary accounts of the location of multiplicity in mind, we will now examine the procedures by which each group of theorists seeks an accommodation with, or of, 'the multiplicity of meaning'.

When Wolfgang Iser, a former student of Gadamer's, and perhaps the literary theorist associated most readily with reader-response criticism, tackles this problem, it emerges very clearly that it is the inexhaustibility of the text which demands that the reader take decisions as to its meaning. Paradoxically, since the imperative to decide in effect *controls* readers' responses, inexhaustibility is precisely that which makes a text determinable. This paradox is worth unfolding further since it demonstrates a crucial aspect of *unitarian criticism* when compared to *difference criticism*.

Controlling readers' responses

Iser's approach to reading is best known for his thesis that all literary texts, particularly those that we esteem highly, contain within them '*Leerstellen*' ('blanks' or 'gaps'), a concept he develops out of Roman Ingarden's '*Unbestimmtheitsstellen*' ('spots of indeterminacy'; Iser 1978: 170). A text, that is, comes with 'instructions' (ibid.: 212) or 'textual signals' (ibid.: 9), except that only some of these have been formulated, while others are left blank; and it is precisely those 'unwritten' parts which, for Iser, are the vital motor of the reader's acts of comprehension, giving space to the exercise of imagination when we read (1974: 283). Even though a text always includes places of indeterminacy, this does not make it a network of unfinished meanings, which it is for Derrida. Instead, Iser follows Ingarden's thesis that a text is a schemata with holes which are to be made whole by the reader, like a skeleton which needs flesh to give it body. In this way, the reader realizes the literary work's meaning. Iser's key essay 'Interaction between Text and Reader' (1980) shows that, although the gaps are pre-structured into the text, they do not have to be filled by a reader in a pre-given way, but make it possible for different readers to produce different meanings for a text, so that 'each individual reader will fill in the gaps in his own way' (1974: 280). In effect, then, gaps of indeterminacy are an indicator of a text's 'inexhaustibility' insofar as, Iser says, 'one text is potentially capable of several different realizations, and no reading can ever exhaust the full potential' (ibid.).

Thus Iser's emancipation of the reader is paradoxical, and at best only partial. Precisely because every decision to fill out the blanks in this or that way also means that the reader has to discard or exclude other options by which the gaps might have been filled, Iser argues that, '[b]y making his decision', the reader 'implicitly acknowledges the inexhaustibility of the text; at the same time it is this very inexhaustibility that forces him to make his decision' (1974: 280). Despite the fact that it is full of 'elements of indeterminacy', the Iserian text is not a network of unfinished meanings, as it is for deconstruction, but a determination of points of 'finishable unfinishedness'. The paradox of Iserian indeterminacy therefore means that reading is determinant not of a text, but only of itself, as *this* reading. Reading is free to the extent that the text determines it thus.

Accordingly, Iser argues that it is the text's 'incompleteness' which 'necessitates syntheses' (1978: 109) on the part of the reader, who is therefore compelled to make the text whole. Whether it is gaps in the plot, or whether a lack of connection at the word-by-word or sentence-by-sentence level, or between paragraphs or even entire narrative viewpoints, the text drives the reader to make and hazard anticipations, inferences, links, selections, projections, etc., until it all adds up and the text gradually takes shape in the reader's mind. As readers, then, '[w]e look forward, we look back, we decide, we change our decisions, we form expectations, we are shocked by their nonfulfillment, we question, we muse, we accept, we reject; this is the process of recreation' (Iser 1974: 288). 'Recreation' forces the reader 'to fit everything together in a consistent pattern' (ibid.: 283), even if 'consistency' is not given.

> If we cannot find (or *impose*) this consistency, sooner or later we will put the text down. The process is virtually hermeneutic. The text provokes certain expectations which in turn we project onto the text in such a way that *we reduce the polysemantic possibilities* to a single interpretation in keeping with the expectations aroused, thus extracting an individual, configurative meaning.
>
> (Ibid.: 285; my emphasis)

Just as Gadamer's notion of the 'anticipation of completion' turned out to be a means of control by which to curb interpretive potential, so what Iser calls 'consistency-building [as] the indispensable basis for all acts of comprehension' (1978: 125) turns out to be a control mechanism, an *imperative* by which what is polysemantic or 'many' becomes consistent and 'one'. Anything that resists reading, or that is unreadable, *must be* cancelled out so as to make it readable.

Reading expectations

Iser therefore shares the orientation of hermeneutics towards consistency and unity but, by locating these in a text necessarily 'richer than any of its individual realisations' (1974: 280), any and all historical, cultural or generally contextual co-determinants are removed from the production of meaning. On this point, Iser's theory of *aesthetic response* is clearly differentiated from the *aesthetics of reception* of his Konstanz school colleague Hans Robert Jauss. Jauss does not focus exclusively on the internal textual structures which guide reading, but on the ways in which the external, literary-historical context informs our readings. Like Gadamer, Jauss therefore addresses the ways in which readers understand texts *similarly* across time and culture, in order 'to forge a link between the past and the present, between the canonical sense of the text and the sense "for us"' (1990: 54). Although critical of Gadamer for merely 'presupposing' rather than 'consciously achieving' his fusion of horizons (1985: 169), Jauss similarly presents the reader's emerging 'understanding' of the text as an 'active synthesis' of two 'horizons' (ibid.: 166). Jauss's synthesis is designed to overcome the antithesis of a 'work-immanent' or *intrinsic* approach to literature (as in formalism) and an extrinsic approach that reduces a text to the expression of its social and/or historical context (as in Marxist criticism). It is by synthesizing the two that readers constitute texts as aesthetic objects within the wider context of literary and extra-literary history (cf. Jauss 1978, 1982b). Jauss's investigations into 'what makes it possible for the reader to understand the text in its otherness' (1985: 157) therefore set out to 'achieve' what Gadamer only 'presupposed':

> [T]he understanding-of-oneself in the otherness of the text and the everyday-understand-ing-of-oneself when one speaks and another replies *have to be anchored in a prejudgment of what has already been said and understood together.*
>
> (Ibid.; my emphasis)

Without such a common 'prejudgment' or 'foreknowledge' (Jauss 1982b: 23), the understanding of literary texts would 'degenerate into a free-floating pro-duction of differences' (Jauss 1985: 157), a criticism often levelled at Derrida. By making understanding thus dependent on 'prejudgment', Jauss implicates the interpreter's historical situatedness in the process of understanding. The question is, therefore, what does this necessary pre-understanding consist in?

In the essay 'Literary History as a Challenge to Literary Theory', Jauss explicates the 'methodological centrepiece' (Holub 1984: 59) of his argu-ment: the concept of the 'horizon of expectation' (Jauss 1982a: 23-8). As 'a "system of references" or a mind-set' that a reader 'might bring to any text' (Holub 1984: 59), the horizon of expectation contains in effect the elements of the reader's pre-understanding:

> first, through familiar norms or the immanent poetics of the genre; second, through the implicit relationship to familiar works of the literary-historical surroundings; and third, through the opposition between fiction and reality, between the poetic and the practical function of language, which is always available to the reflective reader during the reading as a comparison.
>
> (Jauss 1982b: 24)

A particular text, meanwhile, 'predisposes its audience to a very specific kind of reception' by *activating* these elements of pre-understanding through 'announcements, overt and covert signals, familiar characteristics, or implicit allusions' (ibid.: 23). Even innovative and challenging texts can be measured against the horizon of expectation, so that the process of working out pre-understandings consists in translating the variously unfamiliar, from the detective novel to the literary experiment, through the necessary familiarity of pre-understanding.

If this is how the reader comes to understand the text, the literary critic's function is to examine how readers actualize textual meanings both from signals within a given text (the generic markers, for instance, by which a text signals its belonging to detective or to romance fiction) and from within their historically specific store of foreknowledge as to how literary texts shape meaning (how poetry differs from drama, for instance). The critic may thereby assess both the character of the historical specificity of a given horizon of expectation and how the structuration of meaning changes in the course of literary history.

Jauss further argues that whether a work 'at the historical moment of its appearance, satisfies, disappoints, or refutes the expectations of its first audience' (1982b: 25), and the influence a work has been able to exert in the course of the history of its reception (the extent to which it stands the test of time), also therefore provides criteria of literary *value*. That, for instance, a work entirely fulfils its audience's horizon of expectation would mean that it comes 'dangerously close to the irresistably convincing and enjoyable "culinary" art' (ibid.: 26) that neither challenges nor expands an audience's horizons.[8] Meanwhile, an innovative work that, by confuting expectations, establishes new and lasting norms, expands and alters that horizon, marking out its historicity. In this way, Jauss combines the formalist esteem for innovation with the historicist concern with context through the study of reception, conceived as a constant negotiation of the unfamiliar through the familiar. As such, the reader becomes the vehicle articulating literary history. While historically concrete, this reader is nevertheless the effect of a pre-understood horizon of expectations that is theoretically prejudged as consistent and unitary. Yet Jauss's is not the only theoretical attempt to account for the consistency of readers' expectations.

Conventions of reading

With their theories of literary competence or literary conventions, respectively, the North American critics Culler and Fish maintain Jauss's emphasis on the preconditions of intelligibility. As in the case of Jauss, for instance, Jonathan Culler's reader, as presented in *Structuralist Poetics*, is 'guide[d] in the perception and construction' of the literary text by certain foreknowledges, 'expectations about the forms of literary organization, implicit models of literary structures, practice in forming and testing hypotheses about literary works' (1975: 95). These expectations constitute an 'internalized competence' which, just as much as our linguistic competence, is a system we must necessarily have 'mastered' (ibid.: 120) if we are to be able to read and interpret at all. Indeed, the reader cannot approach a work of literature without having learned how to read it *as* literature; we must, that is, have some rudimentary notion of how literature works to be able to recognize a poem as a poem when we see one. It is this same 'literary competence' (ibid.: 113-30), acquired through (tacit or overt) training in the 'institution' of literature, that enables readers to read, and authors to write, literary works. Thus we never read in a vacuum, Culler argues, echoing Jauss, not simply because we cannot read a literary text except 'in connection with or against other texts, which provide a grid through which it is read and structured' (ibid.: 139), but also because our strategies for reading are deeply, and necessarily, embedded in the institution of literature. The 'I' of the reader is not therefore some private essence unique to each individual subject, but an intersection in a system of shared codes, conventions or knowledges, which form that subject through learning, and which now traverse it and are applied in the act of reading (cf. Culler 1975: 29-30).

Culler's structuralist or semiotic approach to reading is interested less in how a particular reader might understand a specific text than in exposing the structures, systems or logics by which readers make texts signify. As Elizabeth Freund argues, this is 'a theory not only of reading, but of the reading of reading' (1987: 72). In *The Pursuit of Signs* (1981), Culler describes his 'semiotic' project as

a theory of reading [whose] object would not be literary works themselves but their intelligibility: the ways in which they make sense, the ways in which readers have made sense of them. Indeed, the semiotic programme may be better expressed by the concepts of 'sense' and 'making sense' than by the concept of 'meaning', for while 'meaning' suggests a property of a text (a text 'has' meaning), and thus encourages one to distinguish an intrinsic (though perhaps ungraspable) meaning from the interpretations of readers, 'sense' links the qualities of a text to the operations one performs on it. [...] If a text which at first did not make sense comes to make sense, it is because someone has made sense of it. 'Making sense' suggests that to investigate literary signification one must analyse interpretive operations.

(1981: 50)

Although therefore in agreement with Jauss in emphasizing context and the conditions of intelligibility, it is evident here that this is a deeply anti-hermeneutic stance, since Culler is not really concerned with *what* a text means (its content), or any 'meaning' a text might *have*, but with the structures and operations whereby readers, who supply these structures in the *performance* of literary competences, *make sense* actual. These structures are in principle open to public observation, *apart* from the content of the readings generated by them. Thus, it follows that the very procedures by which readers make sense, can serve the critic as the basis of what might well be called an ethnography of reading: in readers' performances, these procedures become available to observation and analysis, and tell us everything about the logic according to which literature signifies. In this respect Culler makes reading not just an important *aspect*, but rather the definitive *object* for the study of literature. It is therefore incumbent on 'the study of literature [a]s a discipline' to produce 'a study of the conditions of meaning' not through textual analyses, but rather through 'a study of reading' (1980: 49).[9] What then are the conditions of reading, according to Culler?

Underlying the *descriptive* account of reading performances as events of sense-making, Culler gives literary institutions a *prescriptive* function. Not only does the institution (tacitly) adjudicate what is and is not an 'acceptable' or 'plausible' reading (1975: 127), it also issues an imperative that *sense be made*. Like Jauss, Culler argues that even a work once largely unintelligible (he gives the examples of *The Waste Land* and *Ulysses*) can be made intelligible at a later stage provided 'new ways of reading have been developed' (ibid.: 123). If therefore 'any work can be made intelligible if one invents appropriate conventions' (ibid.), this is not because, as it was for Jauss, the 'otherness' of a text is read against the horizon of the already read. Rather, new ways of reading, new literary competences, are developed 'in order to meet what is the fundamental demand of the system: the demand for sense' (ibid.). Culler's 'demand for sense' therefore transposes the conditions of the unity or consistency of sense-making from text, to reader and, finally, to an institutional imperative: sense is inevitably made because competence is enforced. As Gadamer, Iser, Jauss and Culler argue, even if intelligibility is not immediately handed on a plate to us by an author, it is nevertheless always guaranteed that texts are readable. As Freund suggests, such prejudices, anticipations, horizons and imperatives may, however, be too successful, in that, given them, 'there would be no aberrant texts, just as there are no aberrant readings' (1987: 82).

Interpretive communities

To say that there are *no aberrant texts* and *no aberrant readings* is exactly the standpoint that Stanley Fish assumes in *Is There a Text in this Class?* (1980). For Fish there can be no aberrant texts because there are no texts, but only readers, and there are no aberrant readings because, he says, 'determinacy and decidability are always available' (1980: 268). How so? Completely reversing the New Critical doctrine that the text is the sole source of meaning, because 'everything is *in* it' (ibid.: 158), Fish amply and cheekily demonstrates that there is nothing 'in' the text *at all*. Instead, the reader supplies everything, because texts are not the *source* of interpretation, but 'interpretation is the source of texts' (ibid.: 16). At which point we might well wonder, with Eagleton, '[w]hat it is that Fish believes he is interpreting when he reads?' (1983: 85).[10] Equally, if there is nothing 'in' the text, it follows, as Fish himself concludes, that 'there are no determinate meanings' (1980: 312). Wouldn't this mean that a reader can produce just any meaning whatsoever? And, if so, then are 'determinacy and decidability [...] always available' as options, so to speak, to be rejected or embraced by fiat? Can he have it both ways? In other words, how can Fish make 'the text disappear' (ibid.: 173) and give the reader free interpretive rein, while at the same time asserting the stability of the interpretive process? The answer, if it is not sheer malice to vex his critics, can be found in his notion of 'interpretive communities' (ibid.: 171), that is, 'a community made up of those who share interpretive strategies' (ibid.: 161).

Like Culler, Fish makes use of the concept of 'literary competence' (Fish 1980: 48), which is what an 'informed reader' has learned and brings to the task at hand, the understanding of literature. Such a reader, Fish explains, 'is sufficiently experienced as a reader to have internalized the properties of literary discourses, including everything from the most local devices (figures of speech, and so on) to whole genres' (ibid.). Since such interpretive strategies are nothing other than 'presuppositions' or 'prejudices' (ibid.: 365), in short, pre-understandings, they not only give structure to the interpretive experience, but structure it *in the first place*, because they already exist prior to reading. As Fish tells us, 'interpretive strategies are not put into execution after reading: they are the shape of reading, and because they are the shape of reading, they give texts shape, making them, rather than, as is usually assumed, arising from them' (ibid.: 13). This, then, is at least one of the ways in which Fish makes the text disappear, but also provides an account of that text's genesis, or the means by which it appears. For if interpretive strategies exist prior to the act of reading, then they are clearly neither 'in' the text nor for that matter an effect of the text, and since they 'determine the shape of what is read rather than as is usually assumed, the other way round' (ibid.: 171), then the text has no shape until such strategies are brought to bear upon it, and only appears, so to speak, as a consequence of these strategies having been deployed. Or to put it still more contentiously, the interpretive strategies which readers bring with them do not merely interpret a text, but bring it, as it were, into existence. So conceived, the text is not, contra Iser, a pre-existent entity determining its readers' responses; rather, the text is its reader's reading. The 'end product of this reading', Fish explains, is 'meaning or understanding' (ibid.: 22), which is why '[i]nterpreters do not decode poems: they make them' (ibid.: 327). Fish is as unequivocal as he is apparently perverse on this point: 'making' is intended 'to have its literal force' (ibid.: 162), not taking it simply in the sense of *making* sense but in the sense of *creating* it.

Having made the reader into the 'writer' of literature, what then is the source of readers' interpretive strategies? By arguing that 'the reader's experience is itself the product of a set of interpretive assumptions' (1980: 147), Fish has made this 'making' not a subjective act, as that which arises from the reader's consciousness, but (similar to Culler) subject to the strategies and conventions which through learning produce the reading subject in the first place. If readers, no less than texts, are constituted by conventions (cf. ibid.: 11), this suggests that meaning is the property neither of an object (the text) nor of a subject (the reader). Instead, the meaning of a text, and of literature *per se*, belongs to the institution of literature, a communal system which precedes us, which we inhabit and which inhabits us. It is in this manner, Fish says, that the institution also 'fashions us, furnishing us with categories of understanding, with which we in turn fashion the entities to which we can then point' (ibid.: 331-2). The institution of literature is therefore as much an enabler as it is a control mechanism, giving us options for interpretation while also restricting the range of those options, namely by placing severe limitations on what does or does not count as an acceptable reading within it. This certainly explains why a reader is not 'a free agent' (ibid.: 11) and cannot just give any old meaning to a text, as well as why 'understanding will, in some sense be uniform' (ibid.: 5). However, while this accounts for the stability of the interpretive process as well as for a certain amount of agreement among readers, what it does not account for is why there are disagreements among readers at all, and differences between 'their' readings, if they all draw on a common pool of interpretive strategies which has been vetted, so to speak, by the institution of literature. What Fish must provide, then, is an account of the interpretive community such that variation, rather than conservation (of strategies, warranted or authorized interpretations, and so on), becomes its norm without, however, sacrificing thereby any constancy in that community.

This is the central problem that any conventionalist account of reading, such as Fish and Culler offer, must negotiate: the co-establishment of difference within convention-enforcing institutions, and the convention-enforcing aspects of those institutions with sufficient flexibility such that variation remains possible. This Fish does by introducing the reader as a member of a literary community – itself made up of a potentially infinite number of smaller interpretive communities – each of which is comprised of those who share a set of assumptions, which in turn will determine the kinds of meanings the members in one group will make as opposed to those that belong to another community. Whether a reader reads for unity then (as is the case for hermeneuts) or for difference (as is the case for deconstructionists), according to a Fishian schema, is not the consequence of either unity or difference inhering in a given text, but because a given reader's 'predisposition' to 'execute' (Fish 1980: 169) this or that interpretive strategy depends on the interpretive community to which this reader belongs; in other words, those looking for determinacy and decidability of meaning will draw on interpretive strategies which belong to a different community than those who look to unleash textual indeterminacy.[11] This then is why Fish can presume that any one community is in agreement as to their own concerns and is in unison with itself, and that differences which occur between readers are the result not of textual difference but of the differences between communities.

Fish therefore proposes a mechanism whereby an 'anarchic' interpretation can find a home in the institution of literature. If the impetus for this comes from Culler's conviction that sense be made, thus accommodating both the flexibility and the convention-enforcing dimensions of the literary institution, for Fish intelligibility is not a demand but a given, because 'unintelligibility, in the strict or pure sense, is an impossibility' (1980: 307). For, if off-the-wall interpretations can always be absorbed within the institution as 'on-the-wall', this means that there are *aberrant readings* and there are *no aberrant readings*, because even aberrant readings can be accommodated within a community. What Fish is not saying, however, is that every reading is always aberrant. This is the assumption which, to put it into Fishian terminology, is made by the interpretive community comprised of deconstructionists, to which we now turn.

Failure of reading

For the Yale critics reading cannot help but be aberrant because of 'a built-in fatality of language', as J. Hillis Miller (1989: 157–8) characterizes Paul de Man's theoretical starting point. According to Miller (ibid.: 158), the task of the deconstructionist is to identify and expose moments of undecidability in a text, and to 'bring its aberrancy into the open'. It is this emphasis on linguistic structures which differentiates the work of the Yale critics from that of the reader-response critics. While, for the latter, language remains essentially a transparent medium, for de Man, criticizing this assumption in Jauss's work, 'all the obstacles to understanding belong specifically to language rather than to the phenomenal world' (1982: xvii). Thus, whereas the reader-response critics believe (to varying degrees) in the possibility of determining a text's meaning(s) – and the reader's ability to do so – for the Yale deconstructionists the structure of language frustrates the entire enterprise of interpretation, and with it our sense as readers of our own sense-making capability. Insofar as language is marked by an inherent playful polysemy, it follows that whatever is expressed in language is replete with undecidabilities, making any given text's meanings not just indeterminate but potentially also indeterminable.

Take the phrase '*Die Sprache verspricht (sich)*', a wordplay used by de Man,[12] which goes some way towards illustrating the issue at hand. In German, this phrase performs more than one meaning: language [*Sprache*] promises (itself), speaks the promise [*verspricht*] of its own truth *and* makes a slip of the tongue [*verspricht sich*], speaks with a forked (or with two) tongue(s). Since the verb '*sich versprechen*' signifies more than one thing, its ambiguity is exemplary of the shifting and unstable structure of language, and so demonstrates Miller's insight that 'other meanings are always there as a shimmering in the word which makes it refuse to stay still in a sentence' (1979b: 219). Shimmering in *sich versprechen*, then, are two irreducible, or undecidable, senses, opening up 'a margin of unpredictability' (Miller 1987a: 214) that entails, according to both de Man's *Allegories of Reading* (1979: 205) and Miller's *The Ethics of Reading*, a necessary 'failure to read' (1987b: 53). Generalizing, therefore, from such examples, the Yale critics argue that *all* texts *versprechen (sich)*: texts harbour the *promise* of a truth, hence the promise of a univocal meaning, the promise of their own readability, but equally fall into a *lapsus linguae* which contradicts their claim for readabililty – 'if by "readable"', as Miller stipulates, 'one means a single, definite interpretation' (1979b: 226). Crucially, however, this unreadability is neither the author's deliberate doing, nor the reader's failure, but the result of how language works on and within a text. In direct contrast to reader-response criticism's prejudged unity of meaning, Miller locates unreadability not 'in the reader but in the text itself' (1989: 159). Different readings cannot be considered as the consequence of the particularity of different readers, since any *difference between* readings arises from a *difference within* texts.

How then does a deconstructive reading, illustrating this 'failure to read', proceed? Perhaps Miller's most famous essay, 'The Critic as Host' (1979b), best exemplifies his etymological method of opening up multiple branches, rather than a single root, of a word's meaning. Countering M. H. Abrams's accusation[13] that the deconstructive critic is nothing more than a parasite who leeches on the work of the great literary author, Miller demonstrates that the terms 'parasite' and 'host' are not opposites or adversaries, but are etymologically linked. Since the Greek *parasitos* can be shown to refer to a 'fellow guest', invited to share the host's food, and since 'host' functions equally as 'guest' and 'stranger' in the Latin *hospes*, Miller concludes that 'a host is a guest, and a guest is a host' (1979b: 221), a structure reiterated in every encounter between critic and text, criticism and literature. As he explains this deconstructive endeavour in 'Ariadne's Thread: Repetition and Narrative Line':

Each word inheres in a labyrinth of branching interverbal relationships going back not to a referential source but to something already, at the beginning, a figurative transfer [...] that all words were originally metaphors. Moreover, one often encounters for a given word, not a single root, but forks in the etymological line leading to bifurcated or trifurcated roots [...]. In any case, the effect of etymological retracing is not to ground the word solidly but to render it unstable, equivocal, wavering, abysmal.

(1978: 158-9)

Miller's deconstructive reader/critic does not do this *to* a text, but follows the text's own *undoing* from within. In a nutshell, 'the text performs on itself the act of deconstruction without any help from the critic' (Miller 1975: 31) – and this, according to Miller, is especially true of great literature.[14]

If critics, including the New Critics, have traditionally defined a great work of literature according to criteria such as unity and organic form, Miller reverses these criteria to judge a work's greatness not by its unity, but by its heterogeneity and difference within (cf. Miller 1979a: 11; 1982: 5, 19). Accordingly, the reader's failure to read becomes the criterion for literary judgement. Equally, if critics have traditionally laid great stress on a reader's ability to determine a text's meaning, and have judged the success of a reading (including their own) by the ingenious ways in which a reader has managed to come up with a definite and definitive interpretation, Miller undermines, by turning upside down, this self-assured certainty. For the deconstructive critic, not only does the reader merely identify the ways in which a text always already self-deconstructs, but the insight gained from these identifications never simply betokens a reader's mastery of a text, it also recognizes the limits of any reader's sense-making attempts. The most a reader can do, then, is to realize through reading that reading itself is marked by a difference within, never revealing just one reading, but at least two incompatible, contradictory and irreducible readings.

Neither Miller nor de Man focus in their theories of reading, on the reader as a subject or agent; rather, they concentrate on how language and textuality frustrate the necessary and yet impossible task of reading. Whether it is called the *impossibility of reading*, the *failure to read* or *unreadability*, each of these notions 'names the discomfort of [a] perpetual lack of closure' (Miller 1980: 113) when it comes to a reader's attempts at making sense of a text. This discomfort is a result of what both Miller (1979b: 250) and de Man (1979: 131) see as the 'performative function of language', or what for de Man in particular is a consequence of the tropological or figurative uses of language. Rhetoricity, according to de Man, puts 'an insurmountable obstacle in the way of any reading or understanding' (ibid.), whether we consider the ordinary, literary, or philosophical uses of language. It follows then that, 'far from constituting an objective basis for literary study, rhetoric implies the persistent threat of misreading' (de Man 1983: 285).

This point is perhaps best exemplified via a reading de Man gives of W. B. Yeats's 'Among School Children', a poem which famously ends with the line: 'How can we know the dancer from the dance?' De Man's reading illustrates that this line can, and therefore cannot not, be read both literally and figuratively. Taken figuratively, the line suggests a union, 'the potential unity between form and experience, between creator and creation'; taken literally, the line leaves us not with a rhetorical question, but with a questioning of this very question: 'how can we possibly make the distinctions that would shelter us from the error of identifying what cannot be identified?' (1979: 11). This is the conclusion de Man draws:

> two entirely coherent but entirely incompatible readings can be made to hinge on one line, whose grammatical structure is devoid of ambiguity, but whose rhetorical mode turns the mood as well as the mode of the entire poem upside down. Neither can we say [...] that the poem simply has two meanings that exist side by side. The two readings have to engage each other in direct confrontation, for *the one reading is precisely the error denounced by the other* and has to be undone by it. *Nor can we in any way make a valid decision as to which of the readings can be given priority over the other;* none can exist in the other's absence.
>
> (Ibid.: 12; my emphasis)

The poem's resistance to meaning constitutes a moment of undecidability which de Man calls 'aporia' or 'lack of means': texts, that is, lack the means to say anything univocally.

The text's unreadability presents itself as an impasse to interpretation: there are no grounds for choosing; both readings are perfectly plausible. Yet each reading must decide the undecidable, and therefore betray the text's undecidability. Any and all readings are therefore necessarily misreadings, and any reader seeking to determine a text's meaning becomes a misreader from the first. Since this is precisely what characterizes the history of reading (or criticism) – a series of misreadings performed by a succession of critics eager to determine a text's meaning, and a further series of readings based on those misreadings and compounding therefore the error of these prior (mis)readings in their own misreadings – it follows that reading is impossible. This is not because there is no correct reading (since, as we have just seen, there is such a thing as an undecidability between perfectly plausible readings), but because it is not possible to put an end to reading. The impossibility of reading entailed by irreducibile rhetoricity is as much the impossibility of interpretive closure as it is the impossibility of not misreading.

Misreading

The instability of language is a crucial aspect of both de Man's and Miller's thinking. It complicates our access to a text's meanings, and our relation to the world, since all experience – all consciousness, the reality that surrounds and shapes us, and the history of which we are the products – is mediated through language. Since 'it is impossible to get outside the limits of language by means of language' (Miller 1987b: 59), it follows that language is the only available measure of reality. To conceive of language in those terms is to conceive of linguistic paradoxes in systemic and *a priori* terms. As such, misreading is a necessary condition of textuality imposed on all reading, which act acquires an expanded sense and now includes not only texts or signs, but also systems, history, reality, and so on. In contrast to this de Manian perspective, Harold Bloom, for whom misreading is a central motif running through many of his books, and particularly *A Map of Misreading* (1975), restores misreading to a deliberate act on the part of a subject.

Interested in relations of influence between poets, Bloom delineates a history of literature where misreading functions as the primary motor of canon-formation (cf. 1975b: 63). Best seen as an *agonistic* process, literary history is not a dialogue with the past, as Jauss argues, but 'poetic warfare' (1979: 5), a 'psychic battleground' (1976: 2) between already canonical poets and their successors or 'ephebes'. Since poets, just as much as critics, live *anxiously* and *defensively* under the influence of their precursors, they need to free themselves from this repressive hold so as to carve out a space in history. Hence Bloomian literary history is concerned not, as are Jauss and the hermeneuts, with the preservation or transmission of a literary inheritance, but with the 'wilful revisionism' (1973: 30) whereby the ephebe asserts his 'originality' (1975a: 24) and 'uniqueness' (ibid.: 70) over and against the rival predecessor. The form this revisionism takes, Bloom says, is that of a 'creative correction' (1973: 30) or a 'strong reading that I have called misreading' (1979: 5). The ephebe's quest to become the *Über-poet* characterizes the struggle of literary creation, without which 'modern poetry could not exist' (1973: 30). In Bloom's Freudian lexis, canon-formation involves an Oedipal struggle because, in order '[t]o live, the poet must *misinterpret* the father, by the crucial act of misprision, which is the re-writing of the father' (1975a: 19). It is therefore of less concern to Bloom whether a text is or is not readable than that it is rewritable.

It follows from Bloom's cycle of literary history as the ongoing revision or rewriting of poetry that reading poetry and writing poetry become increasingly blurred. Take the following citation from *Kabbalah and Criticism* (1975), for instance:

> Poetry begins, always, when someone who is going to become a poet *reads a poem*. But I immediately add – when he *begins* to read a poem, for to see how fully he reads that poem we will have to see the poem that he himself will write *as his reading*.
>
> (1975b: 107)

Bloom argues here that 'poems themselves are *acts of reading*' (1976: 26); accordingly, the reader, provided he or she is strong and wilful, becomes a 'poet-reader' (1975a: 69). Moreover, as *Agon: Towards a Theory of Revisionism* (1982) explains, '[n]o one "fathers" or "mothers" his or her own poem, because poems are not "created", but interpreted into existence, and by necessity they are interpreted from other poems' (1982: 244). The ephebe writes his or her readings as new poems. Thus, if writing involves the reading of one's predecessors and this reading turns into the ephebe's writing, then 'reading is mis-writing and writing is mis-reading' (1975b: 64). In addition, therefore, to rewriting the relations between writing and reading, Bloom rewrites the relations between literature (as a primary activity) and criticism (as a secondary operation directed towards this primary). Arguing that a 'theory *of* poetry must belong *to* poetry, must *be* poetry, before it can be of any use in interpreting poems' (1975b: 109), Bloom is proposing not just a new theory of poetry but a new theory of criticism: not only is the critic called upon to read poetry in terms of the rival relations between poets, or to write up the history of literature as a series of deliberate acts of misprision; the critic's own calling is to (mis)read and (mis)write poetry in the same fashion as any strong ephebe would. As he puts it in *The Anxiety of Influence*, '[p]oets' misinterpretations or poems are more drastic than critics' misinterpretations or criticism, but this is only a difference in degree and not at all in kind' (1973: 94-5).

The reader as writer

In terms of this book's concerns, it is simply a logical outcome of an aesthetics of sense-making as opposed to sensation, and of intellect as opposed to body, that criticism is transformed into poetry. Echoing Bloom in this regard, his colleague Geoffrey Hartman begins with the assertion that 'what a literary critic does is literature' (1980: 20). Like Bloom, Hartman seeks to unsettle the rigid demarcations between high art and 'mere' commentary. His confession in *The Fate of Reading* (1975), 'I have a superiority complex vis-à-vis other critics, and an inferiority complex vis-à-vis art' (1975: 3), gives perhaps the best clue as to what propels Hartman to rework, and thus resituate, the secondary status that literary criticism has held in relation to literary creation since after the Romantics. Reacting against the servile critics he associates with a sober Anglo-Saxon formalism, who busily explicate the unique form and organic unity of a work of art behind which, they naturally assume, lies an even bigger genius in the shape of the masterly figure of the author, Hartman sets out in *Criticism in the Wilderness* (1980) to induce a new worth in the critic and the reader, to effect a positive revaluation of criticism as literature very much in Bloom's spirit, and of reading as a 'form of work' in Roland Barthes' sense (1974: 10):

> The division of literary activity into writers and readers, though it may appear to be commonsensical, is neither fortunate nor absolute. It is crass to think of two specialities, one called *reading* and one *writing*; and then to view criticism as a particularly specialized type of reading which uses writing as an 'incidental' aid. Lately, therefore, forms of critical commentary have emerged that challenge the dichotomy of reading and writing.
>
> (Hartman 1980: 19-20)

As examples Hartman cites Nabokov, Borges, Derrida and Bloom himself, whose stylistically playful writings he sees as undermining the traditional assumption that it is only literature, but not criticism, which makes how something is written just as integral to a text's meaning as what is written. He nurses the hope therefore that, although '[w]e have talked for a long time, and unselfconsciously, of the *work of art*; we may come to talk as naturally of the *work of reading*' (ibid.: 162). Accordingly, Hartman seeks to fulfil the very objective he has set himself, 'that literary commentary may cross the line and become as demanding as literature' (ibid.: 201).

On the surface at least, Bloom and Hartman appear to offer a radical empowerment of the critic and the reader, in many respects rivalling the status once reserved solely for those who create or write originals rather than those who merely comment upon or read those originals. But what survives of the reader if indeed he or she becomes a writer? What survives of reading if everything is writing? True, if we approach reading from the perspective of the historian, we surely gain access to how a reader read only by looking at texts (or images) which have survived as a record of such practices of reading. What counts as evidence of reading here is only, therefore, writing. Even the ethnographer's fieldwork among para- or non-literate societies must *transcribe* from notes, or recorded tapes, and thus transform into writing what counts in oral cultures, among people without writing, as evidence of 'reading' (cf. Fabian 1992). But if we approach this question philosophically, then to say that reading is writing is in effect to have made the reader disappear. It is at this juncture that another major difference between reader-response critics and the Yale critics emerges. Whereas the former make the reader a central focus of interpreting literature, and Fish even makes the text disappear in order to put as much onus on the reader as is theoretically possible, the Yale critics, despite the fact that many of their books foreground the importance of reading, in the end say more about writing than reading. So, despite titles such as *A Map of Misreading*, *The Fate of Reading*, *The Ethics of Reading* and *Allegories of Reading*, Bloom as we have seen makes reading into poetry; Hartman makes it into the *work of reading*, transforming it into a form of writing; Miller too makes reading indistinguishable from writing, at least, that is, if we think it through the logic of the parasite; and de Man makes reading into the explication of the logic of language, such that the reader is automatically the text's own '*cellule de lecture*'. So, is there a reader in these texts?

Putting this question slightly differently, we might ask: what are the consequences of there being, as suggested above, no *reader* other than, it would seem, a textual one, that is, a reader who is already written? Deconstructionists, post-structuralists and postmodernists claim, of course, that there is nothing outside the text, other than more text,[15] so that reading itself is a textual act. This is nowhere more clearly expressed than by Roland Barthes, when he writes in *S/Z* that '[t]his 'I' which approaches the text is already itself a plurality of other texts, of codes which are infinite' (1974: 10). Reader-response critics similarly conceive of the 'I' of the reader in textual terms: either the reader is inscribed in the text or readers are 'overwritten' by expectations, competences or strategies prior to reading. What is clear from such descriptions is that the reader is a construct, that is, a reader entirely 'without history, biography, psychology,' as Barthes famously said (1977: 148), and also without race, class and gender, as theorists in the 1980s would have said.

The politics of difference

While the reader in literary theory in the 1970s was textually constructed (an effect of the text, or a textual 'I'), more recently approaches to reading have been directed, as Andrew Bennett sums it up, 'towards the recognition that readers are historically or socially constructed, rather than abstract and eternal essences' (1995: 4). From the 1980s onwards, not least because of the impact of women's studies, post-colonial, ethnic and, latterly, also queer studies, attention shifted away from the textual notion of the reader to the contextually situated reader. The many works published on book history during the 1990s have also contributed towards a greater understanding of how socio-cultural factors impact on reading (chapter 1). Therefore, recent accounts of reading have critiqued earlier ones for their tendency 'to describe a universal "reader"', and have focused instead on 'the differences of reading produced by women, gay or lesbian readers, or readers of ethnic minorities' (Bennett 1995: 4), divisions which theorists have continued to break down into further subdivisions (cf. Sedgwick 1990: 22).

Such approaches exemplify a turn away from 'grand theory' (viewing theory 'as the systematic rationalization of the general presuppositions that underlie the reading of texts as literary texts')[16] towards an engagement with the figure of the reader across a multiplicity of sites and contexts. The questions which are asked by theory now have to do no longer with *a priori* conditions of reading, but with social conditioning, or how *a posteriori* ideological and cultural factors differentiate our readings. This by no means signals the demise of theory; rather, recent developments point towards theory's diversification into particularized theoretical praxes that have given rise to strategies of reading within what might be called cultural politics. Theory here is local in the sense that it is concerned more with contingency than with systematicity, proposing an irreducible localism in place of a universal epistemology. At the level of analysis this favours micro-analyses over macro-analyses, in the terms proposed by Michel Foucault with regard to history,[17] or by Gilles Deleuze and Félix Guattari with regard to 'micro-politics', seizing on the ways in which '[w]e are segmented from all around and in every direction', so that '[t]he human being is a segmentary animal' (1988: 208).

As cultural historians have reminded us, reading too is segmented because it 'was not always and everywhere the same' (Darnton 1990: 187). In a similar vein, cultural theorists demonstrate that readers do not all read in the same way, but are different. Although the former point is derived from a history of reading and the latter from a politics of reading, what is undermined in both instances is the very idea of the ideal reader, a construct that might apply to all readers at all times. To acknowledge, for instance, that women might read differently from men means that identity plays a crucial role in the reading process. Or to appreciate that reading Alice Walker's *The Color Purple* (1982) yields a different experience of reading for a black than for a white reader or is received differently among a black male readership from a black female readership, or how its film version by Steven Spielberg (1985) polarized reactions between black reviewers who criticized the film severely and black women audiences who loved it, becomes the starting point for interrogating how ethnicity, gender and class shape a reader's encounter with a text (cf. Bobo 1995; 1988). However, just as we cannot impose a single identity on the reader, so we cannot assume that all women read in the same way, or that all ethnic minorities share the same experiences and therefore interpret texts along similar lines. Readers are not just different from each other; there is also *difference within* each 'one' reader. Thus, despite the retreat from 'grand theory', we return to the theoretical coordinates established at the outset of this chapter, that is, to what differentiates *unitarian* from *difference critics*.

In the context of feminism, for instance, this means that unitarian critics base their idea of woman on the notion of a shared experience. All women are united, say by 'the bodily experience of menstrual flow'.[18] Difference critics on the other hand reject the idea that a *woman* can be defined by an 'essence', or for that matter that *women* are all 'one' because of an essence that is common to all women. Thus, while the former assume that all women share a similar experience, the latter are mindful that even differences between women, based on age, ethnicity or sexuality, should not be taken as the basis for distinguishing what is common to all women of a similar age, ethnic background or sexuality. For difference critics it is not enough therefore to stress that there are differences between women, or even that there are differences within each group; rather, there are differences within each 'individual'. From the perspective of reading, therefore, the woman reader, like the lesbian reader, is plural not singular (cf. Flynn and Schweickart 1986: xiv). This shift in attention from the 'one' to the 'many', and subsequently the 'many' in the 'one', marks the difference between identity politics and the politics of difference.

When Wayne Koestenbaum warns us, in 'Wilde's Hard Labour and the Birth of Gay Reading', of the risks of embracing gay reading within a single 'interpretive community founded on desire for the same gender', because it comes close to 'submitting to a dangerously comfortable essentialism – as if gayness transcended gender, class, race, nationality, or epoch' (1995: 165), it is clear that as a theorist he rejects identity politics, not just because 'identity is a prison' (ibid.: 178), but because definitions of identity tend to rely on reductive assertions. The fear of falling into the essentialist trap – denying difference and the possibility of change by attributing universal and fixed characteristics to human subjects – is ever present when we assume that identity is something ready-formed which precedes culturation (or reading) rather than being constructed by culture (or during the process of reading). Similarly, Jean E. Kennard's observation, in 'Ourself behind Ourself: A Theory for Lesbian Readers', that it is problematic to assume an 'innate predisposition towards lesbianism', but it is equally problematic not to take into account biology, and as such ignore the body's possibilities (1986: 65), brings to the fore the difficulty feminist theory faces when it asks what difference sexual difference or, as is the case with Kennard and Koestenbaum, sexual orientation makes to the enterprise of reading. Feminist literary theories, precisely because they are concerned with sexual difference, and therefore not just with the politics of difference but also with the physiology of difference, *must* negotiate the essentialist trap.

What feminists do then is to bring the body back into the theoretical arena, something which 1970s theorists resolutely ignored, not merely by postulating the reader as a textual construct, but by concentrating exclusively on the mental processes of reading, how readers make sense of texts. The next chapter, 'Sexual Politics of Reading', outlines the many different approaches to reading within feminist theory, taking as its focus not just the politics of difference, but the physiology of difference, so as to connect the physicalist accounts of reading which dominated criticism indebted to the rhetorical tradition until the eighteenth century (chapter 5), and still made themselves felt in the critiques of mass cultural products such as the novel and film in the nineteenth and early twentieth century (chapters 3 and 4), with theories of bodily reading as articulated within various strands of feminist theory.

7 Sexual Politics of Reading

Figure 8 Ex libris illustrating the correlation between books and bodies.

A politics of reading is necessarily implied across all the dimensions of difference criticism.[1] Fundamentally, its ethos is political, since it aims not to articulate the canonical, the historically continuous and the core, but to empower, through their articulation in theoretical-institutional discourse, the discarded, the revisionist and the marginal. Hence the emphases on recovered texts, forgotten authors and revisionist histories as the literary critical practices most clearly associated with difference criticism. Fundamental, however, to difference criticism in general, and to feminist criticism and theory in particular, is the relation between the theoretical and the actual reader.

    In the previous chapter, we followed the shifts in literary theory, from locating the unity of literary meaning in text, to readings, and to writings, while

questioning the possibility of that unity at all. If the poles of unity and difference articulate literary theory, the difference criticism that, its proponents
claim, succeeds 'grand theory' reorients the problem of unity or difference
from the dimension of meaning to identity and difference in actual readers,
and so poses the political problem of articulating the differences that inflect
actual readers. Feminist criticism is one such attempt to negotiate the relation
between actual and theoretical readers. The present chapter takes feminism as
its focus for two principal reasons. Firstly, the coordinates for this entire book's
investigation of reading are supplied from 'subjugated' terms, such as body,
affect, passion, etc., which conceptually, historically and politically have been
articulated with reference to sexual difference. Secondly, unlike most difference criticism, feminist theories of the reader return us, with a difference, to
the Longinian concerns discussed in chapter 5, insofar as, for feminism, the
physical or somatic dimension of the actual reader necessarily resurfaces. This
means that meaning, while the concern of many feminist literary theorists,
cannot be the sole concern, since the body necessarily inflects the possibility
of meaning (figuratively and actually).

Underlying the presupposition of difference lies the problem of identity.
What is woman? And, by extension, how does she read? Is her identity ready
formed before she begins reading, or is this identity shaped in the process of
reading? If the former, is reading therefore grounded in an experience unique
to woman, or is reading a performance of identity? Is she simply and hope-
lessly interpellated in the texts of a *de facto* male literary history, or can the
woman reader be empowered by resisting such interpellation? Is this resisting
woman reader a critical ideal or an empowered social agent? Is what Laura
Mulvey has called 'passionate detachment' (1975: 18),[2] the destruction of
pleasure in literature, a necessary stage in the progressive liberation of woman
as an agent from she who suffers political and literary subjugation?
Ultimately, the difficulty of providing a clear-cut definition of the woman
reader stems from the problem of defining woman. To define her by her
femaleness, according to the '[d]ata of biology' (de Beauvoir 1972 [1949]: 35),
makes her identity dependent on biological difference, as if anatomy were
destiny. Conversely, to define woman (with or without inverted commas,
with or without capital letters, in the singular or the plural) as a construct is
to bypass biology by 'textualizing' sexual difference, as if the body were solely discursive. While for some feminists a definition is necessary so as to address
effectively the oppression of a class called women, for others any such definition is premature, even dangerous, insofar as woman is a process-of-becom-
ing. Some have even argued that the feminine, because it undermines all
categorization, evades determination, which is why we could not define –
even if we wanted to – what woman *is*, her 'essence'. As these questions and
issues indicate, there are many feminisms.

Therefore, it is a mistake to assume that feminist theory – even if united
in its opposition to patriarchy – constitutes a unified corpus of concerns. And,
just as the presumption that a text is a unified whole remains problematic

(chapter 6), neither can it be assumed that the individual reader presents a unified self, nor that all women readers homogeneously form one readership. When Eve Sedgwick asks us to be attentive to the ways in which '[p]eople are different to each other' (1990: 22), with reference to reading this means that there exist differences not just between but also within groups of readers. Whereas reader-oriented theorists of the 1970s had assumed a universalized reader, which made them blind to identity markers such as gender, feminist theories of reading have sought to address the specificities of sexual and social difference. And yet, many feminist theories can equally be accused of a form of universalism. In 'Under Western Eyes: Feminist Scholarship and Colonial Discourses' (1991) Chandra Talpade Mohanty points to an 'ethnocentric universalism' whereby Western feminist discourses assume 'the cross-cultural validity' of their arguments. A similar criticism has also been levelled against many white feminists who, blind to issues of race, ethnicity or nationality, see gender oppression as overriding all other forms of inequality (cf. Smith 1985: 169). Increasingly therefore, theorists have taken into account additional markers of identity, which is also true of reader-oriented critics such as Patrocinio P. Schweickart and Elizabeth A. Flynn. As editors of *Reading Sites: Social Difference and Reader Response* they urge us not to 'homogenize all differences into the master category of gender', that is, 'to think not of one general other but of particular others, differentiated, among other things, by race, ethnicity, and class' (2004: 18).

The resisting reader

Approaches which pay attention to markers of identity broadly speaking can be divided into three camps: those who use text-based analyses (the preferred mode in literary study, for instance), those who make contextual enquiries (as practised within cultural and media studies), and those who seek to combine both (a model often used within film studies). Textual analyses derive the reader from the text itself (in there), whereas contextual enquiries take as their focus the social audience (out there). What is common to all three approaches is a commitment to read oppositionally (cf. Hall 1992), even if by different methods.

Judith Fetterley, for instance, posits a textually implied reader, which is male. She argues that androcentric works 'co-opt' the female reader 'to identify against herself' (1978: xii). This makes it politically incumbent for a woman to engage with such texts as 'a resisting reader rather than as an assenting reader' (ibid.: xxii) so as to reverse the process of '*immasculation* of women by men' (ibid.: xx). What a text-based approach such as this assumes is that, because readers are positioned by a text in a particular way, they cannot but respond to a text in more or less the same manner: if they are female and/or black, they are either interpellated by the text and become immasculated and/or white or they have to resist interpellation. More recently, feminists have sought solutions which are not negatively defined. Kay Boardman, for instance, has proposed a 'renegade reader [who]

Since *The Color Purple* is a mainstream film, one might have expected a negative rather than a positive reception by black women viewers. One of the reasons
why this was not so is summed up by this comment: '[f]inally somebody says
something about us' (Bobo 1988: 101). As one viewer describes her reactions:

When I went to the movie, I thought, here I am. I grew up looking at Elvis Presley kiss-
ing all those white girls. [...] And it wasn't that I had anything projected before me on the
screen to really give me something that I could grow up to be like. [...] So when I got to
the movie [*The Color Purple*], the first thing I said was 'God, this is good acting.' And I liked
that. I felt a lot of pride in my Black brothers and sisters. [...] By the end of the movie I
was totally emotionally drained [...] Towards the end, when she looks up and sees her sis-
ter Nettie [...] I had gotten so emotionally high at that point [...] when she started to call
her name and to recognise who she was, the hairs on my neck started to stick up. I had
never had a movie do that to me before.

(Ibid.: 102)

The film made a similarly strong impact on a black male columnist from the
Washington Post (18 February 1986), but for very different reasons than those
described by the female viewer above.

Never in my moviegoing experience have I seen whole rows of black women, teens to
elderly, with [...] tears streaming down their faces one moment and eyes bright with
laughter the next. [...] the audience [...] shook me up. Here we were watching the same
screen, but seeing something completely different.

(Courtland Milloy, qtd. Bobo 1995: 88)

Clearly, his viewing experience of the film was unique too, not because of the
film itself, but because of the reactions he observed in the opposite sex.
Whereas many male reviewers had rejected the film for its negative portrayals
of the black male characters, women viewers, by contrast, identified with the
plight of the female characters as victims of male oppression. In addition, Bobo
argues, they found much that was empowering in terms of how the female
characters dealt with this oppression. For Bobo, these reactions illustrate that,
'when a person comes to view a film, she/he does not leave her/his histories,
whether social, cultural, economic, racial, or sexual at the door' (1988: 96).
Insofar as black women occupy a doubly marginalized position in culture,
because they are subjected to 'the twin scourges of sexism and racism' (Gates
1990: 7), this explains why their responses to cultural texts will differ from
those of black male viewers but also from those of white female viewers. This
is borne out by Bobo's research on *The Color Purple*. 'Black women', she concludes, 'have a different history and consequently a different perspective from
other viewers of the film' (1988: 101).
    Bobo's study gives crucial insights into practices of reading among under-
represented groups. Like Elizabeth McHenry, who in her important historical
book *Forgotten Readers* asks us 'to dispense with the idea of a monolithic black
community' (2002: 14), Bobo's work points up differences *within* communities,
not just according to gender, but also according to class and political affiliation.

In addition she draws a connection between practices of reading and practices of everyday life when she equates black women's resistance to a mainstream film such as Spielberg's with their resistance to mainstream culture. As she puts it, '[t]he struggle to resist the pull of the film and to extract progressive meanings' is in effect the 'same struggle that many black women have used to resist domination and oppression in everyday life.' It is precisely for those reasons, she urges us, that 'black women's ability to read against the grain of the film and reconstruct more satisfactory meanings should not be undervalued' (Bobo 1995: 89-90).

What Bobo does undervalue, however, it seems to me, is inadvertently pinpointed by the reviewer from the *Washington Post*. Her approach claims to be investigating 'members of a physical audience' (1995: 24), but she ignores the range of physical responses her ethnographic subjects display. This is to say, Bobo interprets outbursts of tears, or comments such as getting 'emotionally high' or 'the hairs on my neck started to stick up', as an index of reading agency rather than passion. Resistant reading relies on distantiation (Bobo's notion of the Brechtian conception of 'making strange'). Surely, though, tears are an index not of distantiation but closeness? Similarly, if a viewer claims that a film 'took every one of [her] emotions', how can such a statement be interpreted as being illustrative of viewers' 'control over their reactions' (Bobo 1995: 88)? The reason, I suspect, why Bobo prefers to engage with 'the actual empirical viewers who *physically* buy tickets to watch a film' (ibid.: 24) rather than the flesh and blood viewer as a sensuous being – not necessarily always a sense-maker – is that physiology undermines the rationality of the subject, a requisite for a politics of reading, premised on agency. This is to say, affective responses have little place in studies which insist on readers as active construers of meaning, since any notion of undergoing pathos is not easily reconciled with activist politics such as practised within the remit of cultural studies.

Empirical audiences

Perhaps the most striking insights with regard to this issue emerge from Janice Radway's study *Reading the Romance* (1991 [1984]). Like Bobo, Radway is concerned not with a textual reader but with an empirical one. Like Bobo, she ascribes agency to her readers and draws on the tradition of cultural studies. And, crucially also, she shows herself unwilling, just as Bobo was, to pursue the question of affective response.

Interested in the way readers use books, and what they do with them, Radway turns away from a purely textual analysis to an analysis of context, thereby dovetailing with approaches and problems in the historiography of reading. Her focus group from a Midwestern US community, referred to by the fictitious name of Smithton, whom she interviews and provides with questionnaires, is a group of women whose avid reading of romances, Radway argues, is 'a form of individual resistance' (1991: 12) against the self-sacrificing role prescribed for them by a culture in which their husbands' and children's needs take precedence over their own. Since for each of these readers buying books means buying time for herself, this suggests that 'the act of romance reading is oppositional because it allows the women to refuse momentarily their self-negating social roles' (ibid.: 210). The act of romance reading is not just a form of escape, then, but a 'right to escape' (ibid.: 118) from daily routines. Paradoxically, while the kinds of stories which belong to the romance genre provide escapism by compensating for certain needs that remain unfulfilled in these women's lives, they also endorse, as they help them to understand, their roles within that culture. As Radway finds, romances tend not to unsettle their readers by undermining or questioning a woman's role in a patriarchal society; rather, when the romance reader closes her book to return to her daily tasks, she must be 'emotionally reconstituted and replenished, feeling confident of her worth and convinced of her ability and power to deal with the problems she knows she must confront' (ibid.: 184). In this respect, both the act of reading romances (creating time and space for themselves) and the romances these women read (making the female heroine with whom they identify the centre of attention and receiver of affect) have 'therapeutic value' (ibid.: 73), because romance reading creates in them hope and a 'visceral sense of well-being' (ibid.: 12).

Unlike the feminist reader engaging in critical-analytic labour on a text, the Smithton women's engagement is with the text as a vehicle for 'rapture' (Radway 1991: 112), stirring passion and compassion, and not as an occasion for the exercise of critical intellect. This is borne out when Radway examines these women's reading histories. She finds that this group of readers is concerned not with interpretation, what the genre means and how its texts signify, but with the meaning romance reading gives to their lives (ibid.: 86, 190). Given the sheer quantity of romances they consume,[4] it is clear that fiction plays a central part in their lives and that, without romance reading, their lives would be considerably impoverished. It is in this sense that the Smithton women are 'chronic' readers (ibid.: 60) who display an 'emotional dependence on romantic fiction' (ibid.: 119). Dorothy Evans, who runs a bookshop and is one of Radway's key interviewees, even goes so far as to suggest that 'romance reading is a habit that is not very different from "an addiction"' (ibid.: 88). Indeed, 'I know many women', she writes in the first edition of 'Dorothy's Diary of Romance Reading' (April 1980), 'who need to read as an escape as I have done over the years and I believe this is good therapy and much cheaper than tranquilizers, alcohol or addictive T.V. serials' (qtd. ibid.: 52). This suggests that romance reading helps this group of readers to cope with daily life; it also implies that romances are an effective substitute for drugs, or indeed a drug themselves.[5] While their relation to fiction echoes the abundance of late eighteenth- and nineteenth-century treatises on reading as an addiction, as outlined in chapters 3 and 4, it seems that Radway is unwilling to pursue this line of argument further, since it would evoke the kind of effects criticism, or criticism of affect, discussed in chapter 5, which her entire project is designed to disprove. This is to say, the effect/affect tradition of criticism, whereby literature is conceived as a 'unit of force' that acts upon the reader (Tompkins 1980: 204), runs counter to Radway's claim that the Smithton women's engagement with fiction is marked by resistance, and must therefore be understood in terms of a politically oppositional practice. It is here also, of course, that Radway's resistance to considering reading as anything other than a form of resistance echoes Jacqueline Bobo's approach.

While Radway makes it clear that interpretation is not a major concern for these women readers, a claim reminiscent of Jane Tompkins's point that texts have not always, as the history of literary criticism shows, been interpreted for their meaning (1980: 205), here[6] Radway neglects to think through the implications of this comment by Dorothy Evans: 'I think my body is in the room but the rest of me is not (when I am reading)' (qtd. Radway 1991: 87), since this indicates that texts do things to readers, act on them, rather than readers being agents, doing things with texts. This blindness is further underlined by Radway's puzzlement as to why Dorothy, when asked 'What do romances do better than other novels today?', interprets the question as follows:

To my surprise, Dot took my query about 'doing' as a transitive question about the *effects* of romances on the people who read them. She responded to my question with a long and puzzling answer that I found difficult to interpret at this early stage of our discussions.

(Ibid.: 87; emphasis in the original)

Radway's difficulty stems from a desire, motivated by a certain sexual/textual politics, to see reading as involving an *act* of 'participation' (ibid.: 91), since lack of participation entails the elimination of inter*activity*, and therefore passivity on the part of the reader. Thus, when Dorothy Evans elaborates on her ecstatic reading experience and talks about men watching television, making the point that 'they are always consciously aware of where they are', whereas 'a woman in a book isn't', Radway interprets this comment about absorption as an index of reader participation (ibid.: 91). It seems to me that losing oneself in a book is less about participation, which presupposes consciousness of mind, than about switching off one's critical faculties, a temporary loss of self. This marks a crucial difference between the argument I put forward in this book and the argument put forward by critics who work from within the tradition of cultural studies. This difference is worth unfolding further.

It remains one of Radway's great achievements that her ethnography of reading makes it possible 'to distinguish *analytically* between the meaning of the act [of reading] and the meaning of the text read' (1991: 210). Accordingly, Radway focuses not on the textual process but the 'social process' of reading, that is to say, 'what people do with texts and objects rather than on those texts and objects themselves' (1986: 26). By illustrating how audiences make use of texts, and that they use texts for their own ends, Radway's approach comes close to insights also derived from within cultural studies. Her argument, following the tradition set by Richard Hoggart and

Raymond Williams, is that a text – and here she focuses especially on those associated with mass culture – does not 'determine the way it must be used', but that readers 'often remake [mass culture] into something they can use' (ibid.). This exemplification of agency on the part of readers entails that 'consumers of mass culture are apparently neither as passive nor as quiescent as the traditional theory would have it' (ibid.: 27) – in effect, then, the same argument that Bobo put forward. What Radway means by traditional theory is that put forward by the Frankfurt School during the 1930s and 1940s, who, in the face of the rise of fascism, argued that the culture industry, as Radway explains, 'lulled its users into a state of somnolence, indolence, and passive receptivity to the ideological propaganda of others' (ibid.: 10). By contrast, what I have been trying to show in the course of writing this book is what contemporary critics, especially those engaged in a political form of criticism, are loath to pursue, namely that texts also act on readers, physically affect them. In opposition to the Frankfurt School (see chapter 5), but also to approaches influenced by cultural studies, I have sought to point to a whole history of reading where passions *activate* readers' responses. It is a misconception, however, to assume that, because passions act on readers, readers are therefore necessarily passive; rather, it is at the level of the body that passions *activate* responses. It is precisely this that we forget if we see reading solely in terms of a mental activity (in terms of interpretation, or in terms of resistance) at the expense of also seeing reading as activating bodily responses. What this brings to the fore once more is the dichotomy between passive versus active reading (see chapter 3).

Active consumers

A considerable body of recent work, not just from a feminist point of view, and not just from within literary studies, but also from newer disciplines such as film studies and cultural studies, has addressed the issue of the consumer's apparent passivity, of which history has made woman a prime example. On the one hand, this project has involved undermining the notion of the passive female character in fiction, on the other, a related issue has been to undermine the notion of the passive reader or spectator. Despite their differences, feminists working in literary studies (Fetterley), or those associated with cultural studies (Hall, Bobo, Radway), media studies (Brunsdon) or film studies (Stacey), have all in different ways tried to negotiate the issue of passive/active consumption. What these critics share is a political commitment to see readers, screen spectators or TV audiences not in terms of passive dupes but as active reading subjects who are capable of resisting the dominant, or preferred, meanings of a given text – or, as Radway does, to resist the dominant culture by the act of reading. To put this slightly differently, by positing, in one way or another, an active reader/spectator – whether a textual entity or an actual person – these critics seek to undermine the claim that a text masters its readers, that a film masters its spectators, that ideology masters its subjects. These approaches have sought to empower the reader, or the spectator, and crucially also the critic – to turn this figure from a servant into a master. As Jackie Stacey explains:

> Two tendencies in cultural studies are significant here: first, cultural studies has had a strong tradition of interest in 'unrepresented' groups [...] initially in terms of class, and later in terms of ethnicity and gender. Second, and perhaps consequently, cultural studies has a long-standing commitment to understanding popular culture in terms of consumption. In addition, its association with radical politics of resistance in the 1970s and 1980s, together with the influence of the Gramscian model of power which emphasised negotiation and struggle, rather than entirely successful domination, may have made cultural studies particularly receptive to the study of how consumers, rather than producers, make meanings.
>
> (1994: 35)

What a politics of reading must therefore demonstrate is an emancipation of the figure of the reader: not compliant and passive, but resistant and active. The politically engaged reader, spectator or critic must become an agent of change.

Since politics belongs to the world of culture rather than nature, it must reject the unruly passions in favour of the rules of reason.[7] The distinction between reason and passion, the former aligned with culture and the latter with nature, entails an unacknowledged dualism between mind and body. It is precisely for this reason that Radway rejects, as discussed at the end of chapter 3, 'the designation [of reading] as a biological process of ingestion' (1986: 10) found in those approaches which stress that texts can chemically transform readers. Her commitment to a resistant and active reader goes hand in hand with the privileging of mind over body, since the compliant and passive reader would presumably allow herself to be ruled by her passions. And yet, her own findings in *Reading the Romance* suggest that reading for the Smithton women must be understood in terms of a 'visceral sense of well-being' (ibid.: 12). While she concedes therefore that reading has a therapeutic effect on these women, to accept that reading might be opium for this group of readers comes too dangerously close to the Frankfurt School critique of mass culture. In trying to recuperate not just popular culture but a sense of agency for mass audiences, she must reject the apparent elitism implicit in the Frankfurt School argument, whether as regards the devaluation of a particular class of readers as being malleable or as regards a particular class of texts as being unworthy of study.

What is striking about all the approaches discussed so far is that they grapple with the notion of a resisting audience, and that this resistance is as much an issue when it comes to *textual* readers/spectators as it is when it comes to *actual* readers/spectators. While textual approaches such as Fetterley's illustrated the necessity of a resisting reader if feminist politics was to make a difference, in ethnographic studies, such as Radway's and Bobo's, resistance is assumed from the start in order to illustrate that audiences are never just 'passive dupes of an insidious ideology'.[8] It is as if the ideal reader (or film spectator) is one who must and/or does resist (whether resistance takes the form of critique or appropriation).[9] The fact that an ideal reader is assumed at all is problematic, especially with regard to ethnographic approaches, since this would seem to indicate that a theory is in place before ethnographic research begins, as opposed to theory emerging from ethnographic practice. Although Jackie Stacey has complicated the correlation between activity and resistance in her study of film viewers' memories of Hollywood stars, whereby 'activity is necessarily resistant, being the opposite of passivity, which is assumed to mean collusion' (1994: 46), her stance nevertheless indicates just how important audience activity, interactivity or participation – even if not via a resistance model – is for contemporary cultural critics. As she points out, even if a spectator were to collude with, rather than resist, the insidious ideology of a 'politically conservative or patriarchal' text, this would not by any means suggest that such a viewer is necessarily passive, since '"[a]ctivity" in and of itself is not a form of resistance: women may be active viewers in the sense of *actively* investing in oppressive ideologies' (ibid.: 47). So, even if viewers are not resistant, they are not dupes either. The question then of resistance or collusion is secondary, for a cultural politics, to the ascription of agency.

Ethnographic approaches to audience studies, and Stacey's is a case in point here, which in many ways have superseded earlier textual approaches, can be understood – within the context of film studies – as a corrective against theories promulgated in the journal *Screen*, as exemplified by Laura Mulvey – the point being to show that audiences are not passive receivers of meanings but that their encounters with media texts involve an active process of negotiation, thus enabling critics to locate differentiation in response in subjects rather than texts. A primary difference remains, however, between on the one hand the *feminist* reader – or professional critic – resisting a dominant ideology and educating the *passive* female reader to become an *active* feminist reader, and on the other the actual *female* audience presumed to be active in the first place. The assumption in the discourses outlined above is either that the reader is passive and must be activated by feminism to become active (Fetterley) or that we are mistaken in believing that readers are passive in the first place (Boardman, Bobo, Radway, Stacey). While the notion of the active audience was a coup against those who had emphasized an audience's potentially harmful dependence on books or other media, such as is still assumed by film censorship boards for instance, the question of agency remains unresolved.

Agency is the bedrock of empowerment in literary, cultural and film studies, as indeed it was for reader-response criticism (see chapter 6) insofar as reader-response critics shifted the power relations between author, text and reader in favour of the reader as a producer of meaning, away from the author, or the text, as the sole source of meaning. The source of these critics' trouble here is the notion of pleasure, since the pleasures that a woman reader might gain even from reading an androcentric text, giving herself to this text, must be turned into a critical act. Reading here must become an act of 'making strange' (Bobo 1988: 96) or an act of 'passionate detachment' (Mulvey 1975: 18), both strategies necessitating that the reader put a distance between herself and the text. Such a consciousness-raising exercise is vital for a politics of reading, since it alerts the woman reader to the concerns of the feminist reader. As Radway sums up the Smithton women's continual assertions 'that they *are* valuable, that they *have* the right to their pleasures, that women are *not* dumb, that their concerns *aren't* silly and frivolous':

> it seems clear that these indignant defences originate in persistent and nagging feelings of inadequacies and lack of self-worth which are themselves the product of consistent subordination and domination. If romance readers and writers could be brought to see this, it might be possible to transform their utopian longing into actual agitation for social change. In that case, what is now really only a tacit cultural critique might become a more thoroughgoing cultural politics, indeed even active social resistance and opposition.
>
> (1986: 25-6)

My hunch is that this 'passionate detachment' would destroy these women's pleasure in reading romances,[10] although 'other pleasures are possible' of course, to borrow Tania Modleski's words: 'pleasure is involved in analysis itself' (1988: 27). Pleasure for this feminist reader is therefore a confirmation of agency, a *negative pleasure* insofar as it is realized in the distance from the text required, in order to recognize its ideological traps without falling victim to them. Or, to put this differently, the negation in this pleasure is the negation of everything sensible or affective, in favour of alerting the mind to capabilities beyond such enjoyable traps.

'Low-/middle-/highbrow' reading

Resistance understood in those terms is resistance to *pathos*, that is, a refusal to succumb *passively*, perhaps submissively, to what one reads. Reading here is a negative pleasure of self-assertion and self-control, certainly a mastery of self and in many respects a mastery of the text. As such it is linked to a Kantian aesthetic, which Bertolt Brecht turned from a mode of reception into a mode of literary production (chapter 4). So as to avoid passionate attachment from the outset, Brecht rejected realism and wanted to institute the kind of art which made absorption impossible. Mulvey similarly deploys a Kantian aesthetic of 'passionate detachment' as a means by which to counter the male gaze, but she also calls for a Brechtian modernist aesthetic, that is, a new cinema which, unlike classic Hollywood realism, disallows identification and enhances critical distance. The politics implicit in this stance is one which has been analysed by the sociologist Pierre Bourdieu in his book *Distinction: A Social Critique of the Judgement of Taste* (1984). What his thesis brings into focus is the difference, we might say, between the politics of form (as practised by Brecht and Mulvey) and the politics of content (as practised by the realist) – a difference which, Bourdieu would argue, is marked by social difference. Accordingly, Bourdieu differentiates between a 'high' or 'pure aesthetic' (1984: 5), based on a detached and disinterested pleasure in art and which he associates with the Kantian tradition through to Brecht, and a 'popular aesthetic' (ibid.: 4), which is based on '"vulgar" enjoyment' and which is more readily associated with an authentic realism[11] than with a high modernism. The distinction is class-based, since the former pertains to art which is 'demanding' or '*difficile*' (ibid.: 486), expressing the taste of the cultural elite, and the latter is used to designate 'facile' forms of entertainment, encompassing what gratifies the taste of 'the people' (ibid.: 5). Crucially, for Bourdieu, the 'typically intellectualist theory' (ibid.: 3) places a lower value on 'the taste of sense' than on 'the taste of reflection', thus endorsing a hierarchical division between 'facile pleasure, pleasure reduced to a pleasure of the senses, and pure pleasure, pleasure purified of the pleasure' (ibid.: 6).

Ironically, Bourdieu's analysis would suggest that critics who ignore the importance of the pleasures of the senses in favour of analytic pleasures fall within the purview of the tastes of the cultural elite. And, insofar as they insist on dispassionate analysis, they ask their readers to apply a bourgeois rather than a popular aesthetic to popular culture, even if, as Janice Radway does in *Reading the Romance*, they seek to authorize popular cultural forms. This dilemma highlights the connections between reading and class, but also those between social and sexual difference. When Anne G. Berggren asks why the addictive, immersive and affective reading practices of her youth, which she compares with historical reading practices, are not condoned within the academy, which discourages emotional responses, this points to differences between 'middlebrow' and 'highbrow' cultural practices of reading (2004: 166-7). It also raises an issue which is close to the heart of many feminists, namely that an analysis of the ways in which reading is gendered goes hand in hand with an analysis of the ways in which 'reading is *socially framed*' (Long 1992: 192). To emphasize that reading is affective is gendered, because it is woman, history tells us, who shows greater signs of 'affectibility';[12] it is also 'socially framed', because to read affectively, if we adopt Bourdieu's analysis, is to read in accordance with a popular aesthetic tradition, and therefore not to read in accordance with the rules of the academy. While, on a metaphoric level, the threat of mass culture has consistently been linked to femininity in terms of a capacity for reproduction, both biologically and industrially,[13] on a social level, woman's entry to education, and especially the academy, is of course a relatively recent occurrence.

At an institutional level, it would be true to say that literary norms discourage affective reading as much as they frown upon literatures which aim for affect. As Janice Radway notes, those 'who teach reading and control access to it in our society frown with particular dourness on those books that exist solely to produce the pleasures of laughter, tears, shudders, and sexual arousal' (1997: 44). The academic reader – by contrast to the 'general reader',[14] who partakes in the pleasure of the senses – is a professional, whose practices of reading must be aloof and unmoved, practices which historically have been associated with the male rather than the female reader. In Elizabeth Long's view, '[a]cademics tend to repress consideration of variety in reading practices due to our assumption that everyone reads (or ought to) as we do professionally, privileging the cognitive, ideational, and analytic mode' (1992: 192). It is precisely this privileging of the cognitive over the affective which has spurred a number of feminist theorists to revisit the exclusion of the affective from academic discourse. To recognize therefore that reading is 'socially framed' is to acknowledge, according to Long, that 'collective and institutional processes shape reading practices by authoritatively defining what is worth reading and how to read it' (ibid.). In a contemporary critical landscape, this includes, we might add, models of what to read, and how to read, as a feminist.

Practices of reading within institutions of learning clearly differ from those outside, which has to do not just with literary taste but also with 'variable literacies', as Janice Radway calls them; this is to say, different people evaluate books differently 'because they come to them with different backgrounds, different tastes, and different needs' (1997: 6). In Radway's recent book *A Feeling for Books* (1997), which in many ways revises the position she adopted in *Reading the Romance* (first published in 1984), she foregrounds precisely that which remained implicit, even glossed over, in her account of the Smithton women's experience of reading, namely the pleasures attendant on affective reading. The book is a detailed account of the ways in which the editors who worked for the New York-based Book-of-the-Month Club selected books for their subscribers, whose 'middle-brow' literary taste they sought to cater for but also to shape. What she finds again and again is that the Book Club's editors, like their subscribers, did not conceive of reading solely as 'an occasion for interpretation' (Tompkins 1980: 206) but as 'occasions of feeling' (Radway 1997: 43). And it comes as something of a 'revelation' to Radway, but also a liberation from the straitjacket of academically trained reading, that the editors talked of their 'passion of books' in physicalist terms: books were to be 'devoured', they made the 'heart race' and their 'toes tingle' (ibid.: 44). One of the criteria they applied when choosing among the profusion of books available on the literary market was that a book be sufficiently absorbing to 'transport' the reader (ibid.: 72). What most impresses Radway here is that, in selecting books for their subscribers, the editors never lost sight of a modality of reading which engages 'both sense and sensibility, both affect and cognition [...] the body and the brain' (ibid.: 117). In other words,

The Book-of-the-Month Club editors struggled to refuse the familiar categorizing that tends crudely to distinguish entertainment from education and sensual pleasure from cerebral intellection. [...] [They] distinguished themselves alike from those too closely associated with an unthinking body – readers unwilling to perform intellectual work as they read – and those who indulged in rationality and contemplation to such an extent that they denied the sentimental claims of the heart and the sensual demands of the corporeal. The Book-of-the-Month Club editors positioned themselves and those they served in a space *between* – between those who longed for sensations unclouded by reflection and those whose command of intellectual capital had produced nothing but disdain for anyone incapable of understanding their every word.

(Ibid.: 113-14)

From this description it appears that the editors of the Book-of-the-Month Club worked with the classical dictum of *docere–delectare–movere*, and had not removed from the trichotomy its third component, *movere* – the very component which is almost entirely ignored now within academic discourses. Bodily responses to books are deemed inappropriate within the contemporary institution of literature, despite the long history of *movere* as an important aesthetic category in the history of criticism. We remember that in the rhetorical tradition artworks were praised, and therefore worthy of attention, precisely because they affected their beholders (see chapter 5). As such, the 'taste of sense' was not always associated with what Bourdieu calls 'lowly' or 'facile pleasure' (1984: 6, 486). Rather, since attempts to formulate laws for the transmission of the passions were in the mainstream of intellectual preoccupation from antiquity until the eighteenth century, this illustrates that the senses had been core in trying to establish standards of taste. While Bourdieu's analysis of the division of tastes according to social stratification is applicable to a post-Kantian tradition which relegates 'the taste of sense' to popular aesthetics, it is not applicable to a rhetorical tradition; what he ignores is that, historically, 'the taste of sense' was not a form of vulgar enjoyment but belonged to refined pleasure.[15] In this respect, the editors of the Book-of-the-Month Club worked with a canonical conception of aesthetics in the pre-Kantian mould, which they applied to middle-brow literature intended for a middle-brow market. Commenting on the process of book selection, one editor states that 'Swept away is what I want to be by a book', whereas another selects books on the basis of 'what literature is acc. to some, spozed to do, Instruct and Delight' (Lucie Prinz, Joe Savago, qtd. Radway 1997: 117, 31).

That fiction is able to move, delight *and* teach the reader is also what Radway remembers of her own reading experience in her youth and as a young adult. Radway's enchantment with the Book Club is based on the recognition that her own reading history tallies with the Book Club's conception of reading. Not unlike Berggren, Radway feels a division within herself, between how she used to read and how this way of reading came to be displaced in the course of her academic training (cf. Radway 1997: 12, 120). A similar division is also highlighted by Lynne Pearce, who explores this in terms of a self-division which occurs when the academically trained feminist encounters her other self, the self which wishes to give herself to a text. In *Feminism and the Politics of Reading* (1997) Pearce seeks to negotiate the misalignment between reading for cognitive and for emotive pleasure which haunts the professionalized reader caught between the will-to-interpretation and the willingness for *ravissement*. More specifically, Pearce 'looks at the politics of what it is to be a self-conscious feminist reader, and at the politics of what happens when that feminism is "off-duty"'(1997: 3). How can readers 'respond to a text as feminists at the same time as registering their emotional involvement with it'? (ibid.: 23) What happens is 'discomfort' but also confusion. The reader is neither consistent nor reliable, sometimes applying the analytic skills learned as part of her training as a feminist, sometimes seduced by a textual other. In this respect, the reader's relationship with the text is 'structured like a romance' (ibid.: 184), falling in love with the text, falling out of love, passionate, jealous, amorous, devoted – the reader is herself and she is not herself.

The passage between Radway's *Reading the Romance* and Pearce's conception of 'reading as romance' (1997: 20) illustrates how feminist critics have sought either to contest *passionate attachment* by positing a resisting reader, whose relationship with the text is one of *passionate detachment*, or to negotiate, recuperate, even appropriate affective reading on behalf of feminism, despite its negative connotations in the academy, despite its negative associations with the woman reader as a historical configuration, indeed, in spite of those connotations and associations. What is striking about many of the accounts which have re-evaluated affective reading positively is that they have also stressed the 'transformative' nature of reading – in effect, then, bringing together an effects criticism with a criticism of affect.

Rona Kaufman's work on Oprah Winfrey's TV Book Club is a case in point. When participants of this Book Club meet Toni Morrison, whose novel *Paradise* (1997) they struggled to read, the encounter shows up the schism between reading as analytic labour and reading that is 'affective' and 'transformative' (Kaufman 2004: 241). Since Oprah's Book Club places great store on books being able to transform lives, something Winfrey encourages, participants felt that the novel failed them because it emphasized 'the cognitive over the emotive' (ibid.: 245). In the words of one participant: 'I really wanted to read the book and love it and learn some life lessons and when I got into it it was so confusing. I question the value of a book that is hard to understand – and I quit reading' (qtd. ibid.: 244). This comment is illustrative for Kaufman of the division between academic and non-academic modes of reading behaviour. Mindful that the academy provides the reader with useful critical skills, which 'allow for agency in negotiating and crafting one's experience in the world' (ibid.: 250), Kaufman also, however, points to the danger of refusing to acknowledge that the analytic modality of reading constitutes only one among many.

Equally, however, there is a danger which Kaufman does not begin to address (the same is true of Berggren): the act of tying the affective to a reader's sympathetic identification with a given literary character tends to privilege realist over modernist works, that is, fictions which foreground content over form. The difficulty which Morrison's novel presented to participants of the Book Club exemplifies the point, as do the negative comments on modernism expressed repeatedly by editors of the Book-of-the-Month Club (cf. Radway 1997: 279, 288-94). The assumption is that literature affects readers only if it allows them to recognize themselves in the lives of fictional characters. In other words, reading here is not about keeping a distance to the text, but it is the opposite of *disinterestedness* – it is an *interested* pleasure, and one might even say a *self-interested* pleasure, in fiction. However, if affect is indissociable from identification, and if *Paradise* prevented readers of Oprah's Book Club from responding affectively because they found the novel too 'hard to *understand*' (my emphasis), then affect fails not because the cognitive inhibits affect (the argument Radway makes *vis-à-vis* her own reading practice before and after entering the academy), but because not understanding equals not being able to feel affect. According to this logic, the affective is conceived as posterior to the cognitive rather than, as Kaufman, and indeed Berggren and Radway, would be at pains to argue, an anterior response which the academy has driven from readers. This raises the following questions: Do we have to understand in order to be affected? Is readability a necessary condition to experience what Radway calls the 'affective delights of transport' (1997: 72)?

Embodied reading

For the French feminist Hélène Cixous the affirmation of pleasure and affect is of vital importance when it comes to our engagement with literature and art. The pleasure of reading she describes is not limited, however to realism, the privileged genre of the book clubs,[16] as both Kaufman's and Radway's analyses make clear, but is encountered in modernism and the practices of the avant-garde; nor is Cixous a defender of popular culture, but rather what Bourdieu might well call a 'highbrow' theorist. While she refers both to her own and to her students' practices of reading, she does not approach her subject as the ethnographer would, nor does she write as most theorists would. Cixous writes theory as a novelist might. Although she says in *Reading with Clarice Lispector* that '[t]here are thousands of possible relations to a text' (1990: 3), including those of the critic who studies the text's 'construction, its techniques, and its texture', it is the reader who gives herself to a text that catches her attention. In contradistinction to the resisting reader, encountered earlier, Cixous imagines 'a nondefensive, *nonresisting* relationship' between text and reader, whereby 'we are carried off by the text' (ibid.; my emphasis). This echoes the Longinian rapture, which transports the reader to a new realm of passionate experience: the sublimity of 'poetic nourishment' which 'we feel when we read passionately (ibid.: 137). Rather than attaining intellectual distance from the material she reads, Cixous' reader seeks close contact with the text. Describing her own practice of reading, as well as the practice she adopts in seminars with her students, Cixous notes:

> We work very close to the text, as close to the body of the text as possible; we work phonically, listening to the text, as well as graphically and typographically.
>
> Sometimes I look at the design, the geography of the text, as if it were a map, embodying the world. I look at its legs, its thighs, its belly, as well as its trees and rivers: an immense human and earthly cosmos. I like to work like an ant, crawling the entire length of a text and examining all its details, as well as like a bird that flies over it […].
>
> (1988: 148)

What comes across from this passage is a sensuous pleasure in reading. Elsewhere, too, in her work Cixous pays tribute to the physicality of the reading process, such as when she draws attention to the rhythms of a work, or its musical 'pulse', which affects us during reading. Music is paradigmatic for Cixous not of the ideal, as for the Romantics, but of the somatic:

what remains of music in writing, and which exists also in music properly speaking, is indeed that scansion which *also* does its work on the body of the reader. The texts that touch me most strongly, to the point of making me shiver or laugh, are those that have not repressed their musical structure [...].

(Cixous and Calle-Gruber 1997: 64)

In reconnecting the senses with the reception of art through this emphasis on the 'bodily relationship between reader and text' (Cixous 1988: 148), Cixous creates a bridge to a Longinian tradition of aesthetics, bracketing precisely that which Enlightenment ideals had sought to transcend.

The post-Kantian Enlightenment tradition considers aesthetics a science of judgement rather than of sense-experience, already extricating a subject who now judges from the boiling passions underlying it. Where Kant, however, explicitly diagrams the procedure whereby this phase-shift in the structure and environment of subjectivity is to be accomplished, the subject's sacrifice of sensation, receptivity and the passions (as always, in the sense of 'events undergone' or 'suffered') is taken now as a given, an aesthetic *a priori*, to such an extent that even reception studies routinely ask after the *meaning* rather than the *matter* of sense-making. When Cixous draws a parallel between experiencing the rhythms of music and those of a text, she draws out the material connection between an abstract art form (music) and a representational one (literature). If what is abstract, without representational content, can move the reader, *make her shiver*, as Cixous claims, then affect does not rely on meaning. If we assume, however, as Rona Kaufman does (despite the intention of her own argument), that affect depends on cognition, we fail to recognize that literature, like music, 'lets us hear directly that language is produced in an interplay with the body' (Cixous and Calle-Gruber 1997: 64). To borrow Cixous' words from a different context, it could be argued that 'we no longer know how to receive [...] how to hear before comprehension' (1991: 62). This comment suggests that, insofar as we read exclusively for sense, we suppress rather than respond to sensation. The difference between Cixous' project and those outlined in the section on literary taste above could not be clearer. For Cixous the *affective delights of transport* are linked to the sublime, and therefore to a Longinian tradition, where language itself can move the reader to new passionate heights; conversely, Radway uses this phrase not to refer to an awesome experience of the sublime, but humanistically, to describe the emotional involvement between reader and character, as privileged in authentic realism. Affect for Cixous is transformative, but not in the sense of a self-definition, a finding of oneself in the other, as it is the case for the humanistically oriented critic; rather, the self is put under erasure. By urging us 'to hear before comprehension', Cixous shows her 'commitment to moving beyond the categories of the rational and knowable towards [...] the bodily roots of culture' (Shiach 1991: 81), and as such aligns her thinking with Nietzsche, whose own formulations of art as rapture, formulated in his notes 'Toward the Physiology of Art' (1888, discussed in chapter 5), are directed against the Enlightenment ideal of the autonomous rational subject.[17]

What Cixous challenges, then, through her emphasis on the bodily determinants of reading is the primacy of consciousness grounded in Descartes' metaphysics, which provides the basis for subsequent arguments concerning the supremacy of human agency. Insofar as passion acts on the reader, carries her off, Cixous' reader stands as a reminder of 'the illusion of conscious control' (Shiach 1991: 70). She is neither the mistress in her own 'house', or ego, as Freud would say, nor able to master a text. Cixous adopts a similar stance with regard to the writer. Of her own practice she says that 'I undergo writing! [...] I was seized. From where? [...] From some bodily region. I don't know where. "Writing" seized me, gripped me, around the diaphragm, between the stomach and the chest [...]' (1991: 9). Writing – just like reading – is not cut off from the body, disembodied. This somatism is also reflected in Cixous' conception of thinking. As opposed to the rational subject posited by Descartes, that because it thinks, therefore it is, Cixous eliminates mind–body dualism by positing a subject that writes and even *thinks through the body*.[18] 'Language', she tells us, 'is a translation. It speaks through the body. Each time we translate what we are in the process of thinking, it necessarily passes through our bodies' (1988: 151-2). Cixous' willingness to make the body a source of knowledge and creativity, but also her willingness to acknowledge that passions – that is, that undergoing and being acted upon – physically condition thinking, and as such also action, makes a myth of the autonomous rational agency on which modern politics is based.[19] In so doing, Cixous has been accused of offences against feminism as a politics. Therefore, wherein lies the political purchase of her work on behalf of feminism? How might her claim that woman 'physically materializes what she's thinking; she signifies it with her body' (1981: 251) be understood politically? The answer is that Cixous deploys a deconstructive strategy to political ends. Her work has sought to expose the systematic hierarchies that historically have worked to privilege reason over passion, head over heart and, crucially also, man over woman. It is the alignment of woman with the other of reason or, conversely, the alignment of man with rationality that fuels Cixous' distrust of the confirmation of mind, with its concomitant denial of body, in Western thinking.

When Cixous tells us that '[n]early the entire history of writing is confounded with the history of reason' (1981: 249) at the expense of the passions, this could not be more clearly demonstrated than by Freud's explanation of the history of civilization. For Freud, one of the great exposers – and perpetuators – of patriarchy, 'the development of human civilization' depended on 'the matriarchal social order [being] succeeded by the patriarchal one' (1990: 360), in the course of which 'sensuality is gradually overpowered by intellectuality' (ibid.: 365). This is how he justifies his claim:

this turning from the mother to the father points in addition to a victory of intellectuality over sensuality – that is, an advance in civilization, since maternity is proved by the evidence of the senses while paternity is a hypothesis, based on an inference and a premiss. Taking sides in this way with a thought-process in preference to a sense perception has proved to be a momentous step.

(Ibid.: 361)

By aligning woman with 'sensuality' and man with 'the higher intellectual processes' (ibid.: 365), it is as if mankind has managed to climb up the evolutionary and social ladder, and what is left at the bottom is womankind. As a result, Freud tells us, 'he is made proud – so that he feels superior to other people who have remained under the spell of sensuality' (ibid.: 362) and 'the ego feels elevated; it is proud of the instinctual renunciation' (ibid.: 364). This evident privileging of the conceptual over the sensual, or the mental over the corporeal, has as its political correlative the establishment of an asymmetrical distribution of power between the sexes. Whether in public or in private, his sense of superiority operates in tandem with her feelings of inferiority. This is by no means a modern idea.

For ancient thinkers too, such as Aristotle, although humanity is *zoon logon*, it is man who is more a rational animal than woman, since her rational faculty is 'without authority' (1260a). Given that 'lower animals cannot', Aristotle states in *The Politics*, 'apprehend reason, they obey their passions' (1254b). It follows that the human rules over the animal and, just as the rational rules over the irrational, 'the male rules over the female' (1260a). Hence '[t]he male is by nature superior, and the female inferior; and the one rules, and the other is ruled' (1254b). What comes across here, as it did with Freud, is that reason is associated with man, and that woman is the other of reason. The thinker who articulates this association perhaps most explicitly is Philo, an Alexandrian philosopher and rabbi from the first century AD. For Philo, who shared Plato's distrust of sense-perception, reason is superior to passion. The danger perceived by Philo arises when reason becomes slave to passion, when mind submits to body. It is here that the danger of femininity makes itself felt most:

Observe that it is not the woman that cleaves to the man, but conversely the man to the woman. Mind to Sense-perception. For when that which is superior, namely Mind, becomes one with that which is inferior, namely Sense-perception, it revolves itself into the order of the flesh which is inferior, into Sense-perception, the moving cause of the passions. But if Sense the inferior follow Mind the superior, there will be flesh no more, but both of them will be Mind.

(1929: 255-6, qtd. Lloyd 1993: 24)

As this account illustrates, it is not just that 'Mind' is aligned with the male of the species and 'Sense-perception' with the female of the species, but that mind must transcend flesh. It follows that man, but only by resisting passion and reaffirming reason, can and must transcend what is thereafter supposed specific to woman. This is why, in the history of philosophy, as Genevieve Lloyd demonstrates, '[r]ationality has been conceived as transcendence of the feminine'

(1993: 104). Or, to put this argument slightly differently, the feminine confronts man with what he most fears within himself. When he submits to her seductive charms and gives his body to her, he also gives in to the impulses of the flesh which take charge of his mind. At the point at which he is closest to her, he is also closest to that which he seeks to suppress, namely nature (cf. Arneil 1999: 90). Only through what Freud calls 'instinctual renunciation' can he take control of his senses and preserve his superiority, can he take pride in the fact that his ego rules over the id.

Attitudes such as can be discerned in Aristotle and Philo, but also in modern thinkers such as Freud, belong to a long history of hierarchization in Western thought whereby man is associated with the dominant and positive term, and woman with the subordinated and negative term: 'mind over body, culture over nature, self over other, reason over passion' (Grosz 1995: 32). We should not forget, however, that this apparently arbitrary allocation of authority across the axes of gender is not simply or reducibly political, a means by which to keep woman in an inferior social position. Rather, the subordination of the female sex, whether in philosophy or science, whether by a rabbi such as Philo or a neurologist such as Freud, is grounded again and again in the prevailing understanding of physiological factors used for social and political ends.

It is this history of hierarchization which many feminists, including Cixous, have sought to flesh out. In 'Sorties', Cixous gives us this schematic representation of the resultant binary thinking. But even before we can read the schematic list of oppositions, Cixous asks us, 'Where is she?' (1986: 63), thus prompting us to think through the implications of these specific alignments from the point of view of gender:

Activity / Passivity
Sun / Moon
Culture / Nature
Day / Night

Father / Mother
Head / Heart
Intelligible / Palpable
Logos / Pathos.

Form, convex, step, advance, semen, progress.
Matter, concave, ground – where steps are taken, holding- and dumping-ground.

<u>Man</u>
Woman

What is implicit in all such binary oppositions are, of course, structures of hierarchy, which – as has been shown by Derrida, whose work Cixous draws on here – have traditionally informed, organized and ranked Western thinking. Insofar as Freud values 'intellectuality' more highly than its opposite, 'sensuality', or Philo puts a higher value on 'Mind' than on 'Sense-perception', this makes it imperative for feminism to re-examine other binary couplets linked to these particular oppositions. What the privileging of one term above the other, such as 'Head' over 'Heart', reveals, is that the preference for, or the value invested in, one term always works at the expense or exclusion of the *other*, subordinated, term. The same logic is operative too in the privileging, as Bourdieu's analysis exemplifies, of 'the taste of reflection' over 'the taste of sense'. The point here is not just to *expose*, but to *reverse* and *dismantle* – that is, to deconstruct – the system of conceptual oppositions, which has enabled, and still perpetuates, a thinking based on hierarchies, inequalities and exclusions.[20]

What this specific alignment of oppositions and hierarchies also, however, illustrates, as Jonathan Culler has argued, is that 'our notions of the rational are tied to or in complicity with the interests of the male' (1983: 58). Conversely, the passional is the reserved province of woman. As we saw with Philo, man must resist woman so as to resist passion and reaffirm his rational faculty. For a woman to prove herself rational entails that she transcends the feminine, thereby in effect becoming like him, becoming masculine. If we accept this argument, it becomes difficult for feminism to submit to the rule of reason and jettison the unruly passions, for to do so is to be complicit with what Genevieve Lloyd has called the 'historical maleness of Reason' (1993: xix). From the point of view of gender and reading, it would mean that a feminism which 'works to prove itself more rational, serious, and reflective than male readings that omit and distort' (Culler 1983: 58), such as could be said to be the case with Fetterley's re-readings of the male canon, is a feminism which in effect seeks to outreason male reasoning, thereby leaving the hierarchy of reason intact.

The recognition that rationality and its concomitants, mind, logic, intellectuality, consistency, lucidity, unity, etc., are preserves of male authority, not sociologically but conceptually, constitutively, has led many French feminists, Cixous included, to revalorize the previously undervalued terms, turning negative into positive attributes. But rather than basing this revalorization on a validation of women's experience, as a humanist feminist would do, for poststructurally oriented feminists the very categories of woman and experience must be re-evaluated and rethought. Nothing less than thought itself must be unthought; it must be opened to the acts of the body. Thus, Cixous works with, rather than rejects, the excluded other term: the body. Her readings of woman, like those of another French feminist – Luce Irigaray – are *materialist* in all the etymological senses of the word, linking matter with *mater* and the *matrix*. For Irigaray 'she is on the side of the "imperceptible," of "matter"' (1985b: 76), and for Cixous woman is '[m]atter' and 'ground' (1986: 63). Cixous and Irigaray ask us to rethink the relation between the intelligible and the sensible, between the ideal and the material, along a physical continuum that must necessarily subtend the mentalist break.

The task, then, for a feminist 'reception' theory is the physicalization of aesthetics and the exploitation of Philo's nightmare. Like Cixous, who makes the body central to her thinking, indeed makes it a conduit of thought so as to prompt a different mode of thinking altogether, Irigaray too makes the body a starting point of her feminist philosophy. Confronting the Freudian assumption that woman is inferior to man because she lacks the phallus (cf. Freud 1986 [1925]: 405-6; 1979 [1933]), Irigaray's argument demonstrates that woman's *sex is not one*, but *plural*. Compared to the *one* phallus he possesses, '*woman has sex organs more or less everywhere*' (1985b: 28). Since woman is therefore endowed with multiple erogenous zones, this would seem to indicate that she is also endowed with greater 'affectibility'. But, rather than interpreting 'affectibility' as a negative (as Havelock Ellis did when he used the phrase), Irigaray reverses a negative into a positive. She makes physiology work not against women, as Freud or Ellis did, but on behalf of feminism. For Irigaray, woman's body is not a snare or an obstacle to her existence, which must be transcended (as even Simone de Beauvoir's existentialist feminism demanded – so that she might *act* in good faith and deploy her free will), but it enables a different modality of self-expression, whether in terms of sexuality, thinking or writing.

In a similar gesture to Cixous, who had claimed that '[w]e have mouths all over our body. Words come out of our hands, our underarms, our belly, our eyes, our neck' (1999: 79), Irigaray also makes a link between the body and verbal expression. When woman speaks, or by extension writes, there is a correlation between her sexuality and the words which utter from her several lips (mouth *and* labia). She speaks in more than *one* tongue, perhaps even with a forked tongue. Her language is not *one*, but several: '[h]ers are contradictory words, somewhat mad from the standpoint of reason' (1985b: 29), because '*a single word* cannot be pronounced, produced, uttered by our mouths. Between our lips, yours and mine, several voices, several ways of speaking resound endlessly' (ibid.: 209). Irigaray's arguments illustrate that she is not afraid to make biology the starting point of her analysis of woman. One of the critiques of Irigaray – although this might also be applied to Cixous – is that, because she links the body with utterance, she makes speaking and writing indissociable from the sex of the speaker. As Shoshana Felman asks of Irigaray: 'Is it enough to be a woman in order to *speak as* a woman? Is "speaking as a woman" a fact determined by some biological *condition* or by a strategic, theoretical *position*, by anatomy or by culture?' (1975: 3). What is of interest here is the precision with which Felman states the dilemma this chapter has sought to investigate: the authority feminism necessarily accords to politics over biology. This same authority remains evident in a debate which Felman's question initiated when applied to the context of reading.

Reading as/like a woman

The question of whether it is enough to be a woman in order to read as a woman became a key issue in Jonathan Culler's discussion on what is at stake in *reading as a woman*, Robert Scholes's *reading like a man*, and Diana Fuss's *reading like a feminist.*[21] The subject of this debate was the problematic of a core identity and the pitfalls of essentializing the concept of Woman or Man, bringing to the fore differing conceptions of wo/man and of reading. For example, since Jonathan Culler accepts the claim that 'women can read, and have read, as men' (1983: 49), this means that men too can and will read as women. This argument only works if we assume, as Culler does, that '[f]or a woman to read as a woman is not to repeat an identity or an experience that is given but to play a role she constructs with reference to her identity as a woman' (ibid.: 64). For Culler, therefore, reading as a woman is a performance, not grounded in experience, but a hypothesis whereby identity is constructed in the act of reading. As Elaine Showalter among others has pointed out, Culler's reading as a woman in effect involves 'impersonation' (1987: 126): a woman does not read *as* a woman but reads *as if* she were a woman. By contrast, Robert Scholes insists on the importance of experience, which conditions women *as* women and men *as* men. Scholes takes it as a given that women form a real social grouping because they share the same or similar experiences (biological and cultural), which is why a 'male critic, for instance, may work within the feminist paradigm but never be a full-fledged member of the class of feminists' (1987: 207). When we read as women, or as men, we do not slip into a role we have constructed for ourselves, as Culler would have us believe, but we draw on experiences which, because we have had them repeatedly, have left traces 'in our minds and on our bodies' (ibid.: 218). For Scholes, then, experience 'is not just a *construct* but something that *constructs*' (ibid.: 215) and the reason why there is a 'difference between reading about experience and having an experience' (ibid.: 212). This suggests that it is not the text which constructs the reader, but that, whatever the constructing agency may turn out to be, an element of experience must necessarily be involved. If for Scholes identity therefore precedes reading, for Culler identity is a performance staged upon it.

Diana Fuss on the other hand finds troubling Scholes's emphasis on women being members of a class who share a common experience *qua* their position as women in society. In her view, Scholes too readily supposes that, because of a shared set of experiences, men read as men and women as women. This assumption of a common experience among all women, or men, implies a form of cultural essentialism. His argument also, however, comes dangerously close to suggesting that there is something which determines the essence of who we are before we read. Hence Fuss draws attention to the 'hidden appeal to referentiality, to (in this case) the female body' (1994: 100) in Scholes's writing, which lays his thesis open to the charge of biological essentialism. In her own writing, Fuss is careful to avoid the traps of either cultural or biological essentialism. Since for Fuss there is 'little agreement amongst women on exactly what constitutes "a woman's experience"' (ibid.), we cannot take the notion of a 'common' woman's experience as the basis for the claim that women read in a similar way to each other, but read differently from men.[22] In other words, the assumption of unity underlying difference is cognitively and epistemologically unjustified. Although Fuss is critical of Scholes's appeal to experience, she does not ascribe to Culler's notion of reading as performance, whereby a woman reads as if she were a woman. There is, however, a particular aspect of Scholes's thinking which she does adopt in her own formulation of reading.

As we have seen, it is experience which constructs us, in Scholes's view. If this is so, experience also sutures each of us into a particular subject-position. For Scholes it is important that we must become conscious of the way in which we have been conditioned by our experiences, which are always specific to our gender. So, when a man reads, he ought to act in awareness of his conditioning. It is this awareness which will allow him to reflect on what is at stake in *reading as a man*: that is to say, at this juncture he will be *reading like a man*, conscious of his gender and the way in which it has positioned him as a man. This is how Scholes concludes his argument:

> With the best will in the world we shall never read as woman and perhaps not even like women. For me, born when I was born and living where I have lived, the very best I can do is to be conscious of the ground upon which I stand: to read not as but like a man.
>
> (1987: 218)

What Scholes pushes here is the issue of positionality. It is this that Fuss picks up on when she reworks his distinction between reading *as* and *like* a wo/man. Fuss carefully elides the whole issue of essentialism by insisting that she does not read *as a woman* but that she reads from the political position of feminism. She reads 'like a feminist; what it means to read as or even like a woman, I still don't *know*' (1994: 102; my emphasis). For Fuss, then, since there is no determining reference by which we may know our experience, we cannot obey the stricture which, Scholes insists, follows from it, i.e., that we should act in awareness of our conditioned experience. But, because we can know the difference between reading as a feminist and not doing so, it follows that this is what we should do. To read like a feminist is thus to adopt consciously the position from which one speaks.

Since this solves the problem only by eliding it, the question returns: when a woman reads, *is* this 'determined by some biological *condition* or by a strategic, theoretical *position*'? For Fuss it is clearly the latter, since 'sexual categories', she writes, are 'subject-positions' (1994: 112). What interests me especially about this statement is Fuss's following point: namely that these 'subject-positions' are 'subject to change and to historical evolution'. The implication is that subject-positions, unlike biological categories, are fluid. Whence the assumption that biological categories are fixed and determined, rather than similarly subject to change and historical evolution? What if sex as a category were too unstable or changeable to allow us to define across cultures and throughout history his or her being? After all, natural history shows that the only constant in biology is change. To follow this line of argument we have to adopt the tenets of a biological constructivism rather than those of social constructivism. Such an argument also brings us back to the body, taking us to the

heart of the problem as regards a sexual politics of reading. Biology and politics are at odds with each other since, for the former, the human is a molecular process whereas, for the latter, the human is a rational, autonomous entity.
Insofar as feminism is about sexual politics, its biggest bugbear has been biology. This is because biology has been used to substantiate the thesis that anatomy is destiny. If we regard biologism as 'a particular form of essentialism', as
Elizabeth Grosz does, which 'refers to the existence of fixed characteristics,
given attributes, and ahistorical functions that limit the possibilities of change
and thus of social reorganization' (1995: 48), then this definition would bear
out the claim that anatomy is destiny. In which case, this universalist claim
would hold true for 'all women at all times' (ibid.: 49). If, conversely, we regard
biology as contingent on evolution rather than ahistoricity, then we would
have to redefine what we mean by biological determinism. After all, even
Freud argued that 'biology' – while being deterministic and naturalistic – is
also 'truly a land of infinite possibilities' (1991 [1920]: 334). This is precisely
where Sadie Plant, drawing on work more recently done in the life sciences
than Freud was able to, asks us to venture.

The feminization of the reader

Plant is one of the few feminists to give an account of the sexed body that is
not reducibly discursive. Crucially, her approach presents a way out of the
essentialist/anti-essentialist debates. When she substantiates Irigaray's argument as to woman's heightened sense-perception by quoting from a textbook
on biology which, according to Plant, reluctantly concedes that 'the human
female is actually sensitive all over her body', and thus 'appears to be very
much more responsive to tactile stimuli than the male' (Montagu 1971, qtd.
Plant 1997: 189), it is to bring biology closer to feminism rather than to pitch
one against the other. Although we might wish to dismiss the argument of
woman's greater 'affectibility' on the grounds that it merely reinforces the
prejudice that woman is incapable of thought and action independently of
her biology, we should not do so too quickly on the simple grounds that both
sets of arguments deploy biology. Whereas a thesis such as J. G. Millingen's in
*Mind and Matter, illustrated by Considerations on Hereditary Insanity and the
Influence of Temperament in the Development of the Passions* (1847) – which claims
that '[w]oman, with her exalted spiritualism, is more forcibly under the control of matter; her sensations are more vivid and acute, her sympathies more
irresistible. She is less under the influence of the brain than the uterine system, the plexi of abdominal nerves, and irritation of the spinal cord' (qtd. Flint
1993: 57) – is deeply essentialist, Plant knowingly undermines the biological
foundation on which theses of this kind rest. As Irigaray would say, for
Millingen woman clearly cannot 'climb up from the sensible to the intelligible' (1985a: 343): she cannot clamber out from the cave, cavity or crevice
that is her womb,[23] or scale the distance 'from the "lower abdomen" to the
"head"' (ibid.), because she is (in) the cave, tied to earth and nature. His is a

thesis which exploits its essentialism to serve a programme of inferiorizing the female sex. Plant's by contrast is a thesis which gradually builds up a case as to why essentialism is untenable from the perspective of biology itself.

Plant engages biological essentialism – as, I argue, do Irigaray and Cixous – to pluralize biology philosophically (both against received Freudianism, but also against a feminism's account of biology, which early on fixed the latter's account of woman as little more than a womb). Thus, when she uses Gilles Deleuze's and Félix Guattari's insight that human bodies 'imply a multiplicity of molecular combinations bringing into play not only the man in the woman and the woman in the man, but the relation of each to the animal, the plant etc.: a thousand tiny sexes' (1988: 213, qtd. Plant 1997: 204), it is intended to destabilize the notion that there are two distinct and discrete sexes. Indeed, Plant argues a case for literalizing Deleuze's and Guattari's notion of 'becoming-woman' (1988: 275) through current biological research concerning the impact of the environment on the males of many species. The industrialized, technologically saturated, and chemically polluted environment many of us inhabit has had the unforeseen effect, she argues, that

the males of many species are subject to increasing levels of feminization from sources as varied as estrogen processed through the contraceptive pill, agents such as chemical detergents, and a vast number of chemicals which mimic the effects of female hormones which find their way into the water supply.

(Plant 1997: 215)

Effects such as falling sperm count and increasing male infertility are compounded, Plant explains, by 'the feminizing impact of tinned vegetables, cigarettes, and the accelerating collapse of conventional male economic, social, and sexual roles' (ibid.). In other words, Plant predicts, our destiny is being chemically transformed.[24] The larger point Plant reinforces is that sex as a category is not fixed and ahistorical, but is subject to change.

Plant's thesis is contentious because it undermines the assumption that it is only gender, and not sex, which is 'a shifting contextual phenomenon' (Butler 1990: 10). Rather than understanding gender in terms primarily of 'a relative point of convergence among culturally and historically specific set of relations' (ibid.), as Judith Butler does, we must also understand sex as a mobile intersection of biological relations. Indeed, the essentialist claim that biology, and the experiences specific to the biological sexes, determines our socialization, and with it the possibilities of social organization and our cultural environment, is overturned when it is the environment which shapes biology. Insofar as increasing levels of feminization could not have been foreseen, this indicates that our species' biological development is not deterministic in the sense that it is predetermined and permanent but unpredictable. Thus we are mistaken in presupposing both that biology is fixed and ahistorical and that determinism is causal and predictable.

If we apply these insights to the question of reading, and more specifically the issue of reading as a woman or a man, the following scenario suggests itself.

We can either accept Cixous' point that '[i]t is impossible to predict what will become of sexual difference – in another time (in two or three hundred years?)' (1986: 83), or we can make a hypothesis based on Sadie Plant's thesis, and argue that in two or three hundred years reading *as* a man might not be the norm any longer, because men then might read *like* the men they once were, or, indeed, we might all read as women.

In *Zeros + Ones* (1997) Plant offers not just a deconstruction of essentialism but a non-essentialist determinism. Her thesis is not, however, simply metaphorical, since she deals not with representations or social constructions of gender but with biological constructions of the sexes. In this respect she demonstrates a realist deconstruction by which the physico-chemical and technological environment *dismantles* the sexes into a 'thousand tiny sexes', 'each' bearing traces of others. Cultural theorists undertook to diversify the category of gender, now segmented into further categories such as sexual orientation, race, ethnicity, age and education, among others; Plant materializes this diversification not in terms of reducibly social differences, as the former have done, but in terms of biological differences, on the one hand, and technological differentiation, on the other.

Conclusion: *Materialist* Readings

The placing of a chapter on the sexual politics of reading at the end of this book is not coincidental. Chapter 7 is not an afterthought, as if feminism itself were an afterthought to the various theories of reading mapped out in the other six chapters. Rather, as already noted in the introduction, I consistently worked with two terms in this book, including in the last chapter, both of which are inextricably linked with gender: the physiological and the material. However, I also added a third term: the technological, which, although not universally acknowledged as a necessary element in feminist thinking, is the necessary basis for any consideration of reading.

Whereas the conjunction between feminism and politics was the topic of the last pages, then, the feminist politics which has informed this book as a whole has been *materialist*, bringing together − as the word's etymologies do − *materia*, *mater* and *matrix*. Insofar as much of contemporary criticism and theory has ignored the bodily, the technological and the material in general, as though '[m]atter goes underground. It stays there. Imperceptible' (Plant 1997: 179), I have sought to 'make perceptible' not just that readers have bodies, but also that books have bodies, that is, that they are physical, that they enter into physiological relations with other bodies, and that they are technological entities. As such, my approach has involved a re-reading of the history of theories of reading in order to assess which theories have, and which have not, elided the matter of matter.

Of all the contemporary literary theories, feminist theories are unique insofar as, concerned with sexual difference, they foreground the body. For this reason feminist theories have pertinent concerns about the physical relations between readers and books. It is mostly therefore on a feminist terrain that debates about bodily sensations, such as affect, passion, feeling, are being addressed, in contrast to the reader-oriented theories introduced in chapter 6, which deal almost exclusively with the cognitive. This constitutes another reason why feminist theories have had the last word in this book.

By seizing on the reader as a sensuous figure and not solely as a sense-maker, I have deployed the following set of oppositions throughout *Theories of Reading: Books, Bodies, and Bibliomania*:

book as physical object	work as vessel of meaning
texture of the text	text as signifying system

body of the reader	mind of the reader
sensation	sense-making
affect	cognition
passion	reason
occasion for feeling	occasion for interpretation
aesthesis	hermeneutics
flesh and blood reader	reader as abstraction
heart	head
warm	cold
closeness	distance
passive	active
material	ideal
matter	form

I deliberately focused on those terms, or alignment of terms, which many contemporary theories of reading leave untheorized. From the perspective of deconstruction the aim would be to reverse, and then undo, these hierachies. But this is not what I am proposing here. Rather, we have to recognize that binaries such as mind and body, although conceived vertically, as hierarchies, exist horizontally, as a continuum. This is to say, mind does not transcend body (a vertical relation), but mind is subjected to transports by bodies (a horizontal relation): the animal body, of course, but also that of the book and of technologies in gene-ral, and the chemical bodies that constitute them all. If we pose the issue of the relation between mind and body solely in epistemological terms, we fail to acknowledge the body's role as a vehicle in the articulation of knowledge.

Theories exclusively concerned with reading as an 'occasion for interpretation' affirm the cognitive and are thus aligned with the rational at the cost of the passional. If we accept the point that the rational has been strategically deployed as a criterion to distinguish the masculine from the feminine, as we saw Culler and Lloyd argue, it follows that theories concerned with reading as 'occasions of feeling' flatten a transcendentalist history that seeks to affirm interpretation *over* feeling, mind *over* body, man *over* woman. Such theories are co-extensive, then, with a tradition of affective criticism, and are therefore continuous with certain aspects of literary history, unexpectedly bridging the Longinian tradition and contemporary feminism. This suggests, to rephrase Culler's point, that theories which affirm affect are *tied to or in complicity with the interests of the* materialist. Or, translating this insight into the context of this book, it means that hermeneutics as the art of interpretation is complicit with the historical gendering of reason as male, whereas aesthetics as the theory of sense-perception is complicit with transports of passion historically gendered as female.

Reading is clearly not just about sensations, but also about sense-making. This is not to say, however, that involuntary responses during reading, registered by the body before the reader is able to respond intellectually, are not worthy of study. Bodily responses to literature are easily trivialized, as Wimsatt and Beardsley did in 'The Affective Fallacy' when they dismissed from literary enquiry 'tears, prickles, and other physiological symptoms, of feeling angry, joyful, hot, cold, or intense, or of vaguer states of emotional disturbance' (1954 [1949]: 34) – symptoms which for two thousand years had contributed towards a definition of what was attractive and repulsive in art. When understood within the context of this broader history of criticism, bodily responses to literature cannot be written off as unsophisticated. The dictum from antiquity that the dramatic or poetic was to *move* its audience, to release pity, incite passion or fill with horror, is what major thinkers from Aristotle to Longinus, from Sidney to Burke, have all deemed to be a hallmark of great works of art. Once the purpose of art is associated not with the awakening of the senses, but with the powers of reflection, *movere* goes underground. Although as a category it lingers on in critiques of popular art forms, initially the novel and later film, *movere* is no longer part of a high (in the sense of a dominant) aesthetic. Or conversely, as we saw with reference to the preferred reading materials of the book club communities, *movere* becomes part of a popular aesthetic. Such a 'downgrading' of the category already starts in the eighteenth century, and has much to do with the Enlightenment philosophy of art, and especially Kant, who redefines the purpose of art as 'purposiveness without purpose', that is, art as a cognitive *apatheia* emptied of affective pleasure.

We should remember here that critiques of affect as appeared in eighteenth-century educational, literary and medical treatises and the nineteenth-century periodical press, like Kant's own critique, at least acknowledged the role of affect in art, while simultaneously seeking to safeguard the beholder from its powerful effects. For Kant and his popularizers, it was never therefore a question of denying the existence of affect, or of ignoring it, as is the case in much of contemporary literary theory; rather, they pathologized it. One way in which to read this pathologization is to see it linked with the emergence of mass culture and the fear that readers, especially women readers, would indiscriminately and biblio-manically *devour* literature for cheap thrills or vulgar sentiments rather than use it for moral betterment or the refinement of mind. The emergence of mass culture, the result of an unprecedented increase in the production of reading matter catering for an ever increasing literate readership from the lower ranks of society, or those perceived to occupy a lower position within society such as women, marks a turning point in the culture of reading. One way in which to counter reading for self-gratification and turn it into something which enlightens rather than inflames is to insist on dispassionate analysis. In this respect, dispassionate analysis, whether it takes the form of a text-centred formalism or a reader-oriented will-to-interpretation, has a regulatory function: to put the intellect into control so as to bypass the unruly passions.

What the history of theories of reading, as I have told it here, shows is that affect, once meritorious, becomes dangerous before it disappears from critical view almost altogether. Only certain feminist approaches present an exception to this. Since the history of the reader as a sensuous figure is much longer than the conception of the reader as solely a sense-maker, then the whole of literary history lends itself to be re-read, or reclaimed, on behalf of *materialism*. Perhaps the time has come to think what was unthinkable in the heady days of 'grand' theory, so as to reach the unthought: that is, to approach reading from the ground upwards, from the moment of 'sensation which feels the moment in the moment' and not just from the moment of 'cognition which recognizes the moment only after the moment'.[1] Plato urged us to flee the body because its distractions interrupt and disturb thinking, Descartes thought the body incapable of thought, Kant warned us against the body's 'pathological' influences on thinking, and de Beauvoir saw the body as a snare.[2] Following a Nietzschean trajectory, however, where knowledge is not just a will to comprehension but also visceral, Deleuze leaves us with this thought: '"We do not even know what a body can do": in its sleep, in its drunkenness, in its efforts and resistances. To think is to learn what a non-thinking body is capable of, its capacity, its postures' (1989: 189). When it comes to reading, we have a scant understanding of what our body does, but we do know that the body was important in the history of reading. The dis-embodied reader of modern literary theory might well demand, as Deleuze does: 'Give me a body then' – not just historicized and gendered, but also racialized, sexualized, technologized.

Notes

Introduction

1 Hélène Cixous' own work as a literary theorist is a notable exception here (see chapter 7).

2 I am borrowing these words from Janice Radway (1997: 43).

3 My argument here and elsewhere in this book is greatly indebted to Jane Tompkins (1980).

4 For an exploration of cultural anxieties about visual mass media in the twentieth century, echoing anxieties about the novel in the previous century, see Brantlinger (1998: 209-12).

5 For an example of modern bibliomania, see Holbrook Jackson's *The Anatomy of Bibliomania*, originally published in 1950, two years after his death. A rich source of bibliomanic practices, with chapters on the pleasures of books, book-eating, book-drinking, biblioklepts, book worms, book-hunting, bibliophily, etc., as well as symptoms, causes, and a cure for the disease, the endearing Jackson claims that 'I writ of bibliomania, by being busy to avoid bibliomania' (2001: 21).

6 For a revisionist history of the novel, beginning not with Cervantes but in antiquity, and not on the northern shores of the Mediterranean, see Doody (1996).

7 The term 'remediation' is used by Bolter and Grusin (1999) to refer to the way in which one particular medium 'appropriates the techniques, forms, and social significance of other media and attempts to rival or refashion them in the name of the real' (1999: 99). Examples might include how print borrowed features such as paper, layout, or binding from the codex, or how modernist literature borrowed the montage principles of film. As indicated by these examples, new media (print) do not just borrow from older media (codex), but in turn, older media (literature) rise to the challenge and borrow from newer media (film).

8 My thinking here has been inspired by Lüdeke and Greber (2004) and Böhme et al. (2000). The former adopt an intermedial approach with regard to literature, the latter an intercultural and interdisciplinary approach with regard to culture.

9 It is instructive that Mann associates a natural bodily function, such as tears, with gender, and by further association with cultural debasement. This association will be revisited in several chapters.

10 Compare McLuhan's point that 'hot media do not leave so much to be filled in or completed by the audience'; therefore, unlike 'cool media', this makes them 'low in participation' (1964: 31).

11 We should remember that authors are not the only producers of text.The labours of scribes, printers, typesetters and/or editors are also part of the production process.

1   A History of Reading

1 This section of the book is based on research by historians of reading: Chartier (1989c, 1994, 1995); Darnton (1990); Gauger (1994); Martin (1994); Davidson (1989); Flint (1993); Raven et al. (1996); Schön (1987). For a synoptic overview of the history of reading in the Western cultural tradition, similar to the one I present here, see Cavallo and Chartier (1999: 1-36).
2 For accounts of reading in cultural traditions other than the West and in religious traditions other than Christianity, see Boyarin (1992).
3 As Roger Chartier points out, this explains the importance of dictation at that time (cf. 1995: 19).
4 Dramatic works tended to be divided first into acts and then into scenes from the sixteenth century onwards.
5 Printing, and the use of movable type, was widespread in Asian cultures long before Gutenberg's invention (cf. Chartier 1995: 14-15).
6 For a discussion of the shift from *imitation* as an aesthetic principle to that of *innovation*, see Young (1948 [1759]: 14).
7 Historical research has shown not only that Protestants owned more books than Catholics (cf. Chartier 1989c), but also that book reading was strongly encouraged in Protestant areas, while in Catholic quarters it was often associated with heresy (cf. Ducreux 1989).
8 For a distinction in eighteenth-century France between prohibited books which were 'published without authorization', and pirated books which were 'published under false addresses and without printing permission' see Chartier (1988b: 305; 1991: 73).
9 See Davidson (1986: 73) for a critique of Engelsing on these grounds, as well as Darnton (1990: 165-6) and Schön (1987: 299-300); see also chapter 4 for a detailed discussion of the impact of *Werther* on the reading public.

2   The Material Conditions of Reading

1 Textual critics are not to be confused with literary critics; for developments within the discipline of textual criticism (also referred to as critical bibliography), see Davison (1998); Greetham (1992); McGann (1991); and McKenzie (1999); on the relations between textual criticism and the history of the book, see McDonald (1997); and Hall (1986).
2 Pound is an heir to Blake insofar as he too puts into practice a 'bibliographical imagination' (McGann 1991: 142).
3 I am not convinced that McKenzie's point is applicable to the typography of texts, that is, the 'formatting' of a page. I think in this context it would be more apt to say that form *affects* sense.The point is valid, however, with respect to the medium of the book, that is, the object itself which conveys the text. Chartier seems similarly unconvinced by McKenzie's claim. Although he quotes McKenzie's phrase that 'forms effect meaning' (McKenzie 1999: 13; see Chartier

influence

1997: 82), only two pages later, and seemingly in agreement with McKenzie, he
rephrases the point, stating that 'forms *affect* meaning' (my emphasis), thereby
watering down the overtly determinist stance taken by McKenzie. For a further
elaboration on the determinist argument, see chapter 3.

4 This is the case for all so-called conflated editions. Such editions are the product of one of the most common conventions for editing – eclectic editing –
whereby the editor produces an 'ideal text version', conflating or merging
several text sources to create a new version which the editor believes 'represents the fullest extent of authorial intention' (Bowers 1998: 252).

5 It should also be noted that the East German counterpart, although published
as a complete book, does not present an integral or intact text either. It is a
shortened version, but this is mainly owing to censorship, with passages where
Wolf addresses the escalating arms race most frankly struck out by the East
German authorities.

6 Shakespeare's own handwritten drafts are known as *foul papers* on the
grounds that they were probably 'covered in changes and crossings-out, or
"blottings"', while the *fair papers* refer to prompt books, which were also
used 'to obtain the approval of the censors'. As Holderness, Porter and Banks
point out further, despite Heminge's and Condell's claim to have based their
edition of the collected plays on 'fair' copies, 'the close correlation between
many of the plays in the folio and some of the previously unpublished quartos suggests that the editors must also have made use of the printed versions.
In other words they worked with a variety of sources, "fair" and "foul",
"good" and "bad" – some already in public circulation, others still privately
owned – discriminating as they saw fit' (2000: 167-8). In which case, it
would be true to say that Heminge and Condell produced a conflated,
hybrid edition of Shakespeare's plays and not the 'True Originall' they
promised.

7 The example Greetham gives is from *Antony and Cleopatra*, and concerns a
speech by Proculeius (lines 3238 and 3241), where a section of text seems to
have been dropped between pages 364 and 365.

8 Pope and Johnson, for instance, sought to restore the true literary Shakespeare
from deformations by the likes of Heminge and Condell, and therefore
attacked the folio as the work of actors overly concerned 'to make [their
author] just fit for their Stage' (Pope 1725, qtd. Murphy 2000: 198). In
Murphy's view, this 'anti-theatricality of the eighteenth-century editors can be
seen as indicative of an increasing tendency to marginalise the multiplicitous
oral and social lineages of the text, refashioning it as an isolable and wholly
"literary" object' (ibid.: 199). It is ironic then that early twentieth-century
editors (those associated with the New Bibliography), equally concerned with
restoring a true literary Shakespeare, should have privileged the folio edition
to this end. This was a move, however, which according to Murphy 'signalled,
if anything, the onset of a more comprehensive, multifaceted attack on the oral
and social dimension of the Shakespeare canon', for what the New
Bibliographers were most concerned with was to reconfirm 'Shakespeare as
the solitary author of a coherent body of unique proprietary texts assembled
in the Folio in good faith by Shakespeare's colleagues' (ibid.: 202).

9 It could be argued that, if Wolf's *Cassandra* were part of a bygone oral culture,
and not the print culture which we inhabit now, then the orderings of the

narrative would have raised little controversy. The question therefore as to which Cassandra version is the *authentic* one is one which is conditioned largely by the concerns of a print culture, whose medium for communication, the printed book, seeks to institute a degree of fixity and consistency unknown to manuscript culture, where texts circulated unhampered by such dictates. After all, *Cassandra* was first delivered in an oral format, and its final chapter, *Kassandra: Erzählung*, is a monologue by a woman who has finally been given her own voice, even if her stories circulated amply in classical times. But we no longer live in an oral culture. It is ironic therefore that an essential feature of oral culture still lives on in *Cassandra* insofar as editing has shown here that, like story-telling, it involves cutting, pasting and rearrangement.

10 Graham D. Caie points out with reference to Chaucer, for instance, that: 'In the famous manuscript of *The Canterbury Tales*, the Ellesmere Manuscript, the text is off-centre, on the left of the page, to give way to the glosses which are written in the same and as large a hand as the text itself. Visually the glosses are privileged as highly as the text itself, a fact only known to readers who consult the manuscript of facsimile, as no edition has yet presented them side by side' (2000: 35).

3   The Physiology of Consumption

1 This chapter has drawn on invaluable research by Baym (1984: 54-62); de Bolla (1989: 252-78); Darnton (1985: 215-56); Ferris (1991: 35-52); Flint (1993: 43-71); Johns (1998: 380-443); König (1977); Mays (1995: 165-194); Saenger (1997: 1-17); Schenda (1988 [1970]: 40-90); Schön (1987: 63-122); Wittmann (1999). Translations from the German sources are mine.

2 The interrelations between the railways and print are strong in other respects too. The railways not only enabled the large-scale and speedy circulation of print during the nineteenth century, but reading while travelling in a train carriage, so as to avoid the gaze of strangers, was a recommended pastime for ladies. This is why booksellers set up store at railway stations from the 1840s onwards, with W. H. Smith being the most long-standing business to have started this way, and famous at the time for selling cheap 'yellowbacks', also referred to as 'railway fiction'.

3 Excellent sources for writings on the early cinema are Kaes (1978); Güttinger (1984); Schlüpmann (1990); and Hake (1993). Translations from the German are mostly mine.

4 For the phantom ride, a camera was strapped to the front of a moving vehicle (such as a train) to give spectators the illusion of moving through space.

5 For quotations by Beneken and Erwald, see König (1977: 95, 104); for Sellmann, see Schlüpmann (1990: 203); and for Prels, see Hake (1993: 52).

6 The 'cinema of attractions' is Tom Gunning's term for early film features (until 1908) which seek to astonish and thrill their audiences. Early cinema is therefore a 'cinema of instants' which 'favoured direct visual stimulus over narrative development' (1998: 218).

7 The 'cyberspace playhouse' is based on an idea by Randal Walser (1990; see Rheingold 1992: 189-93, 286), and of which similar examples, as Benjamin Woolley points out, could already be found in various pleasure arcades as early as 1990 (1992: 161-2).

8 The most sophisticated argument as to the differences between McLuhan and Williams is offered in Lister et al. (2003). In section 5.2 especially, Iain Grant develops an account of technological determinism that is quite different to that which Williams ascribes to McLuhan, deploying not the logic of mechanical causality but of non-linear causality.

9 This quotation by Orderic Vitalis (qtd. Ong 1982: 95) is on the physicality of writing in the Middle Ages, but is just as applicable to the physiology of reading.

4   The Reader in Fiction

1 On the perceived dangers of fiction as represented within fiction, see Brantlinger (1998); Crosman Wimmers (1988); Flint (1993); Pearson (1999); and Peterson (1986).

2 I am rephrasing a point made by Peter de Bolla in the context of eighteenth-century theorists' fear that the text might '"transport" the reader to dangerous places' (1989: 250).

3 This is also true in Dante. Upon hearing Francesca's tale, the narrator weeps (115-17), adding that 'I swooned for pity like as I were dying, / And, as a dead man falling, down I fell' (141-2).

4 David H. Richter goes so far as to suggest that readers of the Gothic could more readily identify with the 'perils and plight' of the protagonists because they had been prepared for empathetic response by the sentimental novel (1988: 127).

5 In *A Philosophical Enquiry* (1757) Burke develops an understanding of the awe and astonishment by which the sublime in nature or art strikes its perceiver. It is this understanding of the sublime nature of terror which the Gothic also draws on.

6 Isabel Gilbert is the heroine of Mary Elizabeth Braddon's bestseller *The Doctor's Wife* (1864), a rewrite of *Emma Bovary* published before Flaubert's novel became widely known in Britain.

7 This is the question posed by Barthes about Flaubert's irony (1974: 140).

8 Ecstasy, literally *ek-stasis*, means 'standing outside' oneself, in the sense of being in a trance.

9 For a sustained commentary on the differences between Nietzsche's and Kant's aesthetics, see Heidegger (1991: 1.107-14).

10 When critics talk of the passive reader, they tend to ignore, as I argued at the end of chapter 2, that, strictly speaking, reactions such as screams, tears or palpitations do not make readers passive, at least not in a physical sense. This is because, in acting out or performing these responses through body language, the reader is akin to an actor, not because he or she pretends to be moved, but because an actor gives physical expression to the written word.

11 Naomi Schor uses this term with reference to Henry James (1980: 171), whose characters, she argues, 'are perpetually, indeed obsessively, involved in interpretive ventures' (ibid.: 170), and therefore belong to that 'considerable body of (modern) fiction that is explicitly, indeed insistently, concerned with interpretation: its scope and its limits, its necessity and its frustration' (ibid.: 168).

12 For an excellent explication of Heidegger's ideas on the demise of contemporary culture, linked to the mass media, see Petro (1987: 124-7).

13 Morton Heilig, a Hollywood cinematographer, who took out patents for his Telesphere Mask and his Sensorama machine, was the first to envisage what we would now call virtual reality. In his essay 'The Cinema of the Future' he describes his artistic vision of a cinema without the fourth wall, a kind of inhabitable movie, which would 'far surpass the "Feelies"': where we would 'feel physically and mentally transported into a new world' (2002 [1955]: 247).

14 Charney's argument is based on a distinction made by Heidegger with reference to vision (Heidegger 1962: 387-8). Charney borrows Heidegger's distinction to make a point about the cinema, and the way in which it overstimulates its spectators by a continuous assault of moving images. I am using it here to make a point about VR.

5 The Role of Affect in Literary Criticism

1 When I use the term 'literature' in this chapter, I am referring to fictive not factual writing. However, when I use it to refer to imaginative writing before the eighteenth century, my usage of the term is not strictly speaking historical. This is because the term 'literature' is a relatively 'recent phenomenon', as Eagleton points out, 'invented sometime around the eighteenth century' (1983: 18). Although it is now used to designate creative writing in general, in the eighteenth century, for instance, 'there was grave doubt about whether the new upstart form of the novel was literature at all' (ibid.: 17). For a further discussion of the concept of literature and the usage of the term, see Eagleton (ibid.: 1-19).

2 For a discussion of Lady Bradshaigh's tear-stained response to Richardson's *Clarissa*, typical of its time, see Mullan (1996: 247).

3 Distinct from phenomenology, which is the intellectual reflection that takes place on the basis of sense-perception, concerning the fact and structure of sense-perception in order to define the logic of the object as it appears to consciousness, is aesthetics as the study of the feelings which arise in a reader, or spectator, from objects regarded as moving, beautiful, terrifying or sublime. It is this latter approach which is to be mobilized in this chapter.

4 Lyotard's explanation of Boileau draws on Père Bouhours, who takes the same stand as Boileau (1991: 95). See also Abrams on the concept of the 'Le je ne sais quoi' which can be 'recognised only by the intuition of sensibility' (1953: 193-5).

5 The 'eighteenth-century ideal of the Man of Taste', as Patrick Parrinder explains, 'who must have read everything before he can judge of anything' (1977: 145), is no longer possible in Arnold's time given the sheer abundance of print.

6 The reasons why such terms should be excluded from criticism, Ransom says in 'Criticism, Inc.', are as follows:

I have read that some modern Broadway producers of comedy require a reliable person to seat himself in a trial audience and count the laughs; their method of testing is not as subtle as Aristotle's, but both are concerned with the effects. Such concerns seem to reflect the view that art comes into being because the artist, or the employer behind him, has designs upon the public, whether high moral designs or box-office ones. It is an odious view in either case, because it denies the autonomy of the artist as one who interests himself in the artistic object in his own right, and likewise the autonomy of the work itself as existing for its own sake.

(1938: 343)

7 For an in-depth discussion of Holland, and also his relation to Bleich, see Freund (1987: 112-33).

8 I am referring here to Michel Foucault's claim that the function of the author in the Western tradition is regulatory (1986 [1969]: 111, 118-19). That is, our culture uses the author 'to master and control the great proliferation of discourse, in such a way as to relieve its richness of its most dangerous elements; to organise its disorder so as to skate around its most uncontrollable aspects' (1972: 228).

6   The Reader in Theory

1 Excellent accounts of reader-oriented theory are provided in Freund (1987) and Holub (1984). For anthologies of reader-oriented theories, see Suleiman and Crosman (1980); Tompkins (1980); Bennett (1995); Machor and Goldstein (2001); and Schweickart and Flynn (2004).

2 Books on reader-oriented theorists often only touch on deconstruction as an alternative approach to reading, with the exception of Culler (1983) and Bennett (1995). This chapter gives equal weight to the latter perspective.

3 The first quotation is from Hans-Georg Gadamer (Gadamer 1989: 31), who takes it as a given that 'one cannot read what is written without understanding' (ibid.: 118); the second quotation is from J. Hillis Miller, following Paul de Man's insight (Miller 1989: 164).

4 I am not the only one to make this distinction (cf. Suleiman 1980: 38).

5 In German, *Verstehen* (understanding) is related to *Verstand* (reason) and also contains the verbal root *stehen* (to stand), the noun of which is *Stand* (stand or position). To argue, as Gadamer does, that 'to understand means that one is capable of stepping into the place of the other in order to say what one has there understood' (1989: 96) is to emphasize the correlation between *Verstehen* as understanding and as standpoint. As Gadamer himself asks and answers, '[w]hat is the literal meaning of *Verstehen*? It means "to stand in for someone"' (ibid.: 118).

6 This is also why the presupposition that communication will be a success is 'more regulative than constitutive of text and reading', as James Risser quite rightly points out, because it determines in advance what we look for (1989: 182).

7 For a detailed discussion of the Gadamer–Derrida debate on understanding, see Littau (1996).

8 Therefore, the reader must make 'a special effort to read [such works] "against the grain" of the accustomed experience' (Jauss 1982b: 26). This point not only betrays Jauss's formalist orientation, but has also become a useful approach for feminism in terms of reading works by certain male authors against the grain of their implicitly sexist assumptions. I will return to this issue in chapter 7.

9 According to Freund, this means that 'the object of interpretation now becomes the interpretation itself'.

10 Fish is very candid when he says that 'I cannot answer that question, but neither, I would claim, can anyone else' (1980: 165).

11 I have, for instance, given a unified account of Fish's theory, despite the fact that Fish has altered some of his assumptions in the course of his career, as chronicled in *Is There a Text in this Class?*. It could therefore be argued that I have done so to apply a Fishian principle, either because I belong to a community of those who want to make a unity out of a writer's oeuvre or because I put Fish into a community all by himself. I leave it up to my reader, who is equally guided by certain critical assumptions, to decide this.

12 As both Miller (1989: 167) and Werner Hamacher explain (1989: 198), de Man's brief mention of this phrase at the end of his chapter 'Promises (*Social Contract*)' in *Allegories of Reading* (1979: 276) is used to subvert Heidegger's dictum that *Die Sprache spricht* [language speaks].

13 See Abrams's 'The Deconstructive Angel', which, together with Miller's 'The Critic as Host', is reprinted in Lodge and Wood (2000). The two essays form part of a debate which initially took place at the MLA conference in December 1976, and which was subsequently published in *Critical Inquiry*, 3 (1977).

14 Indeed, 'great works of literature', Miller writes, 'are likely to be ahead of their critics. They are there already. They have anticipated explicitly any deconstruction the critic can achieve' (1975: 31). Thus literature subsumes criticism. If this argument were generalized so that writing subsumed reading, then what, from the perspective of reader-response criticism, is there left to do for the reader? We will return to this issue below.

15 I am evoking here, of course, Derrida's phrase '*il n'y a pas de hors-texte*' (1976: 158).

16 This description of theory is Murray Krieger's (1994: 9).

17 Ana-lysis means of course 'breaking-up' or 'dissolution', and it is therefore not surprising that Foucault refers to what he does in *The History of Sexuality: Volume 1* as an 'analytics' and not a theory (1980: 82).

18 For a debate on this issue, see Robert Scholes (1987: 211) and Diana Fuss (1994: 100-1), whose counter-argument that 'not all females, in fact, menstruate' illustrates why it is problematic to 'base the idea of a class of women on "essence" or "experience"'. For a detailed discussion of this debate, see chapter 7.

7   Sexual Politics of Reading

1 Difference criticism is used here as an umbrella term for feminist, race, postcolonial, queer theories.

2 Mulvey made this point with reference to Hollywood film.

3 By contrast, black feminist critics defended both Walker against attacks from black male reviewers and the film's right to exist. They were critical, however, of the way in which the film changed who told the story, transposing what in the novel had been a female perspective into that of a male narrative lead.

4 Some of the women, Radway found, read up to twenty-five romances a week (1991: 60).

5 It was Dorothy Evans's doctor, worried about her physical and mental exhaustion, who advised her to find a suitable leisure pursuit to relax her (Radway 1991: 51).

6 As we shall see, she changes her position in her later work *A Feeling for Books* (1997).

7 A similar point is made by Lynne Pearce: 'readers cannot hold emotion and politics together because they belong to two different systems, or models, of reading' (1997: 23).

8 These are Sara Mills's words, made with reference to Tania Modleski's work on popular romance. As Mills notes about Modleski's argument in *Loving with a Vengeance* (1982), 'the women who read Mills and Boon-type romances are active and questioning and that, far from simply consuming the fiction of the text, they often use it to challenge or develop their own identities and relationships' (1994: 13).

9 Judith Mayne raises a related point as regards ethnographic approaches and the assumption of the ideal reader, namely that this makes it 'difficult to know how much of [actual women's] responses are displaced representations of the critic's own' (1993: 84).

10 It should be noted that Mulvey draws a similar conclusion herself when she writes that 'passionate detachment' would undoubtedly destroy satisfaction and pleasure in the Hollywood film, although this should not be regarded 'with anything much more than sentimental regret' (1975: 18).

11 Since authentic realists hold that the reader seeks communion with the text, and the author behind the text, they reject an aesthetics of disinterestedness. The best explanation of 'authentic realism' as a critical but decidedly anti-theoretical approach is given by Sara Mills (1996). Authentic realists emphasize the experiential nature of literature. Literature should be pleasurable and transformative, and ideally be able to help readers to cope with life, even 'change their life'. Preference is given to the realist tradition, since modernism's foregrounding of textuality and form is felt to be distracting from content.

12 This term is used by Havelock Ellis (1894) to account for sexual difference (cf. Flint 1993: 65)

13 See Radway for a further elucidation of this (1997: 209); see also Andreas Huyssen's thesis on this issue (1986: 191).

14 As Radway explains, the 'general reader' is a serious reader who reads regularly, and is to be distinguished further from the 'common reader', who is an 'occasional reader' and whose readings are 'unfocused' (1997: 103–4; see also 10, 91–2, 112).

15 I am not implying that the distinction between a 'low' and a 'high' aesthetic is applicable to the rhetorical tradition, since the polarization between art and commercial entertainment is an effect of industrialization, on the basis of which a literary marketplace emerged. I am saying, however, that 'the taste of sense' once belonged to elevated pleasure, and it is this that Bourdieu disregards.

16 The preference for realist fiction is perhaps best summed up by Elizabeth Long, who says that 'Reading Groups [...] retain a certain humanistic "innocence" about meaning, and a deep allegiance to the conventions of realism' (1986: 604).

17 Also compare Morag Shiach's point that 'Nietzsche's writings provided a theoretical and stylistic source for Cixous's early work', which is especially evident in this passage from Nietzsche's 'Of the Despisers of the Body' (1885): 'You say "I" and you are proud of this word. But greater than this – although you will

not believe in it – is your body and its great intelligence, which does not say "I" but performs "I"' (Nietzsche 1969: 62, qtd. Shiach 1991: 81).

18 I am echoing the title of Jane Gallop's book *Thinking through the Body* (1988).

19 Compare Cixous' statement on why she prefers poetry to politics: 'I would lie if I said that I am a political woman, not at all. In fact, I have to assemble the two words, political and poetic. Not to lie to you, I must confess that I put the accent on the poetic. I do it so that the political does not repress, because the political is something cruel and hard and so rigorously real that sometimes I feel like consoling myself by crying and shedding poetic tears' (1984: 139-40).

20 See Derrida's elucidation of this procedure in *Positions* (1981: 41).

21 For other contributions to this debate see Showalter (1987), Modleski (1986), Jacobus (1986: 3-24) and Mills (1994: 25-46).

22 Fuss gives the example that not all females menstruate, for instance (1994: 100). However, would it not also be true to say that, necessarily, all who menstruate are female?

23 I am echoing here Irigaray's play on words – *antre/ventre* ('cave'/'womb') – which she uses to re-read the parable of Plato's cave in her chapter on 'Plato's *Hystera*' (1985a: 243).

24 Plant cites here the authors of *Our Stolen Futures*, who argue that, '[b]y disrupting hormones and development, these synthetic chemicals may be changing who we become' (Theo Colborn et al. 1996, qtd. Plant 1997: 218).

Conclusion: *Materialist* Readings

1 This quotation, based on an insight by Heidegger, is from Leo Charney (1995: 279) and was discussed in chapter 4.

2 Plato (1975: 111); Descartes (Principles of Philosophy IV), Kant (1902-:V.209), de Beauvoir (1972: 60-5).

References and Bibliography

Abrams, M. H. (1953) *The Mirror and the Lamp: Romantic Theory and the Critical Tradition*, Oxford: Oxford University Press.

—— (2000) 'The Deconstructive Angel [1977]', in David Lodge and Nigel Wood (eds) *Modern Criticism and Theory: A Reader*, Harlow, Essex: Longman, pp. 242–53.

Adorno, Theodor W. (1970) *Ästhetische Theorie, Gesammelte Schriften*, Vol. 7, Frankfurt am Main: Suhrkamp.

Allen, James Smith (2001) 'Reading the Novel', in James L. Machor and Philip Goldstein (eds) *Reception Study: From Literary Theory to Cultural Studies*, New York: Routledge, pp. 180–202.

Alston, Peter (1998) 'Bibliography in the Computer Age', in Peter Davison (ed.) *The Book Encompassed: Studies in Twentieth-Century Bibliography*, Winchester: St Paul's Bibliographies, pp. 276–89.

Anon. (1812) 'On NOVEL-READING, and the Mischief which Arises from its Indiscriminate Practice', *Lady's Magazine*, 43: 222–4.

Anon. (1867) 'Reading as a Means of Culture', *Sharpe's London Magazine*, 31 (December): 316–23.

Anon. (1978 [1910]) 'Neuland für Kinematographentheater', in Anton Kaes (ed.) *Kino-Debatte: Texte zum Verhältnis von Literatur und Film 1909-1929*, Tübingen: Max Niemayer, p. 41.

Arac, Jonathan, Wlad Godzich and Martin Wallace (eds) (1983) *The Yale Critics: Deconstruction in America*, Minneapolis: Minnesota University Press.

Aristotle (1996a) *Physics*, trans. Robin Waterfield, intro. David Bostock, Oxford: Oxford University Press.

—— (1996b) *The Politics and the Constitution of Athens*, trans. Jonathan Barnes, ed. Stephen Everson, Cambridge: Cambridge University Press.

Arneil, Barbara (1999) *Politics and Feminism*, Oxford: Blackwell.

Arnold, Matthew (1906 [1880]) 'The Study of Poetry', *Essays in Criticism*, 2nd ser., London: Macmillan, pp. 1–55.

—— (1907 [1865]) 'The Function of Criticism at the Present Time', *Essays in Criticism*, 1st ser., London: Macmillan, pp. 1–41.

Ashfield, Andrew, and Peter de Bolla (eds) (1996) *The Sublime: A Reader in British Eighteenth-Century Aesthetic Theory*, Cambridge: Cambridge University Press.

Austen, Jane (1995 [1818]) *Northanger Abbey*, Harmondsworth: Penguin.

Austin, Alfred (1874) 'The Vice of Reading', *Temple Bar*, XLII (September): 251–7.

Barth, John (1981) 'The Literature of Exhaustion', in Raymond Federman (ed.) *Surfiction: Fiction Now and Tomorrow*, Chicago: Swallow Press, pp. 19–33.

Barthes, Roland (1974) *S/Z*, trans. Richard Howard, New York: Hill & Wang.

—— (1975) *The Pleasure of the Text*, trans. Richard Miller, New York: Hill & Wang.

—— (1977) *Image, Music, Text*, trans. Stephen Heath, London: Fontana.

Baudelaire, Charles (1964) *The Painter of Modern Life and Other Essays*, trans. Jonathan Mayne, London: Phaidon Press.

—— (1965 [1857]) 'Madame Bovary by Gustave Flaubert', in Flaubert, *Madame Bovary*, ed. Paul de Man, New York: W. W. Norton, pp. 336–43.

—— (1983 [1857]) 'Further Notes on Edgar Poe', in Eric Warner and Graham Hough (eds) *Strangeness and Beauty: An Anthology of Aesthetic Criticism, 1840-1910*, Vol. 1: *Ruskin to Swinburne*, Cambridge: Cambridge University Press, pp. 186–93.

Baudrillard, Jean (1993) *Symbolic Exchange and Death*, trans. Iain Hamilton Grant, London, Sage.

Baym, Nina (1984) *Novels, Readers and Reviewers: Responses to Fiction in Antebellum America*, Ithaca, NY: Cornell University Press.

Bazin, Patrick (1996) 'Towards Metareading', in Geoffrey Nunberg (ed.) *The Future of the Book*, Berkeley and Los Angeles: University of California Press, pp. 153–68.

de Beauvoir, Simone (1972 [1949]) *The Second Sex*, trans. H. M. Parshley, Harmondsworth: Penguin.

Behne, Adolf (1978 [1926]) 'Die Stellung des Publikums zur modernen deutschen Literatur', in Anton Kaes (ed.) *Kino-Debatte: Texte zum Verhältnis von Literatur und Film 1909-1929*, Tübingen: Max Niemayer, pp. 160–3.

Benjamin, Walter (1973 [1939]) *Charles Baudelaire: A Lyric Poet in the Era of High Capitalism*, trans. Harry Zohn, London: Verso.

Bennett, Andrew (ed.) (1995) *Readers and Reading*, Harlow, Essex: Longman.

Berggren, Anne G. (2004) 'Reading like a Woman', in P. Patrocinio Schweickart and Elizabeth A. Flynn (eds) *Reading Sites: Social Difference and Reader Response*, New York: Modern Language Association, pp. 166–88.

Bergk, Johann Adam (1966 [1799]) *Die Kunst, Bücher zu lessen: nebst Bemerkungen über Schriften und Schriftsteller*, Jena: In der Hempelschen Buchhandlung.

Blair, Hugh (1996 [1763]) *A Critical Dissertation on the Poems of Ossian*, in Andrew Ashfield and Peter de Bolla (eds) *The Sublime: A Reader in British Eighteenth-Century Aesthetic Theory*, Cambridge: Cambridge University Press, pp. 207–12.

Bloch, Ernst (1984 [1914]) 'Die Melodie im Kino oder immanente und transzendentale Musik', in Fritz Güttinger (ed.) *Kein Tag ohne Kino*, Frankfurt am Main: Deutsches Film Museum, pp. 313–19.

Bloch, R. Howard, and Carla Hesse (eds) (1995) *Future Libraries*, Berkeley and Los Angeles: University of California Press.

Bloom, Clive (1996) *Cult Fiction: Popular Reading and Pulp Theory*, London: Macmillan.

Bloom, Harold (1973) *The Anxiety of Influence: A Theory of Poetry*, New York: Oxford University Press.

—— (1975a) *A Map of Misreading*, New York: Oxford University Press.

—— (1975b) *Kabbalah and Criticism*, New York: Seabury Press.

—— (1976) *Poetry and Repression: Revisionism from Blake to Stevens*, New Haven, CT: Yale University Press.

—— (1979) 'The Breaking of Form', in Bloom, Paul de Man, Jacques Derrida, Geoffrey Hartman and J. Hillis Miller, *Deconstruction and Criticism*, New York: Continuum, pp. 1–37.

—— (1982) *Agon: Towards a Theory of Revisionism*, New York: Oxford University Press.

Bloom, Harold, Paul de Man, Jacques Derrida, Geoffrey Hartman and J. Hillis Miller (1979) *Deconstruction and Criticism*, New York: Continuum.

Boardman, Kay (1994) '"The Glass of Gin": Renegade Reading Possibilites in the Classic Realist Text', in Sara Mills (ed.) *Gendering the Reader*, Hemel Hempstead: Harvester Wheatsheaf, pp. 199–216.

Bobo, Jacqueline (1988) '*The Color Purple*: Black Women as Cultural Readers', in E. Deirdre Pribram (ed.) *Female Spectators: Looking at Film and Television*, London: Verso, pp. 90–109.

—— (1995) *Black Women as Cultural Readers*, New York: Columbia University Press.

Böhme, Hartmut, Peter Matussek and Lothar Müller (2000) *Orientierung Kulturwissenschaft: was sie kann, was sie will*, Hamburg: Rowohlt Verlag.

de Bolla, Peter (1989) *The Discourse of the Sublime: Readings in History, Aesthetics and the Subject*, Oxford: Blackwell.

Bolter, Jay David (1991) *Writing Space: The Computer, Hypertext, and the History of Writing*, Hove and London: Lawrence Earlbaum Associates.

—— (1996) 'Ekphrasis, Virtual Reality, and the Future of Writing', in Geoffrey Nunberg (ed.) *The Future of the Book*, Berkeley and Los Angeles: University of California Press, pp. 253–72.

Bolter, Jay David, and Richard Grusin (eds) (1999) *Remediation: Understanding New Media*, Cambridge, MA: MIT Press.

Botting, Fred (1996) *Gothic*, London: Routledge.

Bottomore, Stephen (1999) 'The Panicking Audience? Early Cinema and the "Train Effect"', *Historical Journal of Film, Radio and Television*, 19 (2): 177–216.

Bourdieu, Pierre (1984 [1979]) *Distinction: A Social Critique of the Judgement of Taste*, trans. Richard Nice, London and New York: Routledge.

Bowers, Fredson (1998) 'Notes on Theory and Practice in Editing Texts', in Peter Davison (ed.) *The Book Encompassed: Studies in Twentieth-Century Bibliography*, Winchester: St Paul's Bibliographies, pp. 244–57.

Boyarin, Jonathan (ed.)(1992) *The Ethnography of Reading*, Berkeley and Los Angeles: University of California Press.

Bradbury, Ray (1976 [1954]) *Fahrenheit 451*, London: Panther Granada.

Brantlinger, Patrick (1998) *The Reading Lesson: The Threat of Mass Literacy in Nineteenth-Century Fiction*, Bloomington: Indiana University Press.

Bray, Abigail (2004) *Hélène Cixous, Writing and Sexual Difference*, Basingstoke: Palgrave Macmillan.

Brecht, Bertolt (1978) *Brecht on Theatre*, ed. and trans. John Willet, London: Methuen.

Brunsdon, Charlotte (1989) 'Text and Audience', in Ellen Seiter, Hans Borchers, Gabriele Kreutzner and Eva-Maria Warth (eds) *Remote Control: Television, Audience and Cultural Power*, London and New York: Routledge, pp. 116–29.

Burke, Edmund (1990 [1757]) *A Philosophical Enquiry into the Origin of our Ideas of the Sublime and Beautiful*, Oxford: Oxford University Press.

Butler, Judith (1990) *Gender Trouble: Feminism and the Subversion of Identity*, New York and London: Routledge.

—— (1993) *Bodies that Matter: On the Discursive Limits of 'Sex'*, New York and London: Routledge.

Butterworth, C. H. (1870) 'Overfeeding', *Victoria Magazine*, 14 (November–April): 500–4.

Caie, Graham D. (2000) 'Hypertext and Multiplicity: The Medieval Example', in Andrew Murphy (ed.) *The Renaissance Text: Theory, Editing, Textuality*, Manchester: Manchester University Press, pp. 30–43.

Calinescu, Matei (1993) *Rereading*, New Haven, CT: Yale University Press.

Calvino, Italo (1982 [1979]) *If on a Winter's Night a Traveller*, trans. William Weaver, London: Picador.

Camille, Michael (1997) 'The Book as Flesh and Fetish in Richard de Bury's *Philobiblon*', in Dolores Warwick Frese and Katherine OBrien O'Keeffe (eds) *The Book and the Body*, Notre Dame: University of Notre Dame Press, pp. 34–77.

Caughie, Pamela L. (1988) 'Women Reading/Reading Women: A Review of Some Recent Books on Gender and Reading', *Papers on Language and Literature*, 24: 317–35.

Cavallo, Guglielmo, and Roger Chartier (eds) (1999) *A History of Reading in the West*, trans. Lydia G. Cochrane, Cambridge: Polity.

de Cervantes, Miguel (1992 [1605, 1615]) *Don Quixote*, trans. Charles Jarvis, Oxford: Oxford University Press.

Charney, Leo (1995) 'In a Moment: Film and the Philosophy of Modernity', in Charney and Vanessa R. Schwartz (eds) *Cinema and the Invention of Modern Life*, Berkeley: University of California Press, pp. 279–94.

Chartier, Roger (1988a) *Cultural History: Between Practices and Representations*, Cambridge: Polity.

—— (1988b) 'Frenchness in the History of the Book: From the History of Publishing to the History of Reading', *Proceedings of the American Antiquarian Society*, 97: 299–329.

—— (1989a) 'Texts, Printing, Readings', in Lynn Hunt (ed.) *The New Cultural History*, Berkeley: University of California Press, pp. 154–75.

—— (ed.) (1989b) *The Culture of Print: Power and the Uses of Print in Early Modern Europe*, trans. Lydia G. Cochrane, Princeton, NJ: Princeton University Press.

—— (1989c) 'The Practical Impact of Writing', in Chartier (ed.) *Passions of the Renaissance*, Vol. 3 of Philippe Ariès and Georges Duby (eds) *A History of Private Life*, Cambridge, MA: Harvard University Press, pp. 111–59.

—— (1991) *The Cultural Origins of the French Revolution*, trans. Lydia G. Cochrane, Durham, NC: Duke University Press.

—— (1994) *The Order of Books: Readers, Authors and Libraries in Europe between the Fourteenth and Eighteenth Centuries*, trans. Lydia G. Cochrane, Cambridge: Polity.

—— (1995) *Forms and Meanings: Texts, Performances, and Audiences from Codex to Computer*, Philadelphia, University of Pennsylvania Press.

—— (1997) *On the Edge of the Cliff: History, Language, and Practices*, trans. Lydia G. Cochrane, Baltimore: Johns Hopkins University Press.

Christie, Ian (1994) *The Last Machine: Early Cinema and the Birth of the Modern World*, London: BFI.

Cicero (1988 [ca. 46 BC]) *Orator*, in Raman Selden (ed.) *The Theory of Criticism: From Plato to the Present: A Reader*, Harlow, Essex: Longman, pp. 324–7.

Cixous, Hélène (1981) 'The Laugh of the Medusa', trans. Keith Cohen and Paula Cohen, in Elaine Marks and Isabelle de Courtivron (eds) *New French Feminism*, London: Harvester Wheatsheaf, pp. 245–64.

—— (1984) 'Appendix: An Exchange with Hélène Cixous', in Verena Andermatt Conley, *Hélène Cixous: Writing the Feminine*, Lincoln and London: University of Nebraska Press, pp. 129–61.

—— (1986) 'Sorties: Out and Out: Attacks/Ways Out/Forays', trans. Betsy Wing, in Hélène Cixous and Catherine Clément, *The Newly Born Woman*, Minneapolis: University of Minnesota Press, pp. 63–132.

—— (1988) 'Conversations with Hélène Cixous and Members of the Centre d'Etudes Féminines', in Susan Sellers (ed.) *Writing Differences: Readings from the Seminar of Hélène Cixous*, Milton Keynes: Open University Press, pp. 141–54.

—— (1990) *Reading with Clarice Lispector*, trans. Verena Andermatt Conley, Minneapolis: University of Minnesota Press.

—— (1991) *'Coming to Writing' and Other Essays*, trans. Sarah Cornell, Deborah Jenson, Ann Liddle and Susan Sellers, ed. Deborah Jenson, intro. Susan Suleimann, Cambridge, MA: Harvard University Press.

—— (1999) *Third Body*, trans. Keith Cohen, Evanston, IL: Northwestern University Press.

Cixous, Hélène, and Mireille Calle-Gruber (1997) *Hélène Cixous Rootprints: Memory and Life Writing*, trans. Eric Prenowitz, London: Routledge.

Clarke, Arthur C. (2001 [1954]) *Childhood's End*, London: Pan.

Coleridge, Samuel Taylor (1987) *Lectures 1808-1819 On Literature*, ed. R. A. Foakes, *The Collected Works of Samuel Taylor Coleridge*, Vol. 2, Princeton, NJ: Princeton University Press.

Crosman Wimmers, Inge (1988) *Poetics of Reading: Approaches to the Novel*, Princeton, NJ: Princeton University Press.

Cruse, Amy (1930) *The Englishman and his Books in the Early Nineteenth Century*, London: Harrap.

Culler, Jonathan (1975) *Structuralist Poetics*, London: Routledge & Kegan Paul.

—— (1980) 'Prolegomena to a Theory of Reading', in Susan R. Suleiman and Inge Crosman (eds) *The Reader in the Text*, Princeton, NJ: Princeton University Press, pp. 46–66.

—— (1981) *The Pursuit of Signs*, London: Routledge & Kegan Paul.

—— (1983) *On Deconstruction*, London: Routledge.

Cvetkovich, Ann (1992) *Mixed Feelings: Feminism, Mass Culture, and Victorian Sensationalism*, New Brunswick, NJ: Rutgers University Press.

Daiches, David (1956) *Critical Approaches to Literature*, London: Longmans.

Dante, Alighieri (1949) *The Divine Comedy*, I: *Hell*, trans. Dorothy L. Sayers, Harmondsworth: Penguin.

Darley, Andrew (2000) *Visual Digital Culture: Surface Play and Spectacle in New Media Genres*, London: Routledge.

Darnton, Robert (1985) *The Great Cat Massacre and Other Episodes in French Cultural History*, New York: Vintage.

—— (1990) *The Kiss of Lamourette*, London: Faber & Faber.

Davidson, Cathy N. (1986) *Revolution and the World: The Rise of the Novel in America*, Oxford: Oxford University Press.

—— (1989) 'Towards a History of Books and Readers', in Davidson (ed.) *Reading in America: Literature and Social History*, Baltimore: Johns Hopkins University Press, pp. 1–26.

Davison, Peter (ed.) (1998) *The Book Encompassed: Studies in Twentieth-Century Bibliography*, Winchester: St Paul's Bibliographies.

Dawson, Anthony B. (1995) *Hamlet: Shakespeare in Performance*, Manchester: Manchester University Press.

Deleuze, Gilles (1989 [1985]) *Cinema 2: The Time-Image*, trans. Hugh Tomlinson and Robert Galeta, London: Athlone Press.

Deleuze, Gilles, and Félix Guattari (1988 [1980]) *A Thousand Plateaus: Capitalism and Schizophrenia*, trans. Brian Massumi, London: Athlone Press.

Derrida, Jacques (1976 [1967]) *Of Grammatology*, trans. Gayatri Chakravorty Spivak, Baltimore: Johns Hopkins University Press.

—— (1979 [1976]) *Spurs/Eperons*, trans. Barbara Harlow, Chicago: University of Chicago Press.

—— (1981 [1972]) *Positions*, trans. Alan Bass, Chicago: University of Chicago Press.

—— (1982 [1972]) *Margins of Philosophy*, trans. Alan Bass, Chicago: University of Chicago Press.

—— (1989) 'Three Questions to Hans-Georg Gadamer', pp. 52–4; 'Interpreting Signatures (Nietzsche/Heidegger): Two Questions', pp. 58–71, in Diane P. Michelfelder and Richard E. Palmer (eds) *Dialogue and Deconstruction: The Gadamer–Derrida Encounter*, Albany: State University of New York Press.

Döblin, Alfred (1978 [1909]) 'Das Theater der kleinen Leute', in Anton Kaes (ed.) *Kino-Debatte: Texte zum Verhältnis von Literatur und Film 1909-1929*, Tübingen: Max Niemayer, pp. 37–8.

Doody, Margaret Anne (1996) *The True Story of the Novel*, New Brunswick, NJ: Rutgers University Press.

Doubleday [Ainger, Alfred] (1859) 'Books and their Uses', *Macmillan's Magazine*, 1 (December): 110–13.

Ducreux, Marie-Elisabeth (1989) 'Reading unto Death: Books and Readers in Eighteenth-Century Bohemia', in Roger Chartier (ed.) *The Culture of Print*, Princeton, NJ: Princeton University Press, pp. 191–229.

Duguid, Paul (1996) 'Material Matters: The Past and the Futurology of the Book', in Geoffrey Nunberg (ed.) *The Future of the Book*, Berkeley and Los Angeles: University of California Press, 63–101.

Eagleton, Terry (1983) *Literary Theory: An Introduction*, Oxford: Blackwell.

—— (1990) *The Ideology of the Aesthetic*, Oxford: Blackwell.

Eco, Umberto (1979) *The Role of the Reader*, Bloomington: Indiana University Press.

—— (1994) *Reflections on The Name of the Rose* (1983), trans. William Weaver, London: Minerva.

Eisenstein, Elizabeth L. (1980) *The Printing Revolution in Early Modern Europe*, Cambridge: Cambridge University Press.

Eliot, T. S. (1960 [1920]) *The Sacred Wood: Essays on Poetry and Criticism*, London: Methuen.

Engelsing, Rolf (1974) *Der Bürger als Leser: Lesergeschichte in Deutschland 1500-1800*, Stuttgart: Metzler.

Fabian, Johannes (1992) 'Keep Listening: Ethnography and Reading', in Jonathan Boyarin (ed.) *The Ethnography of Reading*, Berkeley and Los Angeles: University of California Press, pp. 80–97.

Feather, John (1988) *A History of British Publishing*, London: Routledge.

Federman, Raymond (1975/6) 'Playgiarism', *New Literary History*, 7: 563–78.

—— (ed.) (1981) *Surfiction: Fiction Now and Tomorrow*, Chicago: Swallow Press.

Felman, Shoshana (1975) 'Women and Madness: The Critical Phallacy', *Diacritics*, 5 (4): 2–10.

Felski, Rita (1995) *The Gender of Modernity*, Cambridge, MA: Harvard University Press.

Ferris, Ina (1991) *The Achievement of Literary Authority: Gender, History and the Waverley Novels*, Ithaca, NY: Cornell University Press.

Fetterley, Judith (1978) *The Resisting Reader: A Feminist Approach to American Fiction*, Bloomington: Indiana University Press.

Fish, Stanley (1980) *Is There a Text in this Class? The Authority of Interpretive Communities*, Cambridge, MA: Harvard University Press.

Flaubert, Gustave (1992 [1857]) *Madame Bovary*, trans. and intro. Geoffrey Wall, London: Penguin.

Flint, Kate (1993) *The Woman Reader 1837-1914*, Oxford: Clarendon Press.

Flynn, Elizabeth A., and Patrocinio P. Schweickart (eds) (1986) *Gender and Reading: Essays on Readers, Texts and Contexts*, Baltimore: Johns Hopkins University Press.

Foucault, Michel (1972) 'The Discourse on Language', in *The Archeology of Knowledge*, trans. A. Sheridan, New York: Pantheon.

—— (1980) *The History of Sexuality*, Vol. 1: *An Introduction*, trans. Robert Hurley, New York: Vintage.

—— (1986 [1969]) 'What is an Author?', trans. Josué V. Harari, in Paul Rabinow (ed.), *The Foucault Reader*, London: Penguin, pp. 101–20.

Freska, Friedrich (1984 [1912]) 'Vom Werte und Umwerte des Kinos', in Fritz Güttinger (ed.) *Kein Tag ohne Kino*, Frankfurt am Main: Deutsches Film Museum, pp. 98–103.

Freud, Sigmund (1979 [1933]) 'Femininity', *New Introductory Lectures on Psychoanalysis*, trans. James Strachey, Harmondsworth: Penguin.

—— (1986 [1925]) 'Some Psychical Consequences of the Anatomical Distinction between the Sexes', in *The Essentials of Psychoanalysis*, ed. Anna Freud, Harmondsworth: Penguin.

—— (1990 [1939 (1934-8)]) *Moses and Monotheism: Three Essays*, *Origins of Religion*, trans. James Strachey, Harmondsworth: Penguin.

—— (1991 [1920]) 'Beyond the Pleasure Principle', *On Metapsychology: The Theory of Psychoanalysis*, trans. James Strachey, Harmondsworth: Penguin.

Freund, Elizabeth (1987) *The Return of the Reader*, London: Methuen.

Friedlander, Larry (1991) 'The Shakespeare Project', in George P. Landow and Paul Delany (eds) *Hypermedia and Literary Studies*, Cambridge, MA: MIT Press, pp. 257–71.

Fuss, Diana (1994) 'Reading like a Feminist', in Naomi Schor and Elizabeth Weed (eds) *The Essential Difference*, Bloomington: Indiana University Press, pp. 98–115.

Gadamer, Hans-Georg (1975 [1960]) *Truth and Method*, London: Sheed & Ward.

—— (1984) 'Text und Interpretation', in Philippe Forget (ed.) *Text und Interpretation*, Munich: Wilhelm Fink, pp. 24–77.

—— (1989) 'Text and Interpretation', pp. 21–51; 'Reply to Jacques Derrida', pp. 55–7; 'Letter to Dallmayr', pp. 93–101; '*Destruction* and Deconstruction', pp. 102–13; 'Hermeneutics and Logocentrism', pp. 114–25, in Diane P. Michelfelder and Richard E. Palmer (eds) *Dialogue and Deconstruction: The Gadamer–Derrida Encounter*, Albany: State University of New York Press.

Gallop, Jane (1988) *Thinking through the Body*, New York: Columbia University Press.

Gates, Henry Louis Jr. (ed.) (1990) 'Introduction', *Reading Black, Reading Feminist: A Critical Anthology*, New York: Meridian, pp. 1–17.

Gauger, Hans-Martin (1994) 'Die sechs Kulturen in der Geschichte des Lesens', in Paul Goetsch (ed.) *Lesen und Schreiben im 17. und 18. Jahrhundert*, Tübingen: Gunter Narr, pp. 27–47.

Gaupp, Robert, and Helmut Lange (1912) *Der Kinematograph als Volksunterhaltungsmittel*, Munich: Dürerbund.

Gibson, William (1986) *Count Zero*, London: Grafton.

Goethe, Johann Wolfgang von (1949) 'The Writing of Werther', in J. M. Cohen (ed.) *Truth and Fantasy from my Life*, intro. Humphry Trevelyan, trans. Eithne Wilkins and Ernst Kaiser, London: Weidenfeld & Nicolson, pp. 182–92.

—— (1970 [1786]) *The Sufferings of Young Werther*, trans. Harry Steinhauer, New York: W. W. Norton.

Goetsch, Paul (ed.) (1994) *Lesen und Schreiben im 17. und 18. Jahrhundert: Studien zu ihrer Bewertung in Deutschland, England, Frankreich*, Tübingen: Gunter Narr.

Golder, Dave (2000) in *SFX*, 68 (September): 104.

Gorky, Maxim (1983 [1896]) 'A Review of the Lumière Programme at the Nizhni-Novgorod Fair', trans. Leda Swan, in Jay Leyda (ed.) *Kino: A History of the Russian and Soviet Film*, 3rd edn, London: Allen & Unwin, pp. 407–9.

—— (1985) 'Gorky on the Films, 1896', trans. Leonard Mins, in Herbert Kline (ed.) *New Theatre and Film, 1934 to 1937: An Anthology*, London: Harcourt Brace Jovanovich, pp. 227–31.

Grant, Iain (2003) 'Cyberculture: Technology, Nature and Culture', in Martin Lister et al. *New Media: A Critical Introduction*, London and New York: Routledge, pp. 287–382.

Greetham, D. C. (1992) *Textual Scholarship: An Introduction*, New York and London: Garland.

Grosz, Elizabeth (1995) *Space, Time, and Perversion: Essays on the Politics of Bodies*, London: Routledge.

Gunning, Tom (1990 [1986]) 'The Cinema of Attractions: Early Cinema, its Spectator and the Avant Garde', in Thomas Elsaesser (ed.) *Early Cinema: Space Frame Narrative*, London: BFI, pp. 56–62.

—— (1994 [1989]) 'An Aesthetic of Astonishment: Early Film and the (In)Credulous Spectator', in Linda Williams (ed.) *Viewing Positions: Ways of Seeing Film*, New Brunswick, NJ: Rutgers University Press, pp. 114–33.

—— (1998) 'Heard over the Phone: *The Lonely Villa* and the de Lorde Tradition of the Terrors of Technology', in Annette Kuhn and Jackey Stacey (eds) *Screen Histories: A Screen Reader*, Oxford: Clarendon Press, pp. 216–27.

Güttinger, Fritz (1984) *Kein Tag ohne Kino*, Frankfurt am Main: Deutsches Film Museum.
Habermas, Jürgen (1989) *The Structural Transformation of the Public Sphere*, trans. Thomas Burger with Frederick Lawrence, Cambridge: Polity.
Hake, Sabine (1993) *The Cinema's Third Machine: Writing on Film in Germany, 1907-1933*, Lincoln: University of Nebraska Press.
Hall, David D. (1986) 'The History of the Book: New Questions? New Answers?, *Journal of Library History*, 21: 27–38.
Hall, Stuart (1992) 'Encoding/Decoding', in Hall (ed.) *Culture, Media, Language: Working Papers in Cultural Studies 1972-1979*, London: Routledge, pp. 128–38.
Hamacher, Werner (1989) 'LECTIO: de Man's Imperative', in Lindsay Waters and Wlad Godzich (eds) *Reading de Man Reading*, Minneapolis: University of Minnesota Press, pp. 171–201.
Hardekopf, Ferdinand (1984 [1910]) 'Der Kinematograph', in Fritz Güttinger (ed.) *Kein Tag ohne Kino*, Frankfurt am Main: Deutsches Film Museum, pp. 44–6.
Hartman, Geoffrey H. (1975) *The Fate of Reading and Other Essays*, Chicago: University of Chicago Press.
—— (1980) *Criticism in the Wilderness: The Study of Literature Today*, New Haven, CT: Yale University Press.
Heidegger, Martin (1962) *Being and Time*, trans. John Macquarrie and Edward Robinson, New York: Harper & Row.
—— (1991) *Nietzsche*, Vols. 1 and 2, trans. David Farrell Krell, San Francisco: HarperCollins.
Heilig, Morton (2002 [1955]) 'The Cinema of the Future', in Randall Packer and Ken Jordan (ed.) *Multimedia: From Wagner to Virtual Reality*, New York: W. W. Norton, pp. 240–51.
Holderness, Graham, Stanley E. Porter and Carol Banks (2000) 'Biblebable', in Andrew Murphy (ed.) *The Renaissance Text: Theory, Editing, Textuality*, Manchester: Manchester University Press, pp. 154–76.
Holland, Norman (1975) *5 Readers Reading*, New Haven, CT: Yale University Press.
—— (1989 [1968]) *The Dynamics of Literary Response*, New York: Columbia University Press.
Holub, Robert C. (1984) *Reception Theory: A Critical Introduction*, London: Methuen.
Housman, A. E. (1933) *The Name and Nature of Poetry*, New York: Macmillan.
Huxley, Aldous (1983) *Brave New World Revisited*, London: Triad Grafton.
—— (1994 [1932]) *Brave New World*, London: Flamingo.
Huyssen, Andreas (1986) 'Mass Culture as Woman: Modernism's Other', in Tania Modleski (ed.) *Studies in Entertainment: Critical Approaches to Mass Culture*, Bloomington: Indiana University Press, pp. 188–207.
Ingarden, Roman (1974) *The Cognition of the Literary Work of Art*, Evanston, IL: Northwestern University Press.
Irigaray, Luce (1985a) *Speculum of the Other Woman*, trans. Catherine Porter with Carolyn Burke, Ithaca, NY: Cornell University Press.
—— (1985b) *This Sex which is not One*, trans. Catherine Porter with Carolyn Burke, Ithaca, NY: Cornell University Press.
Iser, Wolfgang (1974) *The Implied Reader*, Baltimore: Johns Hopkins University Press.

—— (1978) *The Act of Reading*, Baltimore: Johns Hopkins University Press.

—— (1980) 'Interaction between Text and Reader', in Susan R. Suleiman and Inge Crosman (eds) *The Reader in the Text: Essays on Audience and Interpretation*, Princeton, NJ: Princeton University Press, pp. 106–19.

Jackson, Holbrook (2001 [1950]) *The Anatomy of Bibliomania*, Urbana and Chicago: University of Illinois Press.

Jacobus, Mary (1986) *Reading Woman: Essays on Feminist Criticism*, London: Methuen.

Jardine, Alice, and Paul Smith (eds) (1987) *Men in Feminism*, London: Methuen.

Jauss, Hans Robert (1978) 'Theses on the Transition from the Aesthetics of Literary Works to a Theory of Aesthetic Experience', in Mario J. Valdés and Owen J. Miller (eds) *Interpretation of Narrative*, Toronto: University of Toronto Press, pp. 137–47.

—— (1982a [1977]) *Aesthetic Experience and Literary Hermeneutics*, trans. Michael Shaw, Minneapolis: University of Minnesota Press.

—— (1982b) *Toward an Aesthetic of Reception*, trans. Timothy Bathi, intro. Paul de Man, Brighton: Harvester Press.

—— (1985) 'The Identity of the Poetic Text in the Changing Horizon of Understanding', in Mario J. Valdés and Owen J. Miller (eds) *Identity of the Literary Text*, Toronto: University of Toronto Press, pp. 146–74.

—— (1990) 'The Theory of Reception: A Retrospective of its Unrecognized Prehistory', trans. John Whitlam, in Peter Collier and Helga Geyer-Ryan (eds) *Literary Theory Today*, Cambridge: Polity, pp. 53–73.

Johns, Adrian (1998) *The Nature of the Book: Print and Knowledge in the Making*, Chicago: University of Chicago Press.

Johnson, Barbara (1980) *The Critical Difference: Essays in Contemporary Rhetoric of Reading*, Baltimore: Johns Hopkins University Press.

Johnson, Samuel (1969 [1750]) 'The Modern Form of Romances Preferable to the Ancient: The Necessity of Characters Morally Good', *The Yale Edition of the Works of Samuel Johnson*, Vol. 3: *The Rambler*, ed. W. J. Bate and Albrecht B. Strauss, New Haven, CT: Yale University Press, pp. 19–25.

Jordan, John O., and Robert L. Patten (eds) (1995) *Literature in the Marketplace: Nineteenth Century British Publishing and Reading Practices*, Cambridge: Cambridge University Press.

Kaes, Anton (ed.) (1978) *Kino-Debatte: Texte zum Verhältnis von Literatur und Film 1909-1929*, Tübingen: Max Niemayer.

Kant, Immanuel (1902–) *Kant's Gesammelte Schriften*, Königlich Preussische Akademie der Wissenschaften, Berlin: Walter de Gruyter.

—— (1963) *Kant on History*, ed. Lewis White Beck, New York: Macmillan.

—— (1987 [1790]) *Critique of Judgment*, trans. Werner S. Pluhar, Indianapolis: Hackett.

—— (1992 [1798]) *The Conflict of the Faculties*, trans. Mary J. Gregor, New York: Abaris Books.

Kaufman, Rona (2004) '"That My Dear, Is Called Reading": Oprah's Book Club and the Construction of a Readership', in P. Patrocinio Schweickart and Elizabeth A. Flynn (eds) *Reading Sites: Social Difference and Reader Response*, New York: Modern Language Association, pp. 221–55.

Kaufmann, Michael (1994) *Textual Bodies: Modernism, Postmodernism, and Print*, Lewisburg, PA: Bucknell University Press.

Kennard, Jean E. (1986) 'Ourself behind Ourself: A Theory for Lesbian Readers', in Elizabeth A. Flynn and Patrocinio P. Schweickart (eds) *Gender and Reading*, Baltimore: Johns Hopkins University Press, pp. 63–80.

Kirby, Lynne (1997) *Parallel Tracks: The Railroad and the Silent Cinema*, Exeter: University of Exeter Press.

Kittler, Friedrich A. (1990) *Discourse Networks, 1800/1900*, trans. Michael Metteer with Chris Cullens, Stanford, CA: Stanford University Press.

—— (1999 [1986]) *Gramaphone, Film, Typewriter*, trans. and intro. Geoffrey Winthrop-Young and Michael Wutz, Stanford, CA: Stanford University Press.

Klancher, Jon P. (1987) *The Making of English Reading Audiences, 1790-1832*, Madison: University of Wisconsin Press.

Koestenbaum, Wayne (1995) 'Wilde's Hard Labour and the Birth of Gay Reading', in Andrew Bennett (ed.) *Readers and Reading*, Harlow, Essex: Longman, pp. 164–80.

König, Dominik von (1977) 'Lesesucht und Lesewut', in Herbert G. Göpfert (ed.) *Buch und Leser: Vorträge des 1. Jahrtreffens des Wolfenbütteler Arbeitskreises für Geschichte des Buchswesens, 13. und 14. May 1976*, Hamburg: Hauswedell Verlag, pp. 89–124.

Kracauer, Siegfried (1987 [1926]) 'The Cult of Distraction: On Berlin's Picture Palaces', trans. Thomas Y. Levin, *New German Critique*, 40 (Winter): 91–6.

—— (1997 [1960]) *Theory of Film: The Redemption of Physical Reality*, intro. Miriam Bratu Hansen, Princeton, NJ: Princeton University Press.

Krieger, Murray (1994) *The Institution of Theory*, Baltimore: Johns Hopkins University Press.

Landow, George P. (1991) 'The Rhetoric of Hypermedia: in Landow and Paul Delany (eds) *Hypermedia and Literary Studies*, Cambridge, MA: MIT Press, pp. 81–103.

—— (1992) *Hypertext: The Convergence of Contemporary Critical Theory and Technology*, Baltimore: Johns Hopkins University Press.

—— (1996) 'Twenty Minutes into the Future, or How We are Moving beyond the Book', in Geoffrey Nunberg (ed.) *The Future of the Book*, Berkeley and Los Angeles: University of California Press, pp. 209–37.

Landow, George P., and Paul Delany (eds) (1991) *Hypermedia and Literary Studies*, Cambridge, MA: MIT Press.

Leavis, F. R. (1930) *Mass Civilisation and Minority Culture*, Cambridge: Minority Press.

Leavis, Q. D. (1965 [1932]) *Fiction and the Reading Public*, London: Chatto & Windus.

Lennox, Charlotte (1998 [1752]) *The Female Quixote*, Oxford: Oxford University Press.

Lister, Martin, Jon Dovey, Seth Giddings, Iain Grant and Kieran Kelly (2003) *New Media: A Critical Introduction*, London and New York: Routledge.

Littau, Karin (1996) 'Incommunication: Derrida in Translation', in John Brannigan, Ruth Robbins and Julian Wolfreys (eds) *Applying: To Derrida*, London: Macmillan, pp. 107–23.

—— (2003) 'Eye-Hunger: Physical Pleasure and Non-Narrative Cinema', in Jane Arthurs and Iain Grant (eds) *Crash Cultures: Modernity, Mediation and the Material*, Bristol: Intellect, pp. 35–52.

—— (2005) '*Arrival of a Train at the Ciotat*: Silent Film and Screaming Audiences', in Jeffrey Geiger and R. L. Rutsky (eds) *Film Analysis: A Norton Reader*, New York and London: W. W. Norton, pp. 42–62.

Lloyd, Genevieve (1993) *The Man of Reason: 'Male' and 'Female' in Western Philosophy*, London: Routledge.

Lodge, David (1986) *Working with Structuralism: Essays and Reviews on Nineteenth and Twentieth Century Literature*, London: ARK.

Lodge, David, and Nigel Wood (eds) (2000) *Modern Criticism and Theory: A Reader*, Harlow, Essex: Longman.

Long, Elizabeth (1986) 'Women, Reading, and Cultural Authority: Some Implications of the Audience Perspective in Cultural Studies', *American Quarterly*, 38: 591–612.

—— (1992) 'Textual Interpretation as Collective Action', in Jonathan Boyarin (ed.) *The Ethnography of Reading*, Berkeley and Los Angeles: University of California Press, pp. 180–211.

Longinus (1973) *On the Sublime*, in D. A. Russell and M. Winterbottom (eds) *Ancient Literary Criticism: The Principal Texts in New Translations*, Oxford: Clarendon Press.

Lüdeke, Roger, and Erika Greber (eds) (2004) *Intermedium Literatur: Beiträge zu einer Medientheorie der Literaturwissenschaft*, Göttingen: Wallstein Verlag.

Lux, Joseph August (1978 [1914]) 'Über den Einfluß des Kinos auf Literatur und Buchhandel', in Anton Kaes (ed.) *Kino-Debatte: Texte zum Verhältnis von Literatur und Film 1909-1929*, Tübingen: Max Niemayer, pp. 93–6.

Lyons, Martyn (1999) 'New Readers in the Nineteenth Century', in Guglielmo Cavallo and Roger Chartier (eds) *A History of Reading in the West*, Cambridge: Polity, pp. 313–44.

Lyotard, Jean-François (1988) *The Differend*, trans. Georges Van Den Abbeele, Manchester: Manchester University Press.

—— (1991) *The Inhuman*, trans. Geoffrey Bennington and Rachel Bowlby, Cambridge: Polity.

McDonald, Peter D. (1997) 'Implicit Structures and Explicit Interactions: Pierre Bourdieu and the History of the Book', *The Library*, 19 (2): 105–21.

McGann, Jerome J. (1991) *The Textual Condition*, Princeton, NJ: Princeton University Press.

McHale, Brian (1987) *Postmodern Fiction*, London: Routledge.

McHenry, Elizabeth (2002) *Forgotten Readers: Recovering the Lost History of African American Literary Societies*, Durham, NC, and London: Duke University Press.

Machor, James L. (ed.) (1993) *Readers in History: Nineteenth-Century American Literature and the Contexts of Response*, Baltimore: Johns Hopkins University Press.

Machor, James L., and Philip Goldstein (eds) (2001) *Reception Study: From Literary Theory to Cultural Studies*, London: Routledge.

McKenzie, D. F. (1999 [1986]) *Bibliography and the Sociology of Texts*, Cambridge: Cambridge University Press.

McLuhan, Marshall (1962) *The Gutenberg Galaxy: The Making of Typographic Man*, London: Routledge & Kegan Paul.

—— (1964) *Understanding Media: The Extensions of Man*, London: Routledge & Kegan Paul.

—— (1969) *Counterblast*, London: Rapp & Whiting.

McLuhan, Marshall, and Quentin Fiore (1967) *The Medium is the Massage: An Inventory of Effects*, New York, London and Toronto: Bantam Books.

Mailloux, Steven (2001) 'Interpretation and Rhetorical Hermeneutics', in James L. Machor and Philip Goldstein (eds) *Reception Study: From Literary Theory to Cultural Studies*, London: Routledge, pp. 39–60.

de Man, Paul (trans.) (1965) 'Introduction' to Gustave Flaubert, *Madame Bovary*, New York: W. W. Norton.

—— (1979) *Allegories of Reading*, New Haven, CT: Yale University Press.

—— (1982) 'Introduction' to Hans Robert Jauss, *Toward an Aesthetic of Reception*, Brighton: Harvester Press, pp. vii–xxv.

—— (1983) *Blindness and Insight*, 2nd edn, London: Methuen.

Manguel, Alberto (1996) *A History of Reading*, London: Harper Collins.

Mann, Thomas (1978 [1928]) 'Über den Film', in Anton Kaes (ed.) *Kino-Debatte: Texte zum Verhältnis von Literatur und Film 1909-1929*, Tübingen: Max Niemayer, pp. 164–6.

Martin, Henry-Jean (1994) *The History and Power of Writing*, trans. Lydia G. Cochrane, Chicago: University of Chicago Press.

Mayne, Judith (1993) *Cinema and Spectatorship*, London: Routledge.

Mays, Kelly J. (1995) 'The Disease of Reading and Victorian Periodicals', in John O. Jordan and Robert L. Patten (eds) *Literature in the Marketplace: Nineteenth Century British Publishing and Reading Practices*, Cambridge: Cambridge University Press, pp. 165–94.

Merleau-Ponty, Maurice (1962) *The Phenomenology of Perception*, trans. Colin Smith, London: Routledge & Kegan Paul.

Michelfelder, Diane P., and Richard E. Palmer (eds) (1989) *Dialogue and Deconstruction: The Gadamer–Derrida Encounter*, Albany: State University of New York Press.

Miller, J. Hillis (1975) 'Deconstructing the Deconstructors', *Diacritics* 5 (2): 24–31.

—— (1978) 'Ariadne's Thread: Repetition and the Narrative Line', in Mario J. Valdés and Owen J. Miller (eds) *Interpretation of Narrative*, Toronto: University of Toronto Press, pp.148–66.

—— (1979a) 'A "Buchstäbliches" Reading of *The Elective Affinities*', *Glyph*, 6: 1–23.

—— (1979b) 'The Critic as Host', in Harold Bloom et al. *Deconstruction and Criticism*, New York: Continuum, pp. 217–53.

—— (1980) 'The Figure in the Carpet', *Poetics Today*, 1 (3): 107–18.

—— (1982) *Fiction and Repetition*, Oxford: Blackwell.

—— (1987a) 'Interview', in Imre Salusinszky (ed.) *Criticism in Society*, London: Routledge, pp. 208–40.

—— (1987b) *The Ethics of Reading*, New York: Columbia University Press.

—— (1989) '"Reading" Part of a Paragraph', in Lindsay Waters and Wlad Godzich (eds) *Reading de Man Reading*, Minneapolis: University of Minnesota Press, pp. 155–70.

Mills, Sara (ed.) (1994) *Gendering the Reader*, Hemel Hempstead: Harvester Wheatsheaf.

—— (1996) 'Authentic Realism', in Mills and Lynne Pearce (eds) *Feminist Readings/Feminists Reading*, 2nd edn, London: Prentice Hall, pp. 56–90.

Modleski, Tania (1982) *Loving with a Vengeance: Mass-Produced Fantasies for Women*, London: Methuen.

—— (1986) 'Feminism and the Power of Interpretation: Some Critical Readings', in Teresa de Laurentis (ed.) *Feminist Studies / Criticial Studies*, Bloomington: Indiana University Press, pp. 121–38.

—— (1988) *The Women Who Knew Too Much: Hitchcock and Feminist Theory*, New York and London: Routledge.

Mohanty, Chandra Talpade (1991) 'Under Western Eyes: Feminist Scholarship and Colonial Discourses', in Mohanty, Ann Russo and Lourdes Torres (eds) *Third World Women and the Politics of Feminism*, Bloomington: Indiana University Press, pp. 51–80.

Mudrick, Marvin (1976) 'Irony versus Gothicism', in B. C. Southam (ed.) *Jane Austen, 'Northanger Abbey' and 'Persusasion': A Casebook*, London and Basingstoke: Macmillan, pp. 73–97.

Mullan, John (1996) 'Sentimental Novels', in John Richetti (ed.) *The Cambridge Companion to the Eighteenth Century Novel*, Cambridge: Cambridge University Press, pp. 236–54.

Mulvey, Laura (1975) 'Visual Pleasure and Narrative Cinema', *Screen*, 16 (3): 6–18.

Murphy, Andrew (ed.) (2000) *The Renaissance Text: Theory, Editing, Textuality*, Manchester: Manchester University Press.

Murray, Janet H. (1997) *Hamlet on the Holodeck: The Future of Narrative in Cyberspace*, Cambridge, MA: MIT Press.

Nietzsche, Friedrich (1905–) *Grossoktavausgabe*, Leipzig.

—— (1967 [1887]) *On the Genealogy of Morals*, ed. Walter Kaufman, trans. Kaufmann and R. J. Hollingdale, New York: Vintage.

—— (1967– [1888]) 'Zur Physiologie der Kunst', in *Kritische Gesamtausgabe*, Vol. VIII, 3, ed. Giorgio Colli and Mazzino Montinari, Berlin: Walter de Gruyter, pp. 327–8; trans. David Farrell Krell as 'Toward the Physiology of Art', in Martin Heidegger, *Nietzsche*, Vols. 1 and 2, San Francisco: HarperCollins, 1991, p. 94.

—— (1968 [1887/1888]) *The Will to Power*, ed. Walter Kaufmann, trans. Kaufmann and R. J. Hollingdale, New York: Vintage.

—— (1969) *Thus Spoke Zarathustra*, trans. R. J. Hollingdale, Harmondsworth: Penguin.

—— (1988 [1871]) 'On Truth and Lies in a Nonmoral Sense', *Philosophy and Truth*, trans. Daniel Breazale, Atlantic Highlands, NJ: Humanities Press, pp. 79–91.

Novalis (1997 [1795–6]) 'On Women and Femininity', in Jochen Schulte-Sasse et al. (eds) *Theory as Practice: A Critical Anthology of Early German Romantic Writings*, Minneapolis: University of Minnesota Press, pp. 382–90.

Nunberg, Geoffrey (1995) 'The Places of Books in the Age of Electronic Reproduction', in R. Howard Bloch and Carla Hesse (eds) *Future Libraries*, Berkeley and Los Angeles: University of California Press, pp. 13–37.

—— (ed.) (1996) *The Future of the Book*, Berkeley and Los Angeles: University of California Press.

Ong, Walter (1982) *Orality and Literacy: The Technologizing of the Word*, London: Methuen.

Orgel, Stephen (1981) 'What is a Text?', *Research Opportunities in Renaissance Drama*, 24: 3–6.

Parmar, Pratibha (2000) 'The Moment of Emergence', in E. Ann Kaplan (ed.) *Feminism and Film*, Oxford: Oxford University Press, pp. 375–83.

Parrinder, Patrick (1977) *Authors and Authority: English and American Criticism 1750-1990*, London: Macmillan.

Pearce, Lynne (1997) *Feminism and the Politics of Reading*, London: Arnold.

Pearson, Jacqueline (1999) *Women's Reading in Britain 1750-1835: A Dangerous Recreation*, Cambridge: Cambridge University Press.

Peterson, Clara L. (1986) *The Determined Reader: Gender and Culture in the Novel from Napoleon to Victoria*, New Brunswick, NJ: Rutgers University Press.

Petro, Patrice (1987) 'Modernity and Mass Culture in Weimar: Contours of a Discourse on Sexuality in Early Theories of Perception and Representation', *New German Critique*, 40 (Winter): 115–46.

Philo (1929) *Allegorical Interpretation of Genesis, sec. XIV*, in *Philo*, Vol. 1, trans. F. H. Colson and G. H. Whitaker, London: Heinemann.

Plant, Sadie (1996) 'The Virtual Complexity of Culture', in George Robertson et al. (eds) *Futurenatural: Nature, Science, Culture*, London: Routledge, pp. 203–17.

—— (1997) *Zeros + Ones: Digital Women + the New Technoculture*, London: Fourth Estate.

Plato (1975) *The Last Days of Socrates*, trans. Hugh Tredennick, Harmondsworth: Penguin.

—— (2000), *Ion* and *Republic 2, 3, 10*, in *Classical Literary Criticism*, trans. Penelope Murray and T. S. Dorsch, Harmondsworth: Penguin, pp. 1–56.

Poe, Edgar Allan (1986 [1840]) 'The Man of the Crowd', *The House of Usher and Other Tales*, Harmondsworth: Penguin.

Porter, Roy (2000) *Enlightenment: Britain and the Creation of the Modern World*, London: Penguin.

Radway, Janice (1986) 'Reading is Not Eating: Mass-Produced Literature and the Theoretical, Methodological, and Political Consequences of a Metaphor', *Book Research Quarterly*, 2 (Fall): 7–29.

—— (1991 [1984]) *Reading the Romance: Women, Patriarchy, and Popular Literature*, Chapel Hill: University of North Carolina Press.

—— (1997) *A Feeling for Books: The Book-of-the-Month Club, Literary Taste, and Middle-Class Desire*, Chapel Hill and London: University of North Carolina Press.

Ransom, John Crowe (1938) *The World's Body*, Port Washington, NY: Kennikat Press.

Rapaport, Herman (1989) 'All Ears: Derrida's Response to Gadamer', in Diane P. Michelfelder and Richard E. Palmer (eds) *Dialogue and Deconstruction: The Gadamer–Derrida Encounter*, Albany: State University of New York Press, pp. 199–205.

Raven, James, Helen Small and Naomi Tadmor (eds) (1996) *The Practice and Representation of Reading in England*, Cambridge: Cambridge University Press.

Rees, Edwards (1999 [1913]) 'Rosalie Street and "The Pictures"', *The Guardian* (9 October).

Reeve, Clara (2001 [1785]) *The Progress of Romance*, in Stephen Regan (ed.) *The Nineteenth Century Novel: A Critical Reader*, London: Routledge, pp. 13–22.

Rheingold, Howard (1992) *Virtual Reality*, London: Mandarin.

Richards, I. A. (1929) *Practical Criticism*, London: Harcourt, Brace.

—— (1967 [1924]) *Principles of Literary Criticism*, London: Routledge & Kegan Paul.

—— (1974 [1926]) *Science and Poetry*, New York: Haskell House.

Richter, David H. (1988) 'The Reception of the Gothic Novel in the 1790s', in Robert Uphaus (ed.) *The Idea of the Novel in the Eighteenth Century*, East Lansing, MI: Colleagues Press, pp. 117–37.

Risser, James (1989) 'The Two Faces of Socrates: Gadamer/Derrida Debate', in Diane P. Michelfelder and Richard E. Palmer (eds) *Dialogue and Deconstruction: The Gadamer–Derrida Encounter*, Albany: State University of New York Press, pp. 176–85.

Rorty, Richard (1989) 'Is Derrida a Transcendental Philosopher?' *Yale Journal of Criticism*, 2: 207–17.

Rose, Mark (1993) *Authors and Owners: The Invention of Copyright*, Cambridge, MA: Harvard University Press.

Rothmann, Kurt (2000) *Erläuterungen und Dokumente: Johann Wolfgang Goethe: Die Leiden des Jungen Werthers*, Stuttgart: Reclam.

Saenger, Paul (1997) *Space between Words: The Origins of Silent Reading*, Stanford, CA: Stanford University Press.

Schenda, Rudolf (1988 [1970]) *Volk ohne Buch: Studien zur Sozialgeschichte der populären Lesestoffe 1770-1910*, Frankfurt am Main: Klostermann.

Schiller, Friedrich (1970 [1792]) 'Über die Tragische Kunst', in Klaus L. Berghahn (ed.) *Vom Pathetischen und Erhabenen: Schriften zur Dramentheorie*, Stuttgart: Reclam, pp. 30–54.

Schivelbusch, Wolfgang (1986) *The Railway Journey: The Industrialization of Time and Space in the 19th Century*, Leamington Spa: Berg.

Schlegel, Friedrich (1997 [1794]) 'Theory of Femininity', in Jochen Schulte-Sasse et al. (eds) *Theory as Practice: A Critical Anthology of Early German Romantic Writings*, Minneapolis: University of Minnesota Press, pp. 397–400.

Schlüpmann, Heide (1990) *Unheimlichkeit des Blicks: das Drama des frühen deutschen Kinos*, Frankfurt am Main: Stroemfeld/Roter Stern.

Scholes, Robert (1987) 'Reading like a Man', in Alice Jardine and Paul Smith (eds) *Men in Feminism*, London: Methuen, pp. 204–18.

Schön, Erich (1987) *Der Verlust der Sinnlichkeit oder Die Verwandlungen des Lesers: Mentalitätswechsel um 1800*, Stuttgart: Klett-Cotta.

Schor, Naomi (1980) 'Fiction as Interpretation/Interpretation as Fiction', in Susan R. Suleiman and Inge Crosman (eds) *The Reader in the Text: Essays on Audience and Interpretation*, Princeton, NJ: Princeton University Press, pp. 165–82.

Schulte-Sasse, Jochen et al. (eds) (1997) *Theory as Practice: A Critical Anthology of Early German Romantic Writings*, Minneapolis: University of Minnesota Press.

Schweickart, Patrocinio P., and Elizabeth Flynn (eds) (2004) *Reading Sites: Social Difference and Reader Response*, New York: Modern Language Association.

Sedgwick, Eve Kosofsky (1990) *Epistemology of the Closet*, Berkeley: University of California Press.

—— (2003) *Touching Feeling: Affect, Pedagogy, Performativity*, Durham, NC: Duke University Press.

Selden, Raman (ed.) (1988) *The Theory of Criticism, from Plato to the Present: A Reader*, Harlow: Longman.

Shakespeare, William (1968) *The First Folio of Shakespeare: Based on Folios in the Folger Shakespeare Library Collection*, prepared by Charlton Hinman, London: W. W. Norton.

Shand, A. Innes (1879) 'Contemporary Literature, VII: Readers', *Blackwood's Magazine*, 126 (August): 235–56.

Shelley, Mary (1992 [1831]) 'Author's Introduction to the Standard Novels Edition (1831)', in *Frankenstein or the Modern Prometheus*, ed. Maurice Hindle, Harmondsworth: Penguin, pp. 5–10.

Shelley, Percy (1965 [1821]) 'A Defence of Poetry', in *The Complete Works of Percy Bysshe Shelley*, Vol. 7: *Prose*, ed. Roger Ingpen and Walter E. Peck, London: Ernest Benn; New York: Gordian Press, pp. 109–40.

Shiach, Morag (1991) *Hélène Cixous: A Politics of Writing*, London: Routledge.

Showalter, Elaine   (1987) 'Critical Cross-Dressing: Male Feminists and the Woman of the Year', in Alice Jardine and Paul Smith (eds) *Men in Feminism*, London: Methuen, pp. 116–32.

Sidney, Philip (1973 [1595]) *An Apology for Poetry*, ed. Geoffrey Shepherd, Manchester: Manchester University Press.

Simmel, Georg (1997 [1903]) 'The Metropolis and Mental Life', trans. Hans Gert, in David Frisby and Mike Featherstone (eds) *Simmel on Culture*, London: Sage, pp. 174–85.

Singer, Ben (1995) 'Modernity, Hyperstimulus and the Rise of Popular Sensationalism', in Leo Charney and Vanessa R. Schwartz (eds) *Cinema and the Invention of Modern Life*, Berkeley: University of California Press, pp. 72–99.

Smith, Barbara (1985 [1977]) 'Towards a Black Feminist Criticism', in Elaine Showalter (ed.) *The New Feminist Criticism: Essays on Women, Literature, and Theory*, London: Virago, pp. 168–85.

Sontag, Susan (1987 [1967]) *Against Interpretation*, London: André Deutsch.

Stacey, Jackie (1994) *Star Gazing: Hollywood Cinema and Female Spectatorship*, London: Routledge.

Strobl, Karl Hans (1984 [1911]) 'Der Kinematograph', in Fritz Güttinger (ed.) *Kein Tag ohne Kino*, Frankfurt am Main: Deutsches Film Museum, pp. 51–4.

Suleiman, Susan (1980) 'Introduction: Varieties of Audience-Oriented Criticism', in Suleiman and Inge Crosman (eds) *The Reader in the Text: Essays on Audience and Interpretation*, Princeton, NJ: Princeton University Press, pp. 3–45.

Suleiman, Susan R., and Inge Crosman (eds) (1980) *The Reader in the Text: Essays on Audience and Interpretation*, Princeton, NJ: Princeton University Press.

Swales Martin (1987) *Goethe: The Sorrows of Young Werther*, Cambridge: Cambridge University Press.

Tompkins, Jane P. (1980) 'The Reader in History: The Changing Shape of Literary Response', in Tompkins (ed.) *Reader-Response Criticism: From Formalism to Poststructuralism*, Baltimore: Johns Hopkins University Press, pp. 201–32.

Tsivian, Yuri (1994) *Early Cinema in Russia and its Cultural Reception*, trans. Alan Bodger. London: Routledge.

Valdés, Mario J., and Owen J. Miller (eds) *Interpretation of Narrative*, Toronto: University of Toronto Press.

Waldstein, Edith (1987) 'Prophecy in Search of a Voice: Silence in Christa Wolf's *Kassandra*', *Germanic Review*, 62 (4): 194–8.

Wall, Geoffrey (1992) 'Introduction' to Gustave Flaubert, *Madame Bovary*, London: Penguin, pp. vii–xxvi.

Warnke, Georgia (1987) *Gadamer: Hermeneutics, Tradition and Reason*, Cambridge: Polity.

Waters, Lindsay, and Wlad Godzich (eds) (1989) *Reading de Man Reading*, Minneapolis: University of Minnesota Press.

Watt, Ian (1957) *The Rise of the Novel: Studies in Defoe, Richardson and Fielding*, Harmondsworth: Penguin.

Williams, Raymond (1990 [1974]) *Television, Technology and Cultural Form*, London: Routledge.

Wimsatt, W. K., and Monroe C. Beardsley (1954 [1949]) 'The Affective Fallacy', in Wimsatt, *The Verbal Icon: Studies in the Meaning of Poetry*, Lexington: University of Kentucky Press, pp. 21–39.

Wittmann, Reinhard (1999) 'Was There a Reading Revolution at the End of the Eighteenth Century?', in Guglielmo Cavallo and Roger Chartier (eds) *A History of Printing in the West*, Cambridge: Polity, pp. 284–312.

Wollstonecraft, Mary (1994 [1790, 1792]) *A Vindication of the Rights of Men, A Vindication of the Rights of Woman*, Oxford: Oxford University Press.

Woolley, Benjamin (1992) *Virtual Worlds: A Journey in Hype and Hyperreality*, Oxford: Blackwell.

Wordsworth, William (1974) 'Preface to *Lyrical Ballads* (Versions of 1800 and 1850 Parallel)', in *The Prose of William Wordsworth*, ed. W. J. B. Owen and Jane Worthington Smyser, Oxford: Clarendon Press, pp. 118–59.

Young, Edward (1948 [1759]) 'Conjectures on Original Composition', in Marc Schorer, Josephine Miles and Gordon McKenzie (eds) *Criticism: The Foundations of Modern Literary Judgment*, New York: Harcourt, Brace, pp. 12–30.

Zola, Émile (1977 [1890]) *La Bête Humaine*, trans. Leonard Tancock, Harmondsworth: Penguin.

—— (1995 [1883]) *The Ladies' Paradise*, trans. Brian Nelson, Oxford: Oxford University Press.

Index

a priori conditions of reading 107–8
aberrant readings and texts 113,
    115–16
Abrams, M. H. 85, 88, 91, 117
active–passive consumers 58–61, 76–8, 81,
    134–7
addiction
    reading 42–5, 72–4, 132
    television 79, 81
    to virtual reality 58
Adorno, Theodor 99
aesthetics
    aesthetic response theory 110
    embodied reading 143, 147–8
    history of literary criticism 83–102
    low/middle/highbrow reading 137–8,
        139–40
    of reception 100, 110
affect
    materialist readings 155, 156–7
    pathology of reading 75–6, 156
    production of 2–3, 8–10
        by new technologies 7–9
        tearful readers 66–9, 83–4, 85
        television 81
    role in literary criticism 83–102,
        156–7
        close reading 96–8
        contemplative reading 92–6
        disinterested reading 92–6, 99, 101
        docere–delectare–movere 85, 86–90, 91,
            94, 95–6
        reader–author–text shift 90–2, 97–8,
            101–2
        reading for sense 98–102
        reading with/without pathos
            83–6

sexual politics of reading 131–4, 136–7,
    138–44, 156–7
    see also frightened readers; passionate
        readers
Affective Fallacy 9–10, 96, 156
agency
    active consumers 135–7
    bibliomania and 5–6
    marginalized viewers 129, 131
    the reader in fiction 74, 75
    romance reading 134
Allen, James Smith 74
Alston, Peter 35
anatomy of reading 1–12
Aristotle 11, 63, 86–7, 99, 145, 146
Arnold, Matthew 94–5
art, effects of 62–3, 74–5
    see also affect; dangers, of reading
audience, the *see* reader, the
Austen, Jane 69–72, 76
Austin, Alfred 5, 38, 42, 46, 51, 52, 56
authors, reader–author–text shift 90–2,
    97–8, 101–2, 104
authorship
    history of 16, 18–19
    hypertext 34–5
    materiality of reading 31–2, 33, 34–5
autonomous artwork 81–2

Bakhtin, Mikhail 18
Banks, Carol 160n6
Barth, John 77
Barthes, Roland 76, 103–4, 107, 122
Baudelaire, Charles 45, 46, 47, 74,
    92, 93
Baudrillard, Jean 57
Bauer, Karl Gottfried 38

Baym, Nina 41, 51
Bazin, Patrick 56
Beardsley, Monroe C. 9–10, 96, 97, 101–2, 156
de Beauvoir, Simone 126, 157
Behne, Adolf 49
Beneken, Friedrich Burchard 41, 48, 52
Benjamin, Walter 6, 21, 46
Bennett, Andrew 122
Berggren, Anne G. 138
Bergk, Johann Adam 2, 37, 40, 63
Beyer, Johann Rudolf Gottlieb 42
Bible 18
bibliomania 4–8, 42
    see also reading-fever
biological constructivism 150–1
biological determinism 151, 153
biological essentialism 149–50, 151–3
black women readers 128–31
Blair, Hugh 67
Bleich, David 101
Bloch, Ernst 49
Bloch, Howard 55, 56
Bloom, Clive 21
Bloom, Harold 10, 104, 119–20, 121
Boardman, Kay 127–8, 136
Bobo, Jacqueline 10, 104, 123, 128–31, 134, 135–6
body, the 2–3, 5–6, 10, 11
    feminist theory 124, 126, 142–8, 150–2
    loss of control over 65–77
    *mater*ialist readings 154–6, 157
    see also physiology of consumption
Böhme, Hartmut 158n8
Boileau, Nicolas 90
de Bolla, Peter 5, 46, 65
Bolter, J. David 16, 34, 54, 158n7
book clubs 139–40, 141–2
books 3–4
    danger of future without 77–8
    death of 77
    history of 15–17, 18, 21, 22
    manic amassing of 42
    materiality 23–31, 44
    multisensory media compared 80
Botting, Fred 69, 70
Bottomore, Stephen 50
Bourdieu, Pierre 137–8, 140

Bradbury, Ray 78–9, 80
Brantlinger, Patrick 40, 64, 70
Brave New World (Huxley) 78, 79
Brecht, Bertolt 87, 99, 137
Brunsdon, Charlotte 128, 134
Burke, Edmund 70
Butler, Judith 11, 152
Butterworth, C. H. 48, 53, 55, 56

Caie, Graham D. 161n10
Calinescu, Matei 18, 20, 64, 76
Calvino, Italo 77
Camille, Michael 37
Campe, J. H. 39
canon-formation 119
catharsis 87, 99
Catholicism 18
Cavallo, Guglielmo 25
de Cervantes, Miguel 5, 15, 64, 69
Charney, Leo 80–1
Chartier, Roger 2, 3, 15–16, 17, 18, 24, 25, 31, 32, 34–5, 37
Christie, Ian 47
cinema 3–4, 6–8
    assault on the senses 45, 48–50, 53
    black women audiences 129–30
    contextual enquiries 128–9
    dangers of 7–8, 20, 21–2, 37, 49–52
    special-effects films 52–3
Cixous, Hélène 2, 11, 142–5, 146–8, 153
Clarke, Arthur C. 79–80
class 127, 138
close reading 96–8
cognitive fallacy 9–10
    see also sensation and sense-making
Cohen-Séat, Gilbert 61
Coleridge, Samuel Taylor 44, 63, 65
The Color Purple (Walker) 129–30
computer technology 3, 4, 6–7, 52–8
    see also hypermedia; virtual reality
Condell, Henry 30, 31, 32
consumerism 45, 47
consumption of media 6–7
    passive/active 58–61, 76–8, 81, 134–7
    see also physiology of consumption
contemplative reading 92–6
contextual enquiries 127, 128–9, 131–4, 135–6
controlling readers' responses 108–9

conventions of reading 111–13, 115
copyright 18
Crosman Wimmers, Inge 73
Cruse, Amy 43, 55
Culler, Jonathan 9–10, 104, 105, 107, 111–13, 147, 148–9, 150, 155
cultural history 1–2
  materiality of reading 33
  politics of difference 123
Cvetkovich, Ann 70

Daiches, David 87
dangers
  of cinema 7–8, 20, 21–2, 37, 49–52
  of future without books 77–9
  of hypermedia 56
  of reading 7, 20, 21–2, 37–9, 41, 49–50, 63–77
    affect in literary criticism and 92–3, 156
    frightened readers 69–72
    modernist texts 76–7
    passionate readers 72–4, 75–6
    passive consumption 76–8
    pathology of reading 74–6, 156
    postmodern literature 77
    tearful readers 65–9
  of television 78–9, 81
  of virtual reality 58, 79–81
Dante Alighieri 67
Darley, Andrew 53
Darnton, Robert 3, 18, 38, 39, 123
Davidson, Cathy N. 1, 18
Dawson, Anthony B. 29, 31
deconstructive reading 116–19, 122
Deleuze, Gilles 123, 152, 157
Derrida, Jacques 10, 105, 106, 107, 108, 146
Descartes, René 75, 144, 157
Diderot, Denis 38
difference, politics of 122–4
  see also sexual politics of reading
difference criticism 108, 123, 125, 126
  see also sexual politics of reading
digital technologies 45, 52–8
  see also hypermedia; virtual reality
disinterested reading 92–6, 99, 101
distraction, reading as 48
Döblin, Alfred 51

docere–delectare–movere 85, 86–90, 91, 94, 95–6, 139–40
Donaldson, Peter 33
Doubleday [Ainger, Alfred] 41, 45, 46, 55
Duguid, Paul 54

Eagleton, Terry 19, 89, 97, 99, 113, 163n1
eating
  cinema as form of 51
  reading as form of 40–2, 60
Eco, Umberto 54, 79
Eisenstein, Elizabeth L. 16
electronic libraries 55–6
electronic media *see* computer technology
Eliot, George 72
Eliot, T. S. 96
Elsky, Martin 31
embodied reading 142–8, 150–1, 157
emotion *see* affect
empirical audiences 131–4
Engelsing, Rolf 19–20, 55
Enlightenment, the 65–6, 69–70, 81, 89–90, 143, 156
ephebes 119, 120
epistolary novels 66–7
Erwald, Johann Ludwig 7, 39, 52
essentialism 149–50, 151–3
ethics 89–90
ethnicity 127, 128–31
ethnocentric universalism 127
ethnographic studies 128
  active consumption 135–6
  black women readers 128–31
  romance reading 131–4, 135, 139
expectations, readers' 109–11
experience, reading as/like a woman 149–50
extensive reading 19–22, 55
eye-hunger 51
eye-strain 49–50

Fabian, Johannes 121
Fahrenheit 451 (Bradbury) 78–9
failure of reading 116–19
Feather, John 21, 39, 44
Federman, Raymond 77
Felman, Shoshana 148
Felski, Rita 73, 74

feminist politics 11, 124, 125–53, 154,
  156–7
 active consumers 134–7
 black women readers 128–31
 embodied 142–8, 150–1
 feminization of readers 151–3
 low/middle/highbrow 137–42
 reading as/like a woman 148–51, 152–3
 the resisting reader 127–8, 131–2,
   135–6, 142
 romance reading 131–4, 135, 139
 unitarian criticism 123
feminization of the reader 151–3
Ferris, Ina 74
Fetterley, Judith 10, 127, 134, 135–6, 147
film *see* cinema
Fish, Stanley 9–10, 104, 105, 107, 111,
  113–16, 121
Flaubert, Gustave 72–4, 76, 80
fleeting reading 48, 55
Flint, Kate 20, 38, 69, 70, 72, 151
Flynn, Elizabeth A. 123, 127
formalism 91–2
Foucault, Michel 122–3
Frankfurt School 134, 135
 see also Adorno; Benjamin; Habermas
Freska, Friedrich 51
Freud, Sigmund 144–5, 146, 148, 151
Freund, Elizabeth 103, 112, 113
Friedlander, Larry 33
frightened readers 69–72
Fuss, Diana 148–50

Gadamer, Hans-Georg 10, 105–6, 107–8,
  110, 113
Galle, Roland 20
Gauger, Hans-Martin 14, 18
Gaupp, Robert 49
gay reading 123–4
gendering of novels 69
genius, the sublime and 90
Gibson, William 58
Goethe, Johann Wolfgang von 20, 63,
  65–9, 75
Golder, Dave 49
Gorky, Maxim 49, 50, 51
Gothic fiction 69–71
Grant, Iain 162n8
Greber, Erika 158n8

Greetham, D. C. 30
Grosz, Elizabeth 146, 151
Guattari, Félix 123, 152
Gunning, Tom 50, 52

Habermas, Jürgen 64, 66
Hake, Sabine 7, 49, 50
Hall, Stuart 128
Hardekopf, Ferdinand 51
Hartman, Geoffrey 10, 82, 104, 120–1
head–heart opposition 11
Heidegger, Martin 75, 78
Heilig, Morton 163n13
Heinse, Wilhelm 66
Heinzmann, Johann Georg 38–9
Heminge, John 30, 31, 32
Hepworth, Cecil 50
Hesse, Carla 55, 56
Heylyn, Peter 38
hierarchization 144–7
highbrow reading 137–42
history of literary criticism 83–102, 156–7
history of reading 13–22
Hoche, Johann Gottfried 5, 43, 55
Holderness, Graham 160n6
Holland, Norman 101
Holub, Robert 105, 110
Homer 84
Housman, A. E. 83–5
Hugo, Victor 47
humanism 59, 60–1, 95
Huxley, Aldous 78, 79, 80, 81
hypermedia 53–4
 materiality of reading 33–5
 practices of reading 22
 sense-perception manipulation 54–7

ideal–material opposition 1–2
identification
 affect in literary criticism 100
 multisensory media 79–81
 sexual politics of reading 141–2
identity 123–4, 126
 reading as/like a woman 149
 the resisting reader 127–8
Illich, Ivan 14
individualism 18
industrialization 45–7
inexhaustibility of texts 108–9

Ingarden, Roman 24, 108
institutions of literature 114–15, 139–40
intellect–passion opposition 11, 69, 135,
    144–8, 155
intensive reading 19–20, 55
Intentional Fallacy 96
Internet 4, 55–7
    see also hypermedia
interpretive communities 113–16
Irigaray, Luce 147–8, 151–2
Iser, Wolfgang 10, 104, 107, 108–10, 113

Jackson, Holbrook 158n5
James, Henry 76, 162n11
Jauss, Hans Robert 10, 85, 99–100, 104,
    110–11, 113, 116
Johns, Adrian 38
Johnson, Barbara 108
Johnson, Samuel 4, 5, 37, 64, 70, 74–5
Joyce, James 26

Kant, Immanuel 4, 8, 38, 41, 49, 75, 81,
    92–3, 94, 143, 156, 157
Kaufman, Rona 141–2, 143
Kaufmann, Michael 26
Kennard, Jean E. 104, 124
Kidd, John 26
Kindervater, Christian Viktor 39–40
Kirby, Lynne 49
Kittler, Friedrich 6, 7
Klancher, Jon P. 40
knowledge 56–7
Koestenbaum, Wayne 104, 123–4
von König, Dominik 4, 7, 38, 39, 41,
    42, 48
Konstanz School 104
    see also Iser; Jauss
Kracauer, Siegfried 8, 21, 46, 48, 49, 50,
    61, 78

Landow, George P. 14, 34, 35, 55–6
Lange, Konrad 49
language
    deconstruction 116–19
    instability 116, 119
Laqueur, Thomas 64
Laurel, Brenda 58
learning 56–7
Leavis, F. R. 7, 8, 85, 97, 99

Leavis, Q. D. 2, 36, 85
Lennox, Charlotte 69
lesbian readers 124
Lesk, Michael 35
Leyda, Jay 50
literary competence 112, 113, 114
literary criticism and theory 1–2
    materiality of reading and 25–7, 28–9,
        32–3
    physiology of consumption 37
    the reader in 103–24
        a priori conditions of reading
            107–8
        controlling responses 108–9
        deconstructive reading 116–19
        expectations 109–11
        interpretive communities 113–16
        misreading 106, 118–20
        politics of difference 122–4
        readability 103, 105–6, 107,
            116–17, 118
        reading conventions 111–13, 115
        as writer 104, 114, 120–2
    role of affect 83–102, 156–7
        close reading 96–8
        contemplative reading 92–6
        disinterested reading 92–6, 99, 101
        docere–delectare–movere 85, 86–90, 91,
            94, 95–6
        reader–author–text shift 90–2, 97–8,
            101–2
        reading for sense 98–102
        reading with/without pathos
            83–6
    see also feminist politics
literature, criticism as 120–2
Littau, Karin 50
Lloyd, Genevieve 145–6, 147
Lodge, David 44
Long, Elizabeth 128, 138–9
Longinus 75, 87–8, 90, 93
lowbrow reading 137–42
Lüdeke, Roger 158n8
Lumière brothers 50
Luther, Martin 17
Lutheranism 17–18
Lux, Joseph August 50
Lyons, Martin 40
Lyotard, Jean-François 8, 22, 90

McDonald, Peter D. 24
McGann, Jerome J. 2, 24, 26, 27, 28–9
McHale, Brian 79
McHenry, Elizabeth 130
Machor, James L. 107
McKenzie, D. F. 24, 26–7, 32
McLuhan, Marshall 6, 8, 36, 45, 49, 54, 58
Madame Bovary (Flaubert) 72–4, 76, 80
Mailloux, Steven 107
de Man, Paul 10, 71, 104, 107, 116,
      117–18, 119, 121
Manguel, Alberto 37
Mann, Thomas 7–8
manuscript culture 31–3
marginalized audiences 129–31
Martin, Henri-Jean 15, 16, 17, 21
*mater*ialist readings 147, 154–7
materiality of reading 2, 11–12, 23–35, 44
material–ideal opposition 1–2
Mayne, Judith 166n9
Mays, Kelly 41
meaning production 101–2
   a priori conditions of reading 107–8
   controlling readers' responses 108–9
   deconstructive reading 116–19
   interpretive communities 113–16
   readability 105–6, 116–17, 118
   reading expectations 109–10
media technologies *see* technologies
mediation of texts 29, 30, 31–2
Méliès, George 50
men, politics of difference 123
   see also sexual politics of reading
Merleau-Ponty, Maurice 37, 52
middlebrow reading 137–42
Mill, John Stuart 91–2
Miller, J. Hillis 10, 27, 104, 116–18,
     119, 121
Millingen, J. G. 151–2
Milloy, Courtland 130
Mills, Sara 166n8, 166n11
mind–body binary 144, 155
misreading 106, 118–20
misunderstanding 105, 106
MIT Shakespeare Electronic Archive
     Project 33
mobility 45
modernist novels 76–7, 81–2, 141–2
modernist theatre 87

modernity 45–9, 51
Modleski, Tania 137
Mohanty, Chandra Talpade 127
monastic reading 15
More, Hannah 65, 77
Morrison, Toni 141–2
motion pictures *see* cinema
Mudrick, Marvin 70
Mullan, John 63
multisensory media 79–82
   see also virtual reality
Mulvey, Laura 126, 136, 137
Murphy, Andrew 31, 32
Murray, Janet H. 33, 80, 81

negativity, aesthetics of 99
Nelson, Theodor H. 55
New Criticism 93, 96–8, 117
Nietzsche, Friedrich 5, 6, 8, 41, 45, 46–8,
     75, 93–4, 143–4
Northanger Abbey (Austen) 69–72, 76, 80
Novalis 69
novel reading
   bibliomania 4–5, 39–42
   dangers of 63–77
   decline of 78–9
   modernist texts 76–7, 81–2, 141–2
   postmodern literature 77
   virtual reality and 79–80
Nunberg, Geoffrey 4, 56

Ong, Walter 16, 44
oppositional reading 127–8
Orgel, Stephen 32

Parmar, Pratibha 128
Parrinder, Patrick 163n5
passionate readers 72–4, 75–6
passion–reason opposition 11, 69, 135,
     144–8, 155
   see also affect
passive–active consumers 58–61, 76–8, 81,
     134–7
pathology of reading 74–6, 156
pathos, reading with/without 83–6, 137
Pearce, Lynne 140–1
performance, reading as/like a woman
     149, 150
Philo 145, 146, 147

philosophy, literary criticism and 86, 88–9
physicality of reading 2, 5, 10, 142–3
    see also affect, production of;
        materiality of reading;
        physiology of consumption
physiology, *mate*rialist readings 154
physiology of consumption 36–61
    cinema 45, 48–53
    digital technologies 45, 52–8
    modernist texts 76–7
    modernity 45–9, 51
    passive consumers 58–61, 76–7
    reading addiction 42–5
    reading-fever 39–42
    side-effects of reading 37–9, 41, 49–50
    technology and 43–5, 52–8
Plant, Sadie 56–7, 151–2, 153, 154
Plato 8, 86, 89, 157
Poe, Edgar Allen 47
poetry and the poetic 2–3
    failure of reading 118
    history of literary criticism 83–4,
        86–90, 91–3, 94–8
    misreading 119–20
    print's expressive function 25
    reader as writer 120
    reading conventions 111–12
politics of reading 125
    see also sexual politics of reading
Porter, Roy 64
Porter, Stanley E. 160n6
positionality 150–1
postmodern literature 77
postmodernists 122
poststructuralists 122
Prels, Max 7, 52
print and print technology 3–4, 16–17
    hypermedia compared 54–7
    materiality of reading 25–7, 30–5, 44
    physiology of consumption 43–5, 54–7
    postmodern literature 77
Protestantism 17–18

race 127, 128–31
Radway, Janice 10, 60, 131–4, 135–6, 137,
    138, 139, 140, 141, 142
railway travel 45, 47, 48
Ransom, John Crowe 97–9, 100–1
Rapaport, Herman 106

Raven, James 21
readability 103, 105–6, 107, 116–17,
    118, 141–2
reader, the
    in fiction 62–82
        dangers to 62–76
        modernist 76–7, 81–2
        multisensory media 79–82
        passive consumers 76–8, 81
        postmodernist 77
        television and 77–9, 81
    reader–author–text shift 90–2, 97–8,
        101–2, 104
    in theory 103–24
        a priori conditions of reading 107–8
        active consumption 134–7
        black women 128–31
        controlling responses 108–9
        deconstructive reading 116–19
        embodied reading 142–8, 150–1, 157
        expectations 109–11
        feminization 151–3
        interpretive communities 113–16
        low/middle/highbrow reading
            137–42
        *mate*rialist readings 154–7
        misreading 106, 118–20
        oppositional reading 127–8
        politics of difference 122–4
        readability 103, 105–6, 107,
            116–17, 118
        reading as/like a woman 148–51,
            152–3
        reading conventions 111–13, 115
        romance reading 131–4, 135, 139
        as writer 104, 114, 120–2
reader-response criticism 104–5
    see also reader, the, in theory
'readerly' texts 76
reading addiction 42–5, 72–4, 132
reading aloud 14–15, 37
reading as/like a woman 148–51, 152–3
reading-fever 4–5, 39–42
realism 76
reason–passion opposition 11, 69, 135,
    144–8, 155
reception of meanings 3, 6–7, 10–11, 29
    see also sensation and sense-making
Rees, Edward 51, 52

Reeve, Clara 64, 66
religious reading 15–16, 17–18, 19–21
resisting readers 127–8, 131–2, 135–6, 142
revisionism 119–20
Reynolds, Russell 47
Rheingold, Howard 57, 58
rhetoricity 118
Richards, I. A. 54, 95–7
Richardson, Samuel 38, 66, 85
Richter, David H. 162n4
romance reading
    dangers 20, 64
    sexual politics 131–4, 135, 139
Romantics 90–1, 97
Rorty, Richard 107
Rose, Mark 17, 18
Rost, Hans 50
Rothmann, Kurt 66
Rousseau, Jean-Jacques 38, 39, 66

Saenger, Paul 15, 37
Schenda, Rudolf 5, 39, 40, 42, 43, 55
Schiach, Morag 143, 166–7n17
Schiller, Friedrich 62–3
Schivelbusch, Wolfgang 47
Schlegel, Friedrich 69
Schlüpmann, Heide 49
scholastic reading 15–17
Scholes, Robert 148–9, 150
Schön, Erich 19, 21, 40
Schor, Naomi 162n11
Schweickart, P. Patrocinio 123, 127
secular reading 16, 17, 18–21
Sedgwick, Eve Kosofsky 9, 122, 127
Selden, Raman 16
Sellmann, Adolf 52
semiotic approach 112–13
sensation and sense-making
    anatomy of reading 2–3, 5–6, 10
    dangers of not reading 78–9, 80–1
    dangers of reading 65, 74, 76–7
    history of literary criticism 83–102, 156–7
        close reading 96–8
        contemplative reading 92–6
        disinterested reading 92–6, 99, 101
        docere–delectare–movere 85, 86–90, 91, 94, 95–6

reader–author–text shift 90–2, 97–8, 101–2
        reading for sense 98–102
        reading with/without pathos 83–6
        materialist readings 155–6
        modernist texts 76–7, 81–2, 141–2
        multisensory media 80–1
        the reader in theory 103–4, 105–6, 107, 116–17, 118
        sexual politics of reading 131, 132, 136–44
sense-perception manipulation 54–7
senses
    assaults on 45–50, 51, 53, 56
    impoverishment of 78–9
    see also sensation and sense-making
sentimentalism 68, 81
sexual orientation 124
sexual politics of reading 11, 125–53, 154, 156–7
    active consumers 134–7
    black women readers 128–31
    embodied 142–8, 150–1
    feminization of readers 151–3
    low/middle/highbrow 137–42
    reading as/like a woman 148–51, 152–3
    the resisting reader 127–8, 131–2, 135–6, 142
    romance reading 131–4, 135, 139
Shakespeare, William 29–35
Shand, A. Innes 43–4, 55
Shelley, Mary 49
Shelley, Percy 91
Showalter, Elaine 149
side-effects of reading 7, 20, 21–2, 37–9, 41, 49–50, 63–77
Sidney, Sir Philip 88–9
silent reading 14–15, 37–8
Simmel, Georg 46, 47, 48
Smith, Barbara 127
Smith, Sidney 43, 55
social class 127, 138
socially framed reading 138–9
solitary reading 17–19
Sontag, Susan 10, 99
special-effects films 52–3
Spielberg, Steven 123, 129–30
Stacey, Jackie 134–5, 136
Steele, Richard 46

Sterne, Laurence 26–7
Strobl, Karl Hans 51
structuralist approach 112–13
sublime, the 8, 87–8, 90, 93
The Sufferings of Young Werther (Goethe)
    63, 65–9, 75, 80
suicide, by readers 63–4, 75
Suleiman, Susan R. 104
Swales, Martin 67, 68

'taste of sense' 140
tearful readers 65–9, 83–4, 85
technological determinism 6, 58–9,
    60–1
technologies 3–4, 6–9
  history of reading 14–22
  *materi*alist readings 154
  materiality of reading 33–5, 44
  physiology of consumption 43–5,
    52–9
television consumption 77–9, 81
terror, tales of 69–72
texts
  inexhaustibility 108–9
  instability of 27–9, 116–17
  reader–author–text shift 90–2, 97–8,
    101–2, 104
  text–reader relations *see* reader, the,
    in theory
textual criticism
  feminist theory 127–8, 129, 135
  materiality of reading 24–35
Tieck, Ludwig 67–8
Tilt, E. J. 38
Tompkins, Jane 3, 19, 86, 88, 89, 98, 99,
    104, 133, 139
tragedy, Aristotle's view 86–7
train travel 45, 47, 48
Tsivian, Yuri 50
typographic culture 31–3

understanding
  sexual politics of reading 141–2
  text–reader relations 105–6, 110–11
unitarian criticism 108, 123, 125–6
universities 15–16
(un)readability 103, 105–6, 107, 116–17

verbal expression 148
virtual reality (VR) 7, 21–2, 54, 57–8,
    79–81

Wald, Carl 40
Waldstein, Edith 28
Walker, Alexander 69
Walker, Alice 123, 129
Wall, Geoffrey 73
Walser, Randal 57
Warnke, Georgia 106
Watt, Ian 38, 46
Williams, Raymond 58–9
Wimsatt, W. K. 9–10, 96, 97, 101–2, 156
Wolf, Christa 27–8, 33
Wollstonecraft, Mary 65
women
  dangers of reading 20, 38, 69, 156
  gendering of novels 69
  politics of difference 123
  see also sexual politics of reading
Wordsworth, William 5, 46, 51, 52, 65, 70,
    81, 91, 95
writer, the reader as 104, 114, 120–2
'writerly' texts 76
writing
  history of 14, 15–16, 17, 18–19
  hypermedia and 35

Yale critics 27, 104, 116–19, 121
Yeats, W. B. 118

Zola, Émile 44, 47